D0554686

LITERATURE OF THE CARIBBEAN

Recent Titles in
Literature as Windows to World Cultures

LITERATURE OF THE CARIBBEAN

Lizabeth Paravisini-Gebert

Literature as Windows to World Cultures

GREENWOOD PRESS
Westport, Connecticut • London

Library of Congress Cataloging-in-Publication Data

Paravisini-Gebert, Lizabeth.
   Literature of the Caribbean / Lizabeth Paravisini-Gebert.
     p. cm. — (Literature as windows to world cultures; ISSN 1543–9968)
   Includes bibliographical references and index.
   ISBN 978–0–313–32845–9 (alk. paper)
  1. Caribbean literature—History and criticism. 2. Caribbean literature
(English)—History and criticism. 3. Caribbean literature (Spanish)—History
and criticism. 4. Caribbean literature (French)—History and criticism.
5. National characteristics, Caribbean, in literature. 6. Caribbean
Area—In literature. 7. Caribbean Area—Civilization. 8. Literature and
history—Caribbean Area. I. Title.
   PN849.C3P37 2008
   809'.89729—dc22   2008010293

British Library Cataloguing in Publication Data is available.

Library of Congress Catalog Card Number: 2008010293
ISBN-13: 978–0–313–32845–9
ISSN: 1543–9968

First published in 2008

Greenwood Press, 88 Post Road West, Westport, CT 06881
An imprint of Greenwood Publishing Group, Inc.
www.greenwood.com

Printed in the United States of America

The paper used in this book complies with the
Permanent Paper Standard issued by the National
Information Standards Organization (Z39.48–1984).

10 9 8 7 6 5 4 3 2 1

For my son Gordon Alan Gebert

Contents

Chapter 1

Introduction

The islands of the Caribbean were Europe's first colonies in the New World. Inhabited by an aboriginal population of Arawak and Carib Indians, soon to be joined by hundreds of thousands of African slaves, the region would be the site of the world's first multicultural experiment, the cradle of ethnic and cultural fusion, or syncretism. Discovered by Christopher Columbus on behalf of the Spanish crown in 1492, the islands were not ruled unchallenged by Spain for very long. By the final decades of the sixteenth century, other European powers, thirsting after the riches in gold, silver, spices, and sugar flowing to Spain from its Caribbean and American colonies, had begun to contest its hegemony over the area that would become known as the West Indies. By the early years of the seventeenth century, England, France, Portugal, the Netherlands, and Denmark had taken control of sundry territories in the New World, establishing colonies of their own and bringing their languages, distinct cultures, different religious practices, and particular institutions to the Caribbean cultural mix.

Different as these European powers were in language and culture, they were joined together in their common objective: that of establishing a Caribbean economy based on the development of sugarcane plantations dependent on African slave labor. A very profitable triangular trade was soon established: ships laden with European goods left the ports of London, the Hague, Lisbon, and Cádiz bound for the Caribbean, while others followed the African coast in search of slave traders, reaching the West Indies with their human cargo depleted by the ravages of the Middle Passage. These same ships would return to Europe with their cargos of gold, silver, sugar, indigo, ginger, cotton, and rum, bringing untold wealth to Europe, while leaving the colonies drained of resources and mired in poverty, disease, and incalculable deaths in the sugar fields. The sugar industry had become so widespread by the end of the seventeenth century that Adam Smith, in his book *Wealth of Nations,* would refer to the Caribbean territories as "our sugar islands."

As a result of the establishment of the sugar plantation as the pivot of the region's economy, African slaves became "the most important single ingredient in the economic success of plantation society" (Knight 83). Millions of human beings of diverse racial, geographic, and cultural origins would find themselves pressed into service in the sugar system. However, the heaviest burden was undoubtedly assumed by enslaved Africans, who turned the area into "the historical and geographical core of Afro-America" (Hoetink 55). African slavery in the Caribbean, recorded since 1511, at the very beginning of the conquest and colonization of the region, would not end completely until abolished in Cuba in 1886. It would become the most widespread process of massive transculturation in history (Mintz 9).

Transculturation, a term coined by Cuban anthropologist Fernando Ortiz, describes the process of creation of new cultures initiated by colonialism. It refers to the creative, ongoing process of appropriation, revision, and survival that leads to the mutual transformation of two or more preexisting cultures into a new one. On arriving in the Americas, African slaves experienced multiple levels of transculturation. They had to adapt to new languages and customs in an interchange with slaves of other cultures and with their masters. Food, clothing, religious beliefs and rituals, land use and agricultural practices, patterns of family organization, and relationships between genders were all cultural elements that underwent profound transformations on the plantation. These changes, endured within a brutal exploitative system by the slave population, nonetheless left as profound a mark on the cultures of the European plantation masters and the population that surrounded the system—skilled laborers (white, colored, and free blacks), professionals, and colonial officials. The hierarchies of race and class created a system often described as a pigmentocracy, with those of lighter skin nearer the top of the social pyramid (and with whites at the very top), while the black masses occupied the lowest positions. The breaking of this racialized class system based on skin color has been central to the struggle for social justice in the Caribbean and has become one of the major topics of Caribbean literature.

The plantation, as the crucible of cultural syncretism in the Caribbean, continues to be at the center of the region's literature and culture today. The salient works of Caribbean literature—from Michael Anthony's *The Year in San Fernando* to Derek Walcott's *Omeros*—return to the plantation and its legacy as a master narrative, a foundational tale that permeates any rendering of personal or national history in the region. The continued presence of the plantation in Caribbean literature is easy to understand, given the magnitude of the system of slavery in the West Indies. Of the roughly 5 million Africans transported to the Americas—the United States included—more than half were intended for the sugar plantations of the Caribbean.

The first large-scale plantations of so-called white gold, established in the Caribbean in the middle decades of the seventeenth century, were those in the English-held territories of Barbados, Antigua, and Surinam. By the mid-eighteenth century, British-held Jamaica, until then the region's leading producer of sugar, had surrendered its position to the French colony of St. Domingue, now Haiti. After the Haitian Revolution (1791–1804) brought sugar production to an abrupt halt, creating a void in the market, the French planters who survived the violence fled to Cuba, where they would spearhead levels of production unknown before in the region. Cuba would dominate sugar production in the Caribbean until the end of the twentieth century, when the collapse of the Soviet Union eliminated the last remaining exclusive market for West Indian sugar.

Second to the history of the plantation as a central element in Caribbean literature is the Haitian Revolution of 1791–1804, an event that led to the establishment of the world's first independent black republic. Until the revolution, the French colony of St. Domingue had been the Caribbean's most profitable colony. Its prosperity, however, was built on a violent and systematic exploitation of labor unlike any known in early modern history. It represented the "epitome of the successful exploitation slave society in tropical America" (Knight 149). In 1791, the Haitian slave population of approximately 452,000 rebelled against the brutal conditions of the plantation, beginning the long and violent process that would eventually lead to the establishment of the first independent republic in the Caribbean. The importance of the Haitian Revolution—as a symbol of the struggle against slavery and oppression and as the first black republic in the world on one hand, and of the brutality, death, and dismemberment that could be unleashed on white planters by rebelling slaves on the other—is evident throughout the history of Caribbean literature. Alejo Carpentier's *The Kingdom of This World* (1949), Aimé Cesaire's *La Tragedie du roi Christophe* (1970), Derek Walcott's *Henri Christophe* (1949), and C.L.R. James's *The Black Jacobins* (1938) are among the numerous works of Caribbean literature and history inspired by the revolution.

Like the Obeah-inspired rebellions in the British West Indies, the Haitian Revolution was rooted in the commonality of religious and cultural practices centered on Vodou (or Voodoo, as it is pejoratively called). The beginning of the revolution is said to have been marked by a pact between its leaders and the ancestral spirits that accompanied them on the voyage from Africa (known as *lwa*) at a ceremony held at Bois-Caiman (described by a captured slave during legal proceedings against him at Cap Français). The links between religion and the uprising were established early through the slaves' belief in the powers of their legendary leader Makandal to predict the future, transform himself into various animals, and control the power of the plants to poison planters, attributes that served him well in his clandestine war against the French colonists. These same links between Africa-derived religions and revolts were evident throughout the Caribbean.

African-derived religions—especially Haitian Vodou, Cuban Santería, and Obeah—were among the principal and most lasting legacies of the institution of slavery in the Caribbean. Haitian Vodou—the complex group of practices that Michel Laguerre has described as "the collective memory of the [African] slaves brought to the sugar plantations of Haiti" (129)—is, like Cuban Santería, a religion that worships ancestral spirits known as *lwa* (orishas in Santería), who guide mortals through their struggles in life by offering advice and propitiating solutions to problems. The fundamental elements of Vodou and Santería are systems of divination that make possible communication between spirit and worshipper and possession, a phenomenon through which the spirit can mount or embody a believer and use him or her as the vehicle for direct communication with believers during ceremonies. The possibility of contact with deities that had shared the Middle Passage with their devotees sustained the Haitian and Cuban slave population through the brutal struggles for emancipation and the establishment of independent nations in the nineteenth century. The practices of Vodou, Santería, and Obeah—the set of hybrid or Creolized Caribbean beliefs "which includes such practices as ritual incantation and the use of fetishes or charms" (Richardson 173), together with related practices like Quimbois and Espiritismo, are among the most salient remnants of plantation society in the Caribbean.

The nineteenth century was a century of transition for the region. After the consolidation of the new republic, Haiti's political leaders were unable to establish and sustain a stable regime. The once proud republic sank into the social turmoil, economic and political instability, and environmental degradation that have marked its history into the twentieth century. The wealth derived from sugar production shifted to the Spanish and Anglophone Caribbean.

Prior to the nineteenth century, the Spanish-held territories of Cuba, Puerto Rico, and Santo Domingo had been severely neglected by the Spanish crown, particularly following the discovery of the more profitable territories of Mexico and Peru. The port of Havana had played a key role as supply depot for the Spanish fleet as it made its way between Spain and the colonies of South America. Puerto Rico and Santo Domingo, on the other hand, had been allowed to linger in obscurity, barely surviving as viable colonies through trade in tobacco and indigo, cattle and hides, coffee, and through the operation of small-scale sugar plantations, with production geared for internal consumption, and few African slaves. As a result, the population of both islands—mostly Creoles of mixed European, Amerindian, and African stock—had expanded slowly. Their social and political lives revolved around the fortified garrisons protecting the naval routes between the South

American center of the empire and the metropolis, their economies dependent on the *situado,* a subsidy collected from the Mexican treasury. Their societies would change radically by the destruction of the sugar-producing plantations of Haiti, although they would remain under Cuba's considerable shadow.

The Haitian Revolution transformed Cuba into the greatest of the Spanish sugar islands, creating an enormous demand for additional slave labor to work on the sugar or tobacco fields under conditions and with mortality rates not unlike those the slave population of Haiti had known during the heyday of that country's sugar production. Slave revolts became increasingly frequent, ranging from spontaneous eruptions of violence on individual estates to large, organized uprisings.

Slavery was not abolished in Cuba until 1886, and the tensions and alliances forged during several centuries of racialized labor exploitation featured prominently in the coalitions that joined to wage the Cuban War of Independence from 1895 to 1898. Black and mulatto soldiers fought side by side with the most liberal sectors of Cuban Creole society, hoping to establish a new nation on democratic principles and greater class and race representation. The victory over Spanish forces in 1898—coming in the wake of the United States joining Cuban forces in what would be known as the Spanish-American War—would disappoint the broader social aspirations of the black and mulatto population. When independence was finally granted in 1903, it came under restricted neocolonial conditions, with American sugar corporations taking over sugar plantations previously owned by the Creole elite, and the United States throwing its considerable support behind the most conservative military-backed dictatorships, that of Fulgencio Batista being the most notorious. The brutality and corruption of his regime, in which wealth was tightly held by American corporations and the Cuban entrepreneurs they supported, was particularly evident in the poor infrastructure and lack of social programs for the poorer segments of the population, especially displaced peasants who had moved to the city and had to survive by crime and prostitution. These were the sectors—rural and urban—that supported the 1959 Cuban Revolution, led by Fidel Castro, which opened a new chapter in Caribbean history.

The Cuban Revolution, like the Haitian Revolution in its own historical moment, became the rallying point for discussions of the possibility of radical social change in the Caribbean that would lead to the eradication of the vestiges of the plantation system and its pigmentocracy. As a symbol of the defeat of neocolonialism in the region, it was an event of paramount importance. Its successes in improving social conditions—that is, achieving almost universal literacy and guaranteeing primary health care, education, a social safety net, and the end of the class system based on race—galvanized the many political parties throughout the Caribbean at a crucial moment in the fight for decolonization and independence. On the other hand, the specter of communism it evoked frightened many local governments into severing ties with the Castro regime. It became by far the most radical political experiment in a rapidly changing Caribbean.

Cuba's Spanish-speaking Caribbean neighbors—Puerto Rico and the Dominican Republic—followed significantly different paths during the nineteenth and twentieth centuries. Both intensified their production of sugar in response to the opening of the markets following the Haitian Revolution. Neither would rival Cuban production, although both would see their economies transformed by sugar production. The colony of Santo Domingo opened the decade by joining Haiti, the United States, and Spain's Latin American colonies in wars of independence against continued colonial rule. As the Dominican Republic, it gained its independence from Spain in 1824, only to be invaded by the Haitian army in 1825, in Haiti's bid for the annexation of Santo Domingo and consolidation of the island's complete territory under one flag (Haiti and the Dominican Republic share the island of Hispaniola). The struggle against Haiti, and the humiliation of an almost 20-year occupation by who Dominicans saw with contempt as black former slaves, left deep emotional scars on the young Dominican nation, and a second attempt at occupation by Haiti in 1864 only deepened the already existing animosity between the two nations. As a result, the consolidation of national independence was the salient political and economic intellectual focus of Dominican leaders and writers throughout the nineteenth century. The Dominican Republic, bound as the country had been throughout the century in a seemingly ceaseless struggle to solidify its independence, entered the twentieth century solidly in the orbit of the new neocolonial power in the region, the United States. Like in Cuba, Dominican sugar production, long neglected because of the internecine war against Haiti, and plagued by inefficiency and limited access to new technologies, fell into the hands of American sugar corporations. Its governments, corrupt and greedy for the most part, subordinated the country's independent economic development to serving American interests. Like Haiti, American occupation loomed ahead in the opening decades of the new century; like Cuba, it would see its full share of American-backed dictatorships—that of Rafael Leonidas Trujillo being the most brutal—and would have to defer dreams of racial justice and greater class equality. Following the collapse of sugar production in the 1950s, the Dominican Republic has become a haven for upscale tourism, having become the leader in all-inclusive resort accommodations in the region.

Puerto Rico followed a different path during the nineteenth century. Although it intensified sugar production in the wake of the Haitian Revolution, it maintained a steady production of coffee throughout the century, with coffee production surpassing sugar production after 1850. As a result, it never reached the high percentages of slave populations of other Caribbean islands. At the height of its slave-centered sugar production, only 11 percent of its total population was enslaved. The only Spanish possession in the Caribbean and Latin America not to wage a war of independence against Spain, Puerto Rico, despite a strong separatist movement responsible for at least one serious attempt at independence—the failed 1868 Grito de Lares—would close the century having obtained an Autonomous Charter from Spain, only months before it was ceded to the United States as a new American territory following Spain's loss of the Spanish-American War in 1898. Puerto Rico has remained an American possession, having negotiated an ambiguous status as a U.S. commonwealth. Its sugar production virtually destroyed by the collapse of worldwide sugar prices after World War II, it has established a somewhat precarious economy based on tourism, pharmaceuticals, light industry, and U.S. aid.

The British islands of the Caribbean—Jamaica, Trinidad, and the various islands of the Lesser Antilles such as Barbados, Antigua, and St. Kitts—had experienced the heyday of their sugar production in the eighteenth century. Some of them, like Dominica, had never been efficient producers of sugar, and their economies had been sustained by smaller cash crops such as coffee, indigo, ginger, lemons, and limes. By the dawn of the nineteenth century, West Indian sugar production was becoming increasingly uncompetitive both in the international market and within the British Empire itself. As a result, planters had been philosophical about the cessation of the slave trade and the declaration of emancipation that followed in 1838. The remaining French colonies in the archipelago, Martinique and Guadeloupe, faced similar declining returns from the production of sugar by slave labor, and emancipation was declared in the French colonies in 1848. The second half of the nineteenth century, in both the British and French Caribbean islands, would be characterized by the dynamic growth of a free colored peasantry that followed emancipation and the breakdown of the large formerly slave-run estates. Land became inexpensive, or readily available to occupy as squatters, and a local economy based on the plot system of agriculture, independent from the remaining large sugar estates, began to impact the social, political, and cultural development of the various islands. Those estates that continued large-scale production of sugar had to rely on imported Asian laborers, mostly Chinese and Indian, who arrived in the Antilles in large numbers in the second half of the nineteenth century and brought new languages, cultures, and religious beliefs and practices to the amalgam of the region's Creole religions.

As the postslavery Caribbean looked ahead to the twentieth century, it faced a transformed social and political reality. The plantation, although not a thing of the past, had bowed to the pressures of the international markets and had lost its hegemony. Although the lives of many Caribbean laborers would continue to revolve around the cultivation of sugar, the diversification of the agricultural sector and the introduction of new industries—among them the growing tourist industry—would change forever the nature of work in the region. As the new century dawned, the seeds of the labor and independence movements that would control political development in the first half of the twentieth century had been planted. With the affirmation of the workers' power to define the terms of their relationships with the metropolis would come independent nations whose national identities would be bound with the affirmation of cultures rooted in African-derived cultures.

In the 1950s, the former British colonies in the Caribbean began the process of gaining their independence. Although some remain independent members of the British Commonwealth, others have opted for severing all official ties with their former colonial metropolis. The French colonies of Martinique, Guadeloupe, and French Guyana, on the other hand, became overseas departments of France, a status equivalent to that of an American state, ensuring themselves a range of benefits and services that would otherwise be beyond the scope of their local economies.

As the region enters the twenty-first century in an era of increased globalization, it faces numerous challenges. As small nations in a globalized economy, Caribbean nations are dependent primarily on tourism and foreign remittances for economic growth. Tourism, however, places their environments in increasing jeopardy. These new challenges, like those of the past, have found their way into the literatures of the region, enriching traditions that have always found themselves committed to offering a vivid mirror to the vicissitudes and joys of the islands' histories.

Chapter 2

Michael Anthony's
The Year in San Fernando

Novelist and historian Michael Anthony was born on February 10, 1932, in the region of Mayaro, Trinidad. His mother, Eva Jones Lazarus, belonged to a family that had migrated to Trinidad from the Grenadian island of Carriacou. His father, Nathaniel Anthony, a Trinidadian who died when his son was 10, was a laborer from Moruga. The many challenges of Anthony's youth, from the death of his father to the years of physical labor he was to endure as an adolescent, would become rich material for Anthony's later writings on the complexities of life on his native island.

Michael Anthony received his early education at the Mayaro RC School, but during the academic year 1941–1942 (when he was nine), he attended school in San Fernando, Trinidad's second largest city and industrial capital, a year he would chronicle in his second and most famous novel, *The Year in San Fernando,* now a West Indian classic. At the age of 12, Michael won a scholarship to attend the San Fernando Technical School, the brainchild of the Reverend Streetly, archdeacon of St. Paul's Church. The goal of the school, founded in 1942, was to train youngsters to provide skilled labor for local industry, particularly for the Trinidad Leaseholds Limited, with which it had an agreement. According to Deen, the school trained students in woodworking, metallurgy, mathematics, mechanical engineering, and proficiency in the English language. Shortly before Anthony joined the school, Trinidad Leaseholds Limited had begun building the refinery at the oil fields in Pointe-à-Pitre, which has since become the most important contributor to the San Fernando economy. The building of the refinery during World War II was considered one of the most important contributions to the British war effort by a private company.

Anthony was placed as an apprentice in the foundry, one of the less skill-intensive placements, since, as he lightheartedly described, he was "the only boy who did not have the aptitude for the other callings" (Deen 1). He worked in the foundry throughout his teenage years, enduring his unhappiness with the intense heat, the dirty sand, and the difficult job of casting iron moldings. Despite the difficult time, the training proved useful as both a learning experience and an opportunity to begin practicing the writing that would later open a path to a different career.

In 1953 Michael began submitting poems for publication in the *Trinidad Guardian*. While the paper was glad to include his poems on occasion, they rejected his request for employment, telling him he would first need to travel abroad to gain better qualifications. At the same time, a good friend from his years as an apprentice, Canuth Thomas, was in England on a scholarship, and wrote, encouraging Michael to join him. The timing was right, and in December 1954, Anthony boarded the Dutch liner *Hilderbrandt* on his way to Liverpool.

The new beginning in London brought with it a new perspective on the possibility of a career as a writer. As a housewarming gift on arrival, Thomas presented Anthony with his first typewriter, a Remington, which the latter has kept his entire life. He also began his studies in journalism and started writing with greater fervor than ever before. Thomas, however, presented Anthony with more than just a typewriter. A gifted athlete who had represented Trinidad at the Southern Games—an international competition, since revived, which features track and field, cycling, boxing, tennis, and archery—he served as a model for the protagonist of Anthony's first novel, *The Games Are Coming,* published in 1963, which describes the anticipation and excitement of the Southern Games through the eyes of a cyclist.

Anthony's departure for England had followed on the heels of a separation from his poetess girlfriend, who told him that while she would not follow him, she would await his return. Their relationship continued via letters during his first years in London, until he wrote her in 1956 asking again for her to join him. She declined, sending instead a present to be delivered by a Trinidadian girl on her way to nursing school in London. Anthony fell for the messenger, Yvette Phillip, whom he married in 1959 and with whom he had four children.

In 1965 Anthony published *The Year in San Fernando,* an autobiographical novel strongly influenced by his adolescent experiences. Since then, he has published in excess of 20 books as well as a number of short stories and articles. Other novels include *Green Days by the River* (1967), *Streets of Conflict* (1976), *All That Glitters* (1982) (one of Anthony's own personal favorites), and *Bright Road to El Dorado* (1983). He has also published two collections of short stories, *Sandra Street and Other Stories* (1973) and

Cricket in the Road (1973). He has written a number of profiles and accounts of the history and development of Trinidad and Tobago. Michael's writing is a distinct blend of personal narrative and detailed research. He blends the lyrical perspective of a native Trinidadian with the analytical approach of a trained journalist.

Michael Anthony has lived and worked in the United Kingdom, Brazil, and his home island of Trinidad. He has been the recipient of numerous awards, including the Arts Council of Great Britain Fellowship and Trinidad and Tobago's Hummingbird Gold Medal.

The Year in San Fernando

Michael Anthony's autobiographical novel is one of the classic West Indian bildungsroman of the independence period, the years between 1957 and 1970, during which most of the former British colonies in the Caribbean were negotiating their independence and producing a body of literature closely associated with the process of building a national identity and culture.

The setting of the novel is the city of San Fernando, the second largest of Trinidad and Tobago, located on the southwestern coast of Trinidad. It is there that Francis, a 12-year-old boy from Mayaro, spends a year as a companion and helper to an old woman, Mrs. Chandles. San Fernando is a coastal town—one of Francis's adventures during his year in the city is that of exploring the Wharf—built on the flank of two hills, Alexander Hill and San Fernando or Naparaima Hill. The old town, where Mrs. Chandles's house is located, is built on the flanks of Naparaima, which, on clear days, offers views of western Trinidad and Venezuela on the South American mainland. Its location on the flanks of the 600-foot-high outcrop of limestone accounts for San Fernando's steep streets, which give the old town its character. The Hill, now included in the National Parks and Protected Areas plan, was almost destroyed by the increase in demand for limestone for construction during the oil boom of the 1970s but, during the events narrated in the novel, was still covered in verdant semievergreen forests. Francis is dismayed by his first sight of a geographical marker he had heard so much about in school, which he describes as "towering like a great giant over the town" (27). He will become fascinated by the Hill, which he will watch through the changes of season while he remains in town and see it change slowly until "there were no more open spaces and the whole crown seemed more violently overgrown with trees" (127). He will discover how "in the moments of the sun its outline was sharp and clean-cut, but when the sky grew overcast, it stood dark and forbidding, its head clouded in mist" (127).

The journey from Mayaro to San Fernando—narrated in great detail in chapters 2 and 3 of the novel—follows the picaresque transition from village to city. Mayaro, located in southeastern Trinidad, is now a prosperous vacation destination, lined with seaside villas. More than a village or town, Mayaro refers not only to the bay of that name, but also to the county, which includes a number of villages such as St. Joseph, Beau Sejour, Pierreville, Beaumont, St. Ann's, Radix, Lagon Doux, Grand Lagoon, and Lagon Palmiste. The largest town in the area is Guayaguayare. The area owes its present prosperity to oil and natural gas production, as most of Trinidad's offshore oil fields are to the east of Mayaro. However, in the early 1940s, the novel's historical setting, Mayaro was still a fairly remote area that, until the late nineteenth century, had been accessible only by steamer.

Francis's voyage by bus from Mayaro to San Fernando takes him across the southern end of the island, past Rio Claro and Princes Town, on increasingly modern roads and through noticeably more prosperous rural and urban landscapes. The geographical transition parallels the protagonist's emotional journey, as he moves farther away from his much loved widowed mother and siblings toward an unknown old woman to whom he will be servant and companion and an urban setting unlike the small village that is all he has known in his young life.

The Year in San Fernando is one of the best known Caribbean bildungsroman (defined by Merriam-Webster as novels "dealing with the education and development of their protagonists"), which include George Lamming's *In the Castle of My Skin* (1953), Michelle Cliff's *Abeng* (1984), and Jamaica Kincaid's *Annie John* (1985). The novel depicts the social and ethnic divisions and tensions of Trinidadian society through the eyes of an observant and clear-sighted young boy, Francis. It is an avowedly autobiographical novel, drawn from Anthony's own experiences when, at the age of 12 (from Christmas 1943 to Christmas 1944), he left his family in Mayaro to study in San Fernando. It is, however, as Anthony has insisted, a fictionalized account and not a straightforward autobiography.

The novel is set against the events of World War II, but these play hardly a role in the novel, as they fall outside Francis's perception of his world. Trinidadian soldiers fought on Britain's behalf, and casualties affected many island families. In 1940 the U.S. Navy had negotiated with Great Britain the lease of a naval base on the island that served as one of the coordinating points for American sea operations in the Caribbean. The only references to the war in the book, however, are to Mr. Chandles's weekly purchase of the *Illustrated London News,* which he bought for news about the war, and a conversation he has with Francis about "a great victory against Rommel, the Desert Rat" (151).

The novel is narrated by its protagonist, Francis, and has been particularly praised for its recreation of the voice, outlook, and perspective of its 12-year-old narrator. In their introduction to the 1997 Heinemann edition of the novel, Paul Edwards and Kenneth Ramchand speak of Anthony's particular achievement of adhering "to the boy's point of view in a language that appears simple on the surface but which is sensuous and at times symbolic even while sustaining the illusion of adolescent reportage" (xi). They argue that "it is a source of the novel's irony that people and places can be seen objectively through the boy's observing eyes and subjectively in terms of his response to them" (vii).

As a novel of development, *The Year in San Fernando* may appear truncated, as it only narrates events that took place during one year in Francis's early adolescence. Since the novel is narrated as events develop and exclusively from the character's perspective, there is no attempt in the text at expanding our understanding of Francis's future career beyond the pages of the book (except, of course, what we can glean from the autobiographical connection to the author's own future career as a writer). Its structure is circular, as Francis's trajectory brings him full circle from Mayaro to San Fernando and back again. Its conclusion is open-ended, as we leave the character riding the bus back to Mayaro and contemplating the prospect of a happy reunion with his mother and family, but without a word as to his fate and ultimate career.

This is not to say, however, that there is no character development or transformation during the year Francis spends in San Fernando. Indeed, the year is a transformative one for Francis, but his transformation is presented in subtle and small ways. It is manifested through his increased knowledge and command of the geography of San Fernando and his responsibilities toward Mrs. Chandles. It is also manifested through his nuanced understanding of Mrs. Chandles's character and of the family drama in which she is involved with her children. It is manifested most clearly in his increasing maturity and growing capacity to understand his employer and her dilemma and in his insights into character and human relations.

Given the seasonless tropical environment of Trinidad, the passage of time is marked in the text through the stages of the sugarcane crop and through Francis's growing familiarity with the town and expertise with his routine. Edwards and Ramchand see the cane fields as becoming "an image of the progression of the boy's year in San Fernando, and the 'mystery' of growth and decay" (xiv). The planting and harvesting of the canes, in their reading, "comes to serve an archetypical function in the novel" (xv).

The novel has been criticized for its absence of a clearly discernible plot, and indeed, there is very little plot in the most conventional sense in the novel. This is not to say, however, that there is no organizing principle besides the chronological progress of Francis's year in San Fernando in the text. The novel is organized around 33 chapters arranged chronologically. It is built around a series of themes that develop throughout the novel, and which provide the elements for a plot that leads to a number of resolutions. Of course, the first of these is Francis's own growth as a character, which, as we will see later, provides its own line of development in the text. The second is the progress of a relationship of mutual respect between Francis and

Mrs. Chandles, which builds up in nuanced and subtle ways. The third, and perhaps equally important, is the subplot surrounding Mr. Chandles, his two women, and his struggle to hold on to the family home in San Fernando.

The novel opens with the introduction of Mr. Chandles, a character of a class superior to that of Francis and his family, "as aristocratic as they said he was" (1). He appears in chapter 1 as an enigmatic figure who is not only "well off," as his "manner and bearing, and the condescending look he gave everyone about him" attests to (1), but as one who, in the context of Trinidadian society, must also be understood to be white or light skinned. Francis, on the other hand, as the child of a maid and washerwoman, understands the subtle language of clothing, education, and race.

The opening of the novel already establishes class mobility as one of the salient topics of the book. Mr. Chandles is an aristocrat of sorts, and Mrs. Samuels of the Forestry Office understands the opportunities for social improvement that would be opened to her daughter Marva should she marry such a man. The romance between Mr. Chandles and Marva, on the other hand, introduces a degree of tension into the novel, as the reader must wonder if the romance will prosper and lead to marriage (as Marva expects), or whether Mr. Chandles will seduce and abandon the girl, as we would expect, given the discrepancy in their class status.

The first chapter also establishes the importance of education to achieve any measure of class mobility. What separates Marva from the rest of the girls of her village is the "high culture and education" that she has received, which raises her to the level of Mr. Chandles ("at last some person worthy of Marva had come along" [1]). It accounts for her mother's elation at the prospect of Marva's marriage to Mr. Chandles. It also accounts for the benefits to Francis of having an opportunity to broaden his horizons by travel and greater knowledge. As the novel will reveal as it unfolds, Francis's mother trusts in her children's education to facilitate at least some degree of social mobility.

The first chapter also establishes the family relationships that will sustain (and preoccupy) Francis during his stay in San Fernando. His affection for his siblings is manifest, but it is the relationship with his mother that stands apart in the first chapter. Orphaned by the death of his father, and concerned by the amount of work and worry that his mother faces every day, Francis accedes to her silent entreaty to go. What stands out in his exchanges with his mother is his sensitivity to her moods, desires, and inner thoughts—and his sense of responsibility toward her and his siblings. The acknowledgment to himself that he is indeed going to San Fernando transforms the reality around him, turning him into an acute observer of his surrounding reality and making "Mayaro look very strange" (6).

Chapters 2 and 3 narrate Francis's travel to San Fernando in the company of Mr. Chandles. Here Anthony has Francis explain his ambivalence about his departure through the observed contrast between his elegant, refined, and silent companion and the bus conductor for the first stage of his trip,

Balgobin, whose effervescent freedom and "big cackle of a laugh" both embarrass and attract Francis.

The second stage of his journey (on a yet more comfortable bus) leaves Francis feeling like "a storm of home-sickness [had] swept down on me" (9). Here he mentions for the first time the cane fields that will become the salient way in which Anthony will measure for the reader the passing of time in San Fernando. The voyage, described through landscapes that becomes increasingly urban and populated, becomes "like a carnival…so big and so weird in the night" (11). Francis's arrival in San Fernando is marked by his sense of controlled bewilderment, as he "had never thought there was such a place as this in Trinidad" (13). Amazed at the "maze of streets," he still struggles against "the loneliness closing in round [him]" (14). The arrival also brings a change in the attitude of Mr. Chandles, who becomes one of the puzzles Francis must solve during his stay in San Fernando. He bristles when greeting his mother, and Francis cannot "help thinking something was wrong between these two" (15).

Francis's reaction to his new home underscores the class differences between his own family and that of the Chandles, but also between the latter and Marva's family at the Forestry Office, alerting the reader as to the class ramifications of the changes he must confront. The differences are not subtle, but are reflected in the amount and quality of the furnishing, and above all, on the photographs and oil paintings displayed on walls and tables.

Since Francis is the reader's only informant, we must understand characters and events either through what he explains in the text or through the gaps between what he describes to us and what we perceive to be limitations in his understanding of what he describes. This is particularly true, especially in the early chapters, of his characterization of Mrs. Chandles, the widowed mother of Mr. Chandles, for whom Francis will work while in San Fernando. Mrs. Chandles, in the early chapters, is seen primarily in contrast to two earlier reports: that of Francis's mother, who had described her as "a kind old soul" who was old and would be glad of company, and the impression left by Mr. Chandles, who, while at Mayaro, had always referred to her as "dear," but now behaves as if there were open hostility between them (18). The hostility, as Francis comes to understand in chapter 5, stems from two sources: their dispute about the ownership of the house after Mrs. Chandles's death, and her disapproval of the two women with whom he is involved—Marva in Mayaro and Julia in San Fernando—neither of whom seems suitable for her son's social position and painstaking education.

Chapter 6 introduces Brinetta, the woman Francis has come to replace, and the market in San Fernando where he will from now on buy the food for the household. His walk to the market with Brinetta will serve as his introduction to the mysteries of San Fernando: Mount Naparaima; the Steelband yard, where the bands come to rehearse in preparation for carnival (carnivals in Trinidad have a long and rich tradition, with the bands competing for best original song and performance); the house where Mr. Chandles's other woman lives; the market building, with its "smell of chives and fruit and peppers and roucou and the freshness of the fish and heaven knows what" (29). Francis's growing familiarity with the market, and his growing command of his responsibilities there, constitutes one of the clearest proofs of his development while at San Fernando.

A parallel development is Francis's growing understanding and appreciation of Mrs. Chandles. During his first walk to the market with Brinetta, Francis is puzzled by Brinetta's loyalty to the old woman, despite the gruffness of her manner. He senses that for Brinetta, Mr. Chandles is not the "nice and decent" man he is reputed to be in Mayaro. However, as we glimpse the nuances of loyalties and opinions through Francis's eyes, they reach us in a fragmented way. We must wait for events to unfold and illuminate the situation, as we will only learn more as Francis understands more.

Chapter 6 addresses Francis's feelings a week after his arrival in San Fernando, at a time when Brinetta has returned to her village and he has grown to know the town. He has discovered, for example, the "exhilaration" of going out into the streets early in the morning, the arrival of the vendors from the surrounding countryside, the Indian women from whom he bought food with money he had saved from his shopping, and the best stall from which to buy the red-fish Mrs. Chandles prefers. His confidence boosted by the old lady's approval, he goes as far as to suggest to himself that she could now feel happy to have lost Brinetta.

The narrative of his first week in San Fernando includes an incident whose telling is introduced by an allusion to memory. Francis's speculation that perhaps Mrs. Chandles did not miss Brinetta "the slightest bit" introduces the story of his first meeting with Julia, the young woman who lives in the house Brinetta said would "kill Mrs Chandles" (33). The lovely girl, "so slim and delicate that her dress seemed to drape round her" (33), calls him over and questions him about Mayaro, stirring memories of home and opening a new line of self-questioning about loyalties and the nuances of character. He feels, on one hand, disloyal to Mrs. Chandles in openly speaking to someone who is clearly seen as an enemy, while on the other hand, he is fascinated by the young woman (he does not know whether by age or class she should be referred to as "a lady"), who is both lovely and seemingly kind.

Chapters 8–11 explore Francis's relationship with Mr. Chandles in the light of his changed personality and behavior in his mother's house in San Fernando. There is a subtlety in Francis's apparently naïve assessment of Mr. Chandles that reveals his growing ability to understand the ambiguities involved in the behavior of those around him. In the case of Mr. Chandles, avowedly the only person he really knows in San Fernando, the subtlety of Francis's appraisal is revealed in the clever representation of how the various spaces (geographical and architectural) reveal different aspects of his personality. In Mayaro, he was affable and elegant; in San Fernando, he is gruff and unpleasant to his mother and scolds Francis for small slights (like appearing badly dressed in the front garden of the house), unaware of his mother's increasing approval of the young boy's work and behavior. Mr. Chandles also presents different aspects of his personality in the house (where he accepts his mother's servility without paying the slightest attention to her) and under the house, where he scolds the hardworking youth for his laziness, and where he embraces Julia against the pillars in the darkness.

The puzzle that is Mr. Chandles offers to Francis opportunities for self-analysis. From inquiring as to why he was afraid of Mr. Chandles to pondering how to follow Brinetta's advice to *"take it easy"* (37), Francis devotes many of his leisure hours to introspection. As he seeks to understand the personalities and tensions that surround him, he also begins the process of understanding himself and of applying his newly discovered skills to surviving in his new situation. On the all important issue of the tensions between Mr. Chandles and his mother, for example, he weighs what he knows against what he still does not understand and, heeding Brinetta's advice, wisely decides to hold his judgment: "Although I came to know a lot, I realized there was much I did not know" (38).

Chapter 11 narrates the events leading to March, "the crop-time of the canes" (47). Now in his third month in San Fernando, Francis becomes preoccupied with the world outside the Chandles' home. He continues his occasional chats with Julia, but his attention is caught by the spectacle of the burning canes and the possibility of escaping to play in the school yard next to the house. The hot season takes its toll on Mrs. Chandles's health—a development that Francis interprets as a cyclical reaction to the heat, but which seems to mark the beginning of her decline into the death that marks the end of the novel.

Chapter 12 recalls the unbearable heat of April and the increasing freedom that Mrs. Chandles's ill health offers Francis. Francis's perspective on Mr. Chandles has developed to the point that he divides his perception of contentment between the week, when he is happy in the discharge of his duty, his successes in school, and his developing friendships, and the weekends, when Mr. Chandles was around and time would move "at snail's pace, and it would seem for me a long and dangerous journey to Monday morning" (50–51). The conviction that Mr. Chandles's marriage to Marva is now almost a certainty has only worsened the relationship between mother and son. This contrasts sharply with Francis's description of his own intense longing for his own mother, who was always "in the centre of my mind" and whose vivid memory was enough to bring him "near to tears" (51–52).

Chapters 13–16 cover the four days in April between Holy Thursday and Easter Sunday. Structurally, these chapters, with the two that follow them (chapters 17 and 18), represent the very center of the novel. They cover two events of great thematic importance: Francis's witnessing of the violence and built-up resentment that has poisoned the relationship of the Chandles (the mother and her two sons), and his mother's visit to San Fernando to see him and ascertain whether he is happy and well cared for.

Thematically, the scenes of violence between Mr. Chandles and his mother that Francis witnesses force the latter to rethink the occasional feelings of shame he has experienced at his own poverty and unfamiliarity with the ways of the Chandles and their social class. Feeling that the loud quarrel had made them "a disgrace to Romaine Street" (19), Francis compares their behavior to that of his own family: "And now I thought of our own poverty and of my mother sending me here because she could hardly feed us all. Yet no such row could take place in Ma's house. And we weren't refined or anything. And we had not been to the big college" (55). Mrs. Chandles's withdrawal into her room in anger and distress—forgetting in the process that Francis has not eaten—leaves him feeling abandoned, forsaken, and motherless. In his own distress, he thinks of writing to his mother to tell her that he was starving "and she must come quickly and take [him] away" (57).

Anthony's placement and juxtaposition of these scenes, in what represents in number of chapters and pages the very center of the novel, underscores their importance for understanding the process of growth and maturation experienced by his central character. It posits the values of his family, despite their poverty, as more solid than those of people who had seemed heretofore to represent a higher level of culture and achievement. It is a lesson of the relative value of social position. Emotionally, the character's response to this lesson is to yearn for the comfort and generosity of his own mother. His mother's virtues are enhanced by comparison to Mrs. Chandles, a failed mother to her own children and a questionable mother figure to Francis himself.

Placed between the embarrassing quarrel between the Chandles and the surprise visit Francis receives from his mother, however, is the lengthy description of the events of Easter Sunday, which show Francis that even someone like Mrs. Chandles, who on Holy Thursday seemed almost evil in her violence against her son and her neglect of her responsibilities toward the young boy, can be reborn, can be resurrected as a person of kindness and mirth when in the company of her good friend Mrs. Princet. Francis concludes that "this was an Easter Day beautiful in itself and beautiful because of the strange kindness of Mrs Chandles" (64). He returns to his work that evening "with a joy so new and different that it looked as though the cyder [sic] had really gone to [his] head" (65). Her rebirth in Francis's eyes as the woman capable of thoughtfulness and humanity that she had been on the way to becoming before the fateful quarrel is particularly obvious during his mother's unexpected visit. The mother is received as an equal and treated with kindheartedness and consideration by Mrs. Chandles, a behavior that balances—although it cannot erase—that observed by Francis just days before:

I watched their greeting and their embrace and I was very touched. I was over-joyed that Mrs. Chandles should receive Ma so warmly. Apart from the way she had welcomed Mrs. Princet here, I had never seen her make so much of anyone. (72)

The rebirth ushered in by Easter Sunday, which has such a salutary effect on Mrs. Chandles, includes the land around San Fernando. It coincides with the last of the cane fires and the preparation of the land for the new crop. This provides a way to measure the stages of Francis's experience in San Fernando; he has witnessed a whole planting cycle. "I had seen the planting at the beginning of the year, and then what looked like endless green fields, and lately, the fires every night. And with the fires, the three chimneys of the Usine Ste Madeleine had started puffing smoke. For they were grinding the cane" (79).

The mother's visit, halfway through his sojourn in San Fernando, leaves Francis feeling reassured of his connection to his family and "much more content to stay" (77). It also allows us to see how Francis's stay in San Fernando fits into his mother's plan for her children's future: training as a seamstress for Anna, a job at the St. Joseph factory for Felix, and an educa-tion for Francis. "Stay and take in education, boy," had been her parting words (80). Anchored emotionally by the reassurance of his mother's love, Francis faces the second half of his stay in San Fernando with a greater open-ness to the world around him. His newfound confidence allows him to reach some conclusions about the relationship between Julia and Mr. Chandles, understanding now her vulnerability and the risks of her situation. He felt "he could hurt her badly and send her away," he explains, "and I couldn't stand her being hurt" (87).

Chapters 21–24 focus on the almost giddy camaraderie that develops be-tween Francis and Mrs. Chandles during the rainy season, when the two of them feel semistranded in the house, watching the rain pelting everything outside, with the occasional brilliant rainbow to mark their contentment. This is the period that precedes Mrs. Chandles's physical decay and precipitates the events regarding Mr. Chandles's marriage and the resolution of the conflict over the house. Ironically, this period of calm before the storm is the period of intense rainstorms that turn the streets of San Fernando into streams.

These companionable days of chocolate tea and fry-bakes are marked by Mrs. Chandles's clearest expressions of satisfaction with Francis's work. At one point, Francis remarks, "She had said something I would not easily for-get. She had said I was as good as Brinetta, if not better" (100). It moves him to conclude that the rains, since it had "isolated [them] from everything," had "been making relatives of [them]" (99). The implied affection he has developed toward the old woman, however, also makes him more attentive to her moods and physical condition, and he begins to notice her increased thinness, her lack of tolerance for changes in the weather, concluding that "maybe she was falling away" (100), a metaphor here for her following the path toward death. This period of pleasant companionship comes to an end when Francis is sent to take a note to Mrs. Chandles's younger son Edwin and ventures on to explore the Wharf. It represents his most daring encounter with San Fernando, and it allows him a glimpse of a world far beyond the Trinidadian shores, with its sight of the Venezuelan shores, the ships anchored at bay, and the power of the train as it arrives at the station. His errand, however, is a reminder that there are matters still unsettled in the Chandles household, which Mrs. Chandles's worsening health—and Mr. Chandles's impudence in bringing Marva to the house—will bring to a crisis point.

The last section of the book, especially from chapters 29 to 33, chronicles Mrs. Chandles's fast decline following a serious fall in early December. Her illness provides a long and protracted farewell for Francis, who can leisurely examine the significance of his year in San Fernando and ponder the affection he has developed for his old employer. The novel gives closure to his relationship with Mr. Chandles, with whom Francis develops a sort of truce built in part on Francis's guilt as he realizes that he favors his brother Edwin in what, unbeknownst to Mr. Chandles, has been the transfer of the title to the house to Edwin. Within days of Mr. Chandles's wedding with Marva, after which the couple expects to move to the house on Romaine Street, Francis is told by Edwin of the arrangement and can anticipate Mr. Chandles's ultimate disappointed rage when the news is broken to him. Guilt also plagues Francis for having forgotten to give Mrs. Chandler a dollar sent to her by her son Edwin.

Aided by his leisure once Mrs. Chandles has a nurse to watch over her and there is little for him to do, Francis revisits his old haunts, principally the market, where he has become known and will be missed. This, the beginning of his progress back home, allows Anthony to examine the profound changes that have taken place in Francis's command of his work (his manifest expertise in the market), inclusion in the community (the respect and affection with which he is received in the market), and success in establishing a relationship with Mrs. Chandles (seen in the affection in which he is held by those who have loved her most, Edwin and Mrs. Princet). The detailed description of his journey back parallels that which marked the beginning of the novel and which presented him as naïve, uncertain, and afraid. At the beginning of his journey back home, he is changed, but not in essential values, since his family still occupies his thoughts and heart. He can, however, refuse with certainty and conviction Edwin's invitation to return and live with him in the house, now that it will be his. And he finds himself in a position of being capable of sympathizing with Mr. Chandles, such an aristocratic figure in the opening lines of the book, but who has failed as a person of character, despite the mirage of his social position. Francis, then, returns home in success after his year in San Fernando.

Chapter 3

Alejo Carpentier's

The Kingdom of This World

Alejo Carpentier was born in Lausanne, Switzerland, on December 26, 1904. His father, Jorge Julián Carpentier, was a French architect. His mother, Lina Valmont, of Russian origin, was a professor of languages. Shortly after Carpentier's birth, his parents moved to Havana. As a result, he is widely believed to have been born in Cuba. He spent his childhood on a farm in the outskirts of Havana.

Carpentier lived in Paris during part of his adolescence, where he studied musical theory at the Lycée Jeanson de Sailly before returning to Cuba to complete his secondary education at the Instituto de Segunda Enseñanza. He began his university training at the University of Havana as a student of architecture, but never completed his degree, choosing instead to continue his musical education, a training that would lead to a well-deserved reputation as Cuba's most distinguished twentieth-century musicologist.

Carpentier first made his mark as a writer in 1922, when he embarked on a distinguished career as a journalist, writing for the newspaper *La Discusión*. By 1923, not yet 20, Carpentier had joined the Cuban left, a connection that would lead to his becoming one of the founders of the Cuban Communist Party. In 1923 he had joined a movement of young writers and artists, Los Minoristas, that had protested the Cuban government's fiscal mismanagement.

Carpentier's growing political involvement led to his arrest in 1927 for his opposition to Gerardo Machado's dictatorship. He spent 40 days in jail, during which he started writing his first novel, *Ecué-Yamba-O* (1933), in which he explores the Cuban peasantry's African-derived Santería beliefs. Released in early 1928, he fled Cuba using the passport and identification papers of French journalist and surrealist poet Robert Desnos, who was responsible for introducing Carpentier to European surrealists.

Carpentier's sojourn in France between the two world wars—where he was to spend eight years—had a major impact on his political and literary work. His contact with the surrealist artists to whom he was introduced by Desnos as well as with Spanish and Latin American artists and intellectuals fleeing growing persecution at home led to his interpretation of Caribbean reality as one of magic realism, a notion he would deploy in his early novels, particularly in *The Kingdom of This World* (1949). During frequent visits to Spain, he developed a profound fascination with the Spanish baroque, from which emerged the unique writing style that characterizes his best fiction. He supported himself as a journalist.

Carpentier returned to Cuba at the outbreak of World War II to resume his journalistic career on Cuban radio and begin research on his multivolume work on Cuban music, *La música en Cuba* (1945). He also began working on the short stories that would be collected in *La Guerra del Tiempo* (The War of Time), published in 1958.

In 1943 Carpentier and his wife, Lilia Estéban, traveled to Haiti with a troupe of French actors led by Louis Jouvet. Interested as he was in the Creole religiosities of the Caribbean region, Carpentier was quick to understand the connection between the Haitian Revolution and Vodou practices, which were the very opposite of Cartesian thought:

At the end of 1943 I had the good fortune to visit the...poetic ruins of Sans Souci; the imposing bulk of the Citadel of La Ferrière, intact in spite of thunderbolts and earthquakes—and to discover Cap Haitien, which remains Norman to this day...where a street of very long balconies leads to the stone palace once occupied by Pauline Bonaparte. Having felt the unquestionable charm of the Haitian landscape, having found magical portents in the red roads of the Central Plateau, and heard the drums of the Petro and Rada Voodoo gods, I was moved to compare the marvelous reality I had recently experienced with that exhausting attempt to invoke the marvelous which has characterized certain European literatures of the last thirty years. (Carpentier, *El reino* 14)

The connection between history and a faith deeply linked to magic he found in Haiti inspired Carpentier to write a historical novel that would be grounded on the non-Western, African-derived mythologies and rituals that remained vital elements in the cultures and practices of the New World.

In 1945, for reasons related to his political ideas and support of the anti-Batista movement that would culminate in the Cuban Revolution, Carpentier moved to Caracas, Venezuela, where he lived until 1959 and where he wrote a column on literature and music for the newspaper *El Nacional* until 1961. The deeply forested interior of Venezuela served as the setting for *The Lost Steps,* his well-received novel about a Western musicologist's confrontation with the culture and worldview of an indigenous group uncontaminated by contact with the West. Published in 1953, it won a number of prestigious prizes in Latin America and Europe and is considered by many to be his masterpiece. His novella *El acoso (The Chase)*, published in 1956, linked his interests in fiction and music through its conceit of having been written to be read to the exact measures of Beethoven Symphony no. 3, the *Eroica* Symphony.

Carpentier returned to Cuba in 1959 as a gesture of support for the Cuban Revolution. From 1966 to his death from cancer on April 24, 1980, he lived in Paris as Cuban ambassador to France. His years in France were years of great productivity and recognition, during which he became one of the most widely read and translated of the authors of the Latin American literary *Boom*. His 1962 novel, *El siglo de las luces (Explosion in the Cathedral)*, which examines the impact of the Enlightenment and the French Revolution on the intellectual and political life of the Caribbean, was published to international acclaim. To these were added collections of essays like *Tientos y diferencias*, and several novels, among them his meditation on dictatorship and reason (*El recurso del método [Reasons of State]*, 1974), his historical novel about the efforts to canonize Christopher Columbus titled *El arpa y la sombra (The Harp and the Shadow)*, and *Concierto barroco* (1974). He was awarded an honorary doctorate by the University of Havana in 1975 and earned a number of prizes, among them the Cino del Duca Prize (Italy), the Miguel de Cervantes Prize (Spain), the Medici Prize (France), and the title of Honorary Fellow at the University of Kansas. Carpentier's last novel, *La consagración de la primavera*, based on Stravinsky's "Le Sacré du printemps," appeared shortly before his death in 1979.

The Kingdom of This World

More than half a century after its publication in 1949, Alejo Carpentier's *The Kingdom of This World* remains the only sustained account of the Haitian Revolution in Spanish-Caribbean literature. Known as well for its fictional treatment of Haitian history from a slave's perspective as for the preface that claimed for that history the distinction of epitomizing marvelous realism in the Americas, the novel is committed to narrating one of the salient foundational narratives of Caribbean history.

In his preface to the novel, Carpentier outlines his meticulous research in preparation for the novel:

For it must be remembered that the story about to be read is based on extremely rigorous documentation. A documentation that not only respects the truth of events, the names of characters—including minor ones—of places and streets, but that also conceals, beneath its apparent atemporality, a minute correspondence of dates and chronology. (*El reino* 16)

The events narrated in the novel are indeed familiar to those acquainted with Haitian history: the campaign of poison against the planters unleashed by Makandal the slave in 1757, his execution in 1758, the uprising initiated by Bouckman in Bois Caïman in 1791, the flight of the French planters to Santiago de Cuba, Napoleon Bonaparte's attempt to regain the colony of St. Domingue (1801–1804), Pauline Bonaparte's own peculiar career as an ersatz Creole (1801–1802), Rochambeau's campaign of terror (1803), the defeat of the French at the hands of Dessalines (1803), the troubled reign of King Christophe (1807–1820), and the impact of Haitian president Jean-Pierre Boyer's *Code Rural* (1826), which restored slaverylike conditions for the Haitian peasantry. The characters that people the tale—even less central ones like Pére Labat, Moreau de Saint-Méry, Corneille Breille, Esteban Salas, and the Duchess of Abrantès—have their counterpart in historical documents, or had themselves produced contemporary texts that have become primary historical sources. Even Monsieur Lenormand de Mézy, Carpentier's archetypal planter, lived as a rich landowner in the Limbé region of northern Haiti, where he owned the plantation where Makandal's 1757 rebellion began.

The novel follows the events of the revolution chronologically through the eyes of a slave, Ti-Noël. Part 1 (seven chapters) moves from the introduction of Ti-Noël and his master, the planter Lenormand de Mézy, to the execution of Makandal in 1758. Part 2 (seven chapters) covers from the solemn pact at Bois Caïman that begins the revolution in 1791 to Rochambeau's campaign of terror after the death of General Leclerc in 1802 and Pauline Bonaparte's return to France. The centerpiece of these chapters is Pauline Bonaparte's mimicry of a Creole. Part 3 (seven chapters) opens with Ti-Noël's return to Haiti during the last months of Henri Christophe's reign and follows him to his glimpse of Sans Souci as a symbol of the passing of power into black hands. It narrates how he is forced into labor to build Christophe's Citadelle and ends with the king's suicide and burial in the wet cement of the fortress.

Part 4 (four chapters) opens in Rome, where Soliman (Pauline Bonaparte's former masseur) discovers Canova's sculpture of the then Princess Borghese and is driven into a despairing nostalgia for Haiti. His madness is echoed by Ti-Noël's own, as he finds himself living in the ruins of Lenormand de Mézy's plantation, imagining himself king, until the land surveyors sent under the Rural Code of 1826 arrive to dispossess him of his land and home. He, like Makandal before him, metamorphoses himself into an animal and slips into death, not before learning that the meaning of his toil in the kingdom of this world is that of understanding that action (revolution, in the case of Haiti) is the most appropriate response to the human predicament.

Ti-Noël serves in the text as Carpentier's privileged witness to Haitian history. As a slave, Ti-Noël's perspective is that of the folk whose culture and faith Carpentier seeks to support in the text. Ti-Noël is a believer in the

African gods, or *lwa,* and works alongside Makandal, both on Lenormand de Mézy's plantation and in his subversive campaign. He was present at the ceremony at Bois Caïman and was later forced into labor in the construction of Henri Christophe's Citadelle. Carpentier's Ti-Noël, however, is no Maroon, but a slave who—despite his share of active participation in the revolution—never sheds his oppression throughout the text. Through his gaze, Carpentier seeks to show the progress of history as a series of cycles that take his character from exploitation to freedom and back to exploitation so he can begin the cycle yet again. He lives past the early months of the revolution only because he is saved from execution by his master, and lived through the struggle for independence in Santiago de Cuba, only free to return to Haiti after the revolution has consolidated its power. He remains in the periphery of history.

Part 1 opens with an epigraph from Félix Lope de Vega y Carpio's *Famous Comedy of the New World Discovered by Christopher Columbus* (1600). In this comedy, Lope de Vega (1562–1635)—a Spanish playwright of legendary literary output, believed to have written about 2,000 full-length plays—addresses the contemporary debate over Columbus's discovery of the New World through the exploration of the profound and primarily negative impact of the discovery on balances of power, sex, faith, and nationality.

Chapter 1, "The Wax Heads," introduces Ti-Noël and Lenormand de Mézy amid reminders of the revolution brewing in France. These reminders—from the barber's subscription to the *Leyden Gazette* (a French-language journal of radical political commentary) to a display of wax heads reminiscent of the bewigged heads that will soon fall in France—set up a narrative technique that works contrapuntally. Like musical counterpoint, Carpentier establishes a relationship between voices and worldviews, which although independent in their understanding of history and approach to philosophical and spiritual matters, are nonetheless intertwined through colonialism and the plantation. Counterpoint is a dominant aspect of baroque music.

The first chapter of *The Kingdom of This World* deploys this point-counterpoint from the opening pages. The juxtaposition of the calves' heads at the tripe shop and the four bewigged wax heads introduces the dual perspective that will show how the summary of recent historical events in France (narrated through the brief description of the prints for sale at the booksellers) are countered by the alternative view of history offered by Makandal, stories of the great African kingdoms of Popo, Arada, Nagos, or the Fulah. The kings of Europe sent their generals to fight in their stead and produced "some puling prince who could not bring down a deer without the help of stalkers," whereas African princes were leopards who "knew the language of the forest" (*Kingdom* 15). In the context of two revolutions about to take place, Carpentier's contrapuntal techniques announce the coming victory of the descendants of African kings. Carpentier finishes the chapter by writing overtly of this counterpoint, as the music that serves as a background to their

voyage out of the city—from his master's fife march to Ti-Noël's antiroyal
chanty—encapsulates the various political positions and conflicts of interest
that characterize a plantation society. Ti-Noël will return to the song, ironically, toward the end of the novel, when he sings it to express his dismay at
the return of forced labor under king Henri Christophe.

Chapter 2, "The Amputation," introduces the legendary Makandal, an am-
putee and leader of the first stage of the Haitian insurrection. François Mac-
kandal (Franswe Makandal in Creole) was a slave brought to St. Domingue
(as the French colony was then known) from West Africa. Brought to the Lenormand plantation in north Haiti, near the city of Cap Français (now Cap
Haitïen), he became the leader of a Maroon community and was reported to
be a powerful *oungan*, or Vodou priest. His plan to start a broad-based rebellion by carrying out a mass poisoning of whites was betrayed by a slave, and
he was captured and burned at the stake on January 20, 1758. Carpentier
builds part 1 of his novel on the persistent legend that Makandal, as one of
Haiti's earliest and most powerful *oungan*, drew his knowledge of poisons
from an ability to communicate freely with the African *lwa* and had gained
the power to transform himself at will into all sorts of animals, a power that
allowed him to escape the flames in which he was to burn, so that his spirit
could roam through Haiti and sustain its people.

Chapter 3, "What the Hand Found," shows Makandal in his role of
oungan, which is primarily that of skilled herbalist. Through Ti-Noël's apprenticeship as an herbalist in the Haitian forest, Carpentier depicts the links
between the knowledge of the power of herbs he and Makandal collect and
the African spirits who guide them in their use. The character of Maman Loi
(pronounced "lwa" and standing for both the French word for "law" and
the African spirits, or *lwa*), although constructed as a stereotypical version
of a medieval witch, translates between the spirits and the slaves who need
to learn the secrets of the plants as the means toward freedom. Carpentier's
sensationalistic portrayal of Maman Loi as a witch hints at the possibility that
despite his best intentions, he remains dependent on problematic representa-
tions of Haiti as a land of exotic, African otherness, as her practices (such as
putting her hands in a pot of boiling oil) are not necessarily characteristic of
Vodou practitioners.

In *The Kingdom of this World*, Makandal is portrayed as an *oungan* of the
Rada rite, the Lord of Poison, "invested with superhuman powers as the result
of his possession by the major gods" (*Kingdom* 36). As the embodiment
of the power of faith in the African *lwa*, he is the perfect character for
the representation of the link between the life of the spirit and history
Carpentier envisages in the novel. Endowed with "the supreme authority by
the Rulers of the Other Shore" (*Kingdom* 36), he had been chosen to exter-
minate the whites and create a great empire of free blacks in St. Domingue.
The results of his campaign of extermination are narrated in chapter 5, "De
Profundis," which concludes with the betrayal of Makandal.

Makandal emerges from Carpentier's text as the true heir of Loco and Osain (the first *oungan* and *manbo* priests of Vodou), having mastered the herbs and fungi of the forest—"the secret life of strange species given to disguise, confusion, and camouflage, protectors of the little armored beings that avoid the pathways of the ants" (*Kingdom* 23)—which become weapons in his struggle against the planters' power and terror during the so-called great fear of 1757, which led to the death of more than 6,000 people. In this portrayal, knowledge of the powers hidden in nature is bestowed on him as a sign of his blessing by the gods of Africa, who have followed those who serve them across the waters to a new land. For Ti-Noël, he serves as the vital link with the ancestral gods and with African history.

In chapter 4, "The Reckoning," Carpentier presents a gathering of Makandal's supporters in a guano-covered cave full of the paraphernalia of Vodou practices, albeit highly sensationalized. As in his characterization of Maman Loi, Carpentier shows that despite his commitment to an alternative depiction of Haitian history that emphasizes the people's enduring faith in Vodou and the *lwa,* he is not unwilling to fetishize aspects of that faith in his text in his quest for the magic-realist unveiling of that history required by the new literature he envisioned.

Carpentier's approach to Haitian history had been influenced by Jean Price-Mars's seminal text *Ainsi parla l'oncle* (1928). Price-Mars had been one of the founders of Les Griots, Haitian intellectuals who aimed to recover the African sources of Haitian culture. Their task was predicated on the validation of the Creole language and of the practices of Vodou, crucial steps in the vindication of a revolution that had made independence possible without substantially changing the social and economic systems. In *Ainsi parla l'oncle,* Price-Mars presents two fundamental arguments that Carpentier will incorporate into his historical approach in *The Kingdom of This World.* First and foremost is the notion that from the perspective of the Haitian peasant, the revolution simply replaced the French planters with political leaders who assumed the former rulers' wealth and privileges, continuing the established colonial pattern of exploitation of the Haitian worker—a perception that fitted well into Carpentier's concept of history as a cyclical repetition of a pattern of oppression, revolution, and renewed oppression. Second, Price-Mars posits the authenticity of the people's communion with the African gods (or *lwa*) and the *lwa*'s function in sustaining the peasantry through a history of deprivation and turmoil.

If Price-Mars offered a conceptual framework for the links between religion and history, Carpentier found an equally compelling vision—albeit a decidedly sensationalistic one—in William Seabrook's *The Magic Island* (1929). Seabrook's best-selling book was one of many such texts written during the American occupation of Haiti (1915–1934)—John Huston Craige's *Black Bagdad* (1933) and *Cannibal Cousins* (1934) and Richard Loederer's *Voodoo Fire in Haiti* (1935), among them—whose unstated aim was that of justifying the U.S. Marine presence in a savage land in need of a firm civilizing hand. Carpentier had reviewed the book for the journal *Carteles* (1931), calling it "one of the most beautiful books written in recent years" (46). The book was controversial because of its lurid tales of necromancy, blood sucking by *soucouyants*, and zombification.

Chapter 4, "The Metamorphoses," narrates the search for Makandal through dual perspectives: that of the soldiers engaged in the somewhat dispirited search, and that of the slaves who believe that Makandal is undergoing a cycle of metamorphoses to evade capture and will return to his human form when the time is ripe for revolt. The soldiers, lazy and imbued with the indolent sensuality that Carpentier portrays as characteristic of the tropics, fill their hours with tales of the island's history of piracy, whose most glorious moment was the sack of Cartagena de las Indias, Colombia (1697). The fortified city was attacked by a great force of pirates and privateers led by French privateer Bernard Desjean, Baron de Pointis. The Spanish defenses, not ready for an attack on such a scale, quickly surrendered, and the French looted the city, accumulating the largest loot in the history of Caribbean piracy.

The soldiers celebrate in their talks the history of the great pirates and privateers that founded the colony of St. Domingue or were responsible for daring attacks on the Spanish fleet carrying the gold and silver of America to Spain, such as Pierre Belain d'Esnambuc (1585–1636), a privateer who founder the colony of Martinique; Piet Pieterszoon Hein (1577–1629), the Dutch privateer famous for having deprived the Spanish fleet of the largest treasure in history; Bertrand D'Ogeron (1665–1675), first governor of St. Domingue, who administered a population composed mainly of buccaneers and filibusters; and Jérémie Deschamps du Rausset, first lieutenant governor of the Île de la Tortue, north of Haiti. They trade stories of elusive dancing negroes, of *oungans*, and of zombies who "tilled the land as long as they were kept from tasting salt" (*Kingdom* 41). The slaves, in their turn, watch a variety of the tropical fauna for signs of Makandal's presence and work with a zeal inspired by the hopes of freedom fostered by his example. Carpentier underscores here Makandal's legendary role in keeping alive the slaves' dreams of a freedom that will be attained through his connection to the *lwa*: "One day he would give the sign for the great uprising, and the Lords of Back There, headed by Damballah, the Master of the Roads, and Ogoun, Master of the Swords, would bring the thunder and lightning and unleash the cyclone that would round out the work of men's hands" (*Kingdom* 42). When Makandal completes his cycle of metamorphoses and returns to a human form, as he does in chapter 7, "Human Guise," he appears, significantly, during a Vodou ceremony, in which the slaves intone a *yenvaló*, or dance of supplication, an entreaty to the *lwa* to come to the aid of their people. The *yenvaló* dance is normally accompanied by the sacred Rada drums and the *ogan*, or irons. The chapter offers the reader the first mention of the prerevolutionary Toussaint L'Ouverture, here seen as a cabinetmaker carving images of the Three Wise Kings for a holiday crèche.

In chapter 8, "The Great Flight," which offers a description of Makandal's execution, Carpentier returns to the counterpoint technique he has used before in the novel to show how an event can have different meanings and interpretations to two different groups of people. The narrator's description follows the events in vivid realistic detail, while the slaves' response—which stems from their belief in Makandal's powers of transformation—denies the reality of what they have witnessed and imposes an alternative truth on the events observed. From the slaves' perspective, "once more the whites [had] been outwitted by the Mighty Powers of the Other Shore" (*Kingdom* 52). The counterpoint reminds us, however, that even in his depiction of Makandal's execution, which is intended to signal the extraordinary power of the slaves to maintain their faith, Carpentier still inscribes the scene with their otherness. After all, the slaves may be deluded by faith into believing Makandal has survived. The planters and soldiers of the text—and most important, Carpentier and his readers—*know* he has not.

Part 2 opens with a quotation from Laura Junot, Duchesse d'Abrantès (1784–1838), a member of the Napoleonic court famous for her best-selling memoirs, in which she describes her conversations with Pauline Bonaparte before the latter leaves France for Haiti. Pauline's husband, General Charles Leclerc, was to assume control of the forces sent to restore French control over the new republic. The section, which opens on the eve of the beginning of the Haitian Revolution in 1791, closes with Pauline Bonaparte's return to France, after Napoleon's venture to regain France's most profitable colony is defeated by Haiti's untrained armies and an epidemic of yellow fever.

In chapter 1, "The Daughter of Minos and Pasiphaë," Carpentier again counterpoints two visions of what constitutes reality to underscore the differences in the way masters and slaves perceive and understand the reality around them. The chapter opens with a brief discussion of how the city of Cap Français had developed in the years between the death of Makandal in 1758 and the eve of the revolution, a timing underscored by the reference to the *Gazette de Saint-Domingue,* which had begun publication in 1764. The city's prosperity had fostered the growing fame of the Auberge de la Couronne, an inn owned by its former master chef, Henri Christophe, soon to find himself crowned king of a new nation. Life in the Cap is characterized by indulgence and licentiousness among the planters, exemplified by Lenormand de Mézy's erotomania and sexual abuse of adolescent slave girls and his wife's abuse of her servants, whom she had "whipped on the slightest pretense" (*Kingdom* 60).

The title of the chapter, "The Daughter of Minos and Pasiphaë," refers to M. Lenormand de Mézy's new wife, a "graceless" and untalented actress fond of performing scenes from Jean Racine's *Phèdre* (1677; the excerpts quoted in the text are from Act 4). Phèdre was the daughter of King Minos II of Crete and his wife, Pasiphaë, daughter of Helios, the Sun, and the eldest of the Oceanids, Perse. Married to Theseus, the legendary king of Athens, she falls in love with her stepson Hippolyte, to whom she makes an involuntary confession when she believes Theseus to have died. On Theseus's return, and to protect Phèdre from Hippolyte, who had been horrified by her confession, Phèdre's maid accuses the young man of attempted rape. Theseus curses his son, who goes on to his death in combat with a sea monster, and Phèdre, in her despair, confesses her guilt to Theseus and poisons herself.

As in the preceding chapter, where Carpentier juxtaposed a description of the reality of the execution against the slaves' response to the events, here he presents the slaves again as an audience unaware of the performance aspects of what they are watching and responding to her drunken rendition of Racine's "bravura passages" performance as if witnessing a confession. While the reader is amused at the naïveté, their literal understanding of their mistress's "sins" appears logical given their experience of a white population that lives in licentiousness, adultery, and violence of the worst kind. Racine's dramatic passages, in turn, are contrasted by the "simple little songs [Ti-Noël] had made up in Macandal's honor while currying and brushing the horses" (*Kingdom* 63).

In chapter 2, "The Solemn Pact," Carpentier narrates the legendary Vodou ceremony believed to have taken place at Bois Caïman, a forest in the northern Morne Rouge region, southwest of Cap Français (now Cap Haïtien), on August 14, 1791. The ceremony, presided over by slave leaders Boukman Dutty and Cecile Fatiman, is widely accepted as marking the start of the Haitian Revolution. Present had been some of the early leaders of the revolt, like Georges Biassou, Jeannot Bullet, and Jean-François Papillon. To these Carpentier adds Ti-Noël, present there as the representative from his plantation.

In the novel, as historical records claim, the ceremony is presided by Boukman, a Maroon from Morne Rouge who had come to Haiti by way of Jamaica. A fierce-looking and powerful man, with "'a terrible countenance,' a face like an exaggerated African carving" (Parkinson 39), he was captured and beheaded in the early months of the revolution. Traditional accounts of the ceremony include an address from Boukman to the assembled slaves claiming the aid and support of the *lwa*. Carpentier renders Boukman's words as a reminder that the African gods "demand vengeance from us" and "will guide our arms and give us help" (*Kingdom* 67).

Carpentier underscores the religious elements of the meeting, over which Cecile Fatiman presided as a Vodou priestess. Fatiman was the wife of Louis Michel Pierrot, one of the victorious leaders of the Battle of Vertières of November 18, 1803, the defining campaign of the revolution, in which the Haitians, led by Jean-Jacques Dessalines and Alexandre Pétion, defeated the French troops under General Rochambeau. She died at Cap Haitïen at the age of 112.

The ceremony over which Fatiman presided in the text was dedicated to the *lwa* Ogoun, who presides over fire, iron, politics, and war in the Yoruba mythology. The patron saints of warriors and smiths, his attributes are the cutlass or machete, and his favorite offerings are rum and tobacco. Ogoun is credited with giving the St. Domingue slaves the inspiration for the revolt and with having sustained them through the campaign to defeat the planters and, later, the Napoleonic forces. Fatiman's invocations to Ogoun, as rendered by Carpentier, address the multiple avatars or manifestations of the *lwa* and precede a sacrifice of a black pig to the *lwa*.

In Carpentier's account, the responsibility for drafting a proclamation—given the slaves' illiteracy—fell to the priest of the town of Dondon, the Abbé de la Haye, described in the text as having given unequivocal support to the slaves since he had read the Declaration of the Rights of Man. An admirer of Voltaire (François-Marie Arouet, 1694–1778) and his ideas about civil liberties and citizens' rights, the abbé was a friend and confessor to Jean-François and Biassou, slaves who had been present at the Bois Caïman ceremony and, in 1803, was drowned in the Cap Français harbor under orders from General Rochambeau.

The immediate impact of the Bois Caïman ceremony is described in chapter 3, "The Call of the Conch Shells," with the sudden beginning of the attack on the plantations in response to the reverberating calls of conch shell trumpets echoing across the plains. Carpentier establishes the timing of the attack by having Lenormand de Mézy reminisce on the folly of the Constituent Assembly's vote in May 1791 to grant political rights to the sons of manumitted slaves. As representative of the planters' perspective, Lenormand de Mézy describes—through a description of a series of prints by artists such as Abraham Brunias (1730–1796), as he had already done in the first chapter—the ideological gap existing between the "Utopian imbeciles in Paris whose hearts bled for the black slaves" (*Kingdom* 71) and the planters whose lives and property were threatened by imminent revolt.

Carpentier's description of the initial days of the revolt focuses on the former slaves' undisciplined, drunken rampage through the plantations and their great houses. Ti-Noël's rape of Mlle Floridor is emblematic of this violence and may appear to be gratuitous. Carpentier, however, uses the episode as the means to close a thematic and formal cycle in the novel. The incident is described as stemming from Mlle Floridor's "nights of tragic declamations," which had shown that her breasts were "undamaged by the irreversible outrage of the years" (*Kingdom* 74) and thus is presented as emblematic of the gap in understanding between slaves and their masters. It is also balanced by the allusion in the early paragraphs of the chapter to Lenormand de Mézy's strolling out to the tobacco shed in the hope of finding and raping "one of the girls who had slipped in at this hour to steal some leaves for their fathers to chew" (*Kingdom* 72).

The "Dagon inside the Ark," who gives its title to chapter 4, is a Philistine deity whose name is a diminutive of the Semitic root *dag,* and means, accordingly, "little fish." It is thought to refer to a fish-shaped god popular in maritime cities or to the god of agriculture. Carpentier here refers to a story linking Dagon with the Ark of the Covenant, which was meant to contain the tables of the Law (Exodus 40:18; Deuteronomy 10:5). The story claims that the Ark had fallen into the hands of the Philistines (1 Samuel 4) and was set as a trophy in the temple of Dagon. The next morning, the statue of Dagon was found lying on its face in front of the Ark; on the second morning, Dagon was found again lying on the floor before the Ark, but with hands and feet mutilated. An epidemic of bubonic plague followed these events, a scourge that was attributed to the presence of the Ark in the city and that forced its return.

Carpentier's allusion to Dagon and the Ark comes from a reading of Père Jean-Baptiste Labat's *Nouveau Voyage aux isles Françaises de l'Amérique (New Voyage to the French Islands of America)* (1722). Labat (1663–1738) was a Dominican priest who made a career in the West Indies as a botanist, writer, explorer, and ethnographer. In his *New Voyage,* he discusses the religious creolization brought about by colonization: "The Negroes do without scruple what the Philistines attempted; they associate the ark with Dagon and secretly preserve all their old idolatrous worship with the ceremonies of the Christian religion" (94). This creolization, which led to the interweaving of Catholic and African-derived practices to produce the religion we know as Vodou, had been described in some detail by Mederic Louis Elie Moreau de Saint-Mery (1750–1819), author of (among other titles) the *Description topographique, physique, civile, politique et historique de la partie française de Saint-Domingue* (1796).

In this chapter, Carpentier follows Lenormand de Mézy after he survives the massacre of whites at his plantation and seeks to come to terms with the devastation of an entire way of life. Afraid and bewildered, he uses the respite provided by a temporary defeat of the slaves—during which Boukman is executed, and he succeeds in saving Ti-Noël and others among his slaves from a similar fate—to take the reader on a stroll through Cap Français after the first wave of the growing revolt. A meeting with the French governor, his office adorned with images of Louis XVI, Marie-Antoinette, and the Dauphin (they would die in 1793), reminds us of the planters' profoundly royalist stance. The closing of the Auberge de la Couronne forces him into wistful nostalgia for the pleasures of food, while also reminding the reader that the apparent defeat of the rebellion only marks the calm before the storm.

As with Ti-Noël's rape of Mlle Floridor, sexual assault becomes the true marker of the profound changes in who holds power in the colony. Anarchy and ruin are signaled by the radical change in who possesses the power of sexual assault. "The Negroes had violated nearly all the well-born girls of the Plaine," Carpentier writes. "After ripping away so much lace, after rolling among so many linen sheets and cutting the throats of so many overseers, they could no longer be held down" (*Kingdom* 78).

Lenormand de Mézy's departure for Santiago de Cuba with Ti-Noël turns our perspective away from events in Cap Français and to the French émigré community in Santiago de Cuba, gathered around the Tívoli Café. Chapter 5 quickly narrates the impact of the French émigrés on this quiet city, which blossomed under the influence of the rich and rather decadent newcomers. It was in Tívoli that the French *quadrille* evolved into the world famous Cuban *danzón*. Their coffee plantations became a major economic resource for the whole area. The Tívoli Quarter, with its gracious hotels, famous schools, luxury shops, and cafés, remains one of the most elegant of Santiago.

Lenormand, ruined by the loss of his plantations in Haiti, gives himself to a life of dissipation, while Ti-Noël discovers the close correlation between Cuban Catholicism and the Vodou practices of St. Domingue. This correlation is most clear through the city's veneration of its patron, Santiago or the Apostle James, syncretized in Vodou and Cuban Santería with Ogoun, the tutelary *lwa* of the rebelling slaves. Santiago has a special place in African-derived devotions through his association with the Christianization of the central African kingdom of Kongo by Portuguese sailors in the late fifteenth century. Kongolese slaves carried their devotions to the Caribbean (particularly to Haiti, Cuba, and Puerto Rico), where it merged with the worship of Santiago, associated with the pilgrimage to Santiago de Compostela in northern Spain.

In Santiago de Cuba, Ti-Noël also encounters the religious music of Esteban Salas y Castro (1725–1803), Latin America's most important composer of late baroque vocal music. Salas, the musical director of the Cathedral of Santiago, became widely known in the 1940s following the rediscovery of many of his scores by Carpentier himself. Music fills this chapter, as there are allusions to a number of composers and musical styles such as the sonatas of Johann Friedrich Edelmann (1749–1794), who would be guillotined within a few years of the events narrated in the text. A matron signs "Sous ses lois l'Amour veut qu'on jouisse" from *Acis et Galatée* (1686) by baroque composer Jean-Baptiste Lully (1632–1687). Lenormand, when drunk, breaks into renditions of the "Hymne de St. Louis" (1747) by French composer Louis-Nicolas Clérambault (1676–1749), uncontested master of the French cantata, and the "Marseillaise," by Claude Joseph Rouget de Lisle (1760–1836). Composed as the "Chant de guerre de l'Armée du Rhin" in 1792, it became the rallying cry of the French Revolution and later the French national anthem. Carpentier, however, privileges Ti-Noël's song to Ogoun, which he had learned from Makandal, which calls to Santiago to aid in the war he has left behind.

Chapters 6 and 7, "The Ship of Dogs" and "Saint Calamity," move forward in time to 1802, when Pauline Bonaparte (1780–1825) arrives with her husband, General Charles Victor Emmanuel Leclerc (1772–1802), who has been given the task of defeating the Haitian armies and restoring French power and slavery to St. Domingue. Leclerc arrived in St. Domingue with about 40,000 troops and became infamous for tricking Toussaint L'Ouverture into captivity and exile to the Jura Mountains, where he would die in 1803. His treachery is considered to have turned the tide against him, and within months, his army, decimated by an epidemic of yellow fever, came near complete defeat. Leclerc himself succumbed to the epidemic in 1802 and was replaced by General Donatien Marie Joseph de Vimeur, Vicomte de Rochambeau, the most brutal of French commanders, whose defeat on November 18, 1803, at the Battle of Vertières effectively gave the victory to the rebel armies. Jean-Jacques Dessalines would proclaim the independence of Haiti on January 1, 1804.

Despite Dessalines's negligible presence in *The Kingdom of This World*— and particularly his absence from those segments of the text that chronicle Rochambeau's viciousness—readers of Carpentier's novels with even a cursory knowledge of the history of the revolution must continually strive to reinsert him into the text. Dessalines (1758–1806), Toussaint L'Ouverture's principal lieutenant, became the revolution's leader after the betrayal and capture of Toussaint. After his triumph at Vertières, he became Haiti's first ruler under the 1801 constitution. He was assassinated in 1806. Dessalines became infamous for his brutal tactics against his enemies.

The vacuum left by Dessalines—those very pages of the novel on which one would naturally have expected to find the narrative of his military feats— is filled, somewhat paradoxically, by Pauline Bonaparte. Early chroniclers of the Haitian Revolution seem as fascinated by Pauline Bonaparte's peculiar sojourn in St. Domingue as contemporary authors. Madiou commemorates her in an ode to beauty "reminiscent of Burke's apotheosis of Marie Antoinette, but moved to the tropics, where 'murderous climate, the sadness of our country, the somber and monotonous aspect of our mountains' makes her languorous and takes the rosiness from her cheeks, leaving only a melancholy face girt by a bandeau ornamented with jewels" (Dayan 168). In Carpentier's version, Pauline is childlike and almost fey in her lascivious excess. She arrives in Haiti determined to live a fantasy of queenly splendor culled from readings of Jacques-Henri Bernardin de Saint-Pierre's sentimental novel *Paul et Virginie* (1787), Joseph Lavallée's abolitionist text *Le Nègre comme il y a peu de Blancs* (1789), and Alexander Olivier Esquemelin's *Buccaneers of America* (1684), ready to surrender to the languorous sensuality of a debauched land, enjoying affairs with handsome young officers, displaying her naked body as a temptation to those who could not possess her, and delighting in the massages of Soliman, a former attendant at a bathhouse who "rubbed her with almond cream, depilated her, and polished her toenails"

(*Kingdom* 94–95). Once again, here Carpentier draws from the historical record, which speaks of Pauline's life in Haiti amid orgies, bacchanals, and what Jacques Marquet de Norvins, Leclerc's secretary, described as "indefatigable Corybantes" performed for Pauline at her estate at Isle de la Tortue (see Dayan 247). Terrorized by the plague that eventually kills her husband, she surrenders herself to the protection afforded by her masseur's faith and furtive rituals, which "stirred up in her the lees of old Corsican blood, which was more akin to the living cosmogony of the Negro than to the lies of the Directory, in whose disbelief she had grown up" (*Kingdom* 99).

Critics have found Pauline's function in Carpentier's text most intriguing, as the following sampling of critical perspectives indicates. Emma Susana Speratti-Piñero finds that Pauline became for Carpentier the connecting thread to give cohesion to the feminine collage that personifies the immorality of the colony of the time, which had become the center of a legend of depravity created and accentuated by the slander characteristic of the times (580). Alexis Márquez Rodríguez identifies in Pauline a technical resource to attenuate the temporal historical bent of the narrative. She argues that the inclusion of Pauline fits very well within the atmosphere of the marvelous thanks to what there is of strange and magical in Pauline's life (49). Donald Shaw finds that "Pauline's frivolity, sensuality, luxury, and cowardice when the plague strikes, followed by her renewed self-indulgence while escorting her husband's body . . . caps Carpentier's presentation of white decadence in contrast to the virility and vitality of the blacks" (30). Emir Rodríguez Monegal finds that Pauline articulates Carpentier's political position, in as much as her character represents historical marginality in the fictionalized world. For Santos Torres-Rosado, Pauline's sexuality allows Carpentier to establish a dialogue about natural, spontaneous sensuality and the wantonness that takes control of women when they become free of social mores that repress such instincts.

To Pauline's wantonness Carpentier adds a travesty of faith, a "mockery of piety" that signals her despairing embrace of "the world of the powers called up by the spells of Soliman" when the plague threatens and Leclerc surrenders to an agonizing death:

One morning the horrified French maids came upon the Negro circling in a strange dance around Pauline, who was kneeling on the floor with her hair hanging loose. Soliman, wearing only a belt from which a white handkerchief hung as a *cache-sexe,* his neck adorned with blue and red beads, was hopping around like a bird and brandishing a machete. Both were uttering deep groans which, as though wrenched from inside, sounded like the baying of dogs when the moon is full. A decapitated rooster was still fluttering amid scattered grains of corn. (*Kingdom* 99–100)

This caricaturesque metamorphosis of Pauline into a Vodou *serviteur* is indeed more significant than her surrender to indolence and sensuality in the tropics. Inspired by terror and not by faith, it speaks of the practices of Vodou as superstitious mumbo jumbo, practiced—with positive results in as much as she survives—by a harebrained coquette and her manipulative servant. Pauline's scatty impersonation of Ezili Freda, the flirtacious light-skinned Creole *lwa*, "coquettish, sensual, pleasure loving, and extravagant" (Métraux 110), subverts Carpentier's project and sabotages Carpentier's intended privileging of the connection between history and faith in his account of the Haitian Revolution.

Part 3 opens with a quotation from Karl Ritter (1779–1859), one of the founders of modern geography, who narrates in *Naturhistorische Reise nach der westindischen Insel Hayti* (Natural History Travels to the West Indian Island of Haiti) (1836) his experiences while visiting Haiti during the rebellion against Henri Christophe in 1820.

Chapters 1–4 of part 3, "The Portents," "Sans Souci," "The Sacrifice of the Bulls," and "The Immured," describe Ti-Noël's return to Haiti after an absence of almost 20 years. He returns during the last stages of the completion of Henri Christophe's fortress of La Citadelle Laferrière and shortly before Christophe committed suicide after suffering a stroke. The Citadelle, a massive mountaintop fortress near the town of Millot in northern Haiti, was part of a system of fortifications designed to protect the new nation from French assaults. It is the largest fortress in the western hemisphere, and since 1982, it has been a UNESCO World Heritage site. Below the Citadelle stood the palace of Sans Souci, Christophe's administrative center, built between 1810 and 1813 and seriously damaged by the earthquake that destroyed the Cap in 1842.

Ti-Noël returns to Haiti at a time when Christophe's feudalistic policies—which restricted the population's mobility and imposed a regime of hard labor—had led to increasing discontent. Opposition was growing against his Dahomets, an elite military force trained in administration that enforced Christophe's Code Henri. Perceived as an egocentric tyrant whose rule had become repressive, he was facing growing rebellions, particularly to the south of the country, ruled by Alexandre Pétion. Carpentier, through Ti-Noël's eyes, describes the land as only slowly recovering from the devastation of the revolution. His descriptions of the landscape underscore the ecological wreckage the plantation and the revolution have left in their wake and prefigure Haiti's twenty-first-century ecological dilemma.

In chapter 5, "Chronicle of August 15," Carpentier links Christophe's debilitating stroke and subsequent suicide to his feelings of guilt about the death of Corneille Breille, the Duke of Anse and Christophe's own confessor. Immured in the oratory of his archbishop's palace and allowed only the barest substance, the old Capuchin priest had died in his captivity. In the novel, Breille's ghost appears to Christophe during a requiem Mass celebrated by his successor. The requiem Mass links this grotesque episode in Christophe's career to another gruesome moment in 1814, when he had forced Breille to conduct a similar mass for a Colonel Medina, who had been sentenced to death and who was forced to attend the Mass, standing next to an empty coffin, before he was executed. In the novel, it is while the priest is intoning the Dies Irae—the hymn chanted before the proclamation of the Gospel in the Catholic requiem Mass and which describes the Day of Judgment, the last trumpet summoning the souls before the throne of God—that Christophe has the stroke that will lead to his suicide.

"Ultima Ratio Regum" (chapter 6) is a phrase referring to war as "the last argument of kings" and was engraved on a French cannon by order of Louis XIV. This chapter narrates Christophe's awareness of the end of his reign through the beatings of drums. Beginning with the *mandoucouman,* which signals the retreat of his troops, and growing to encompass the drums of Vodou (of the rada and congo rites), the drums of Bouckman and the alliance between slaves and *lwa,* "the night grew dense with drums" (*Kingdom* 147). The drumming, which can be read as pushing Christophe to his death, is a reminder to Christophe of his abandonment of the *lwa,* of his turning his back on the religion of his ancestors in favor of the Christian God. His interment in the Citadelle—described in chapter 7, "Strait Is the Gate," as his Escorial (the burial site for most of the Spanish kings for the last five centuries)—closes part 4 by bringing it full circle. It has opened with Ti-Noël being forced into hard labor for the construction of the Citadellle, as an example of the corruption of power.

Part 4 opens with a quotation from the works of Pedro Calderón de la Barca (1600–1681), the foremost dramatist of the Spanish Golden Age and author of *La vida es sueño* (1636), one of the masterpieces of the Spanish baroque. The focus of the first chapter of this section, however, is the portrait sculpture of Pauline Bonaparte as Venus Victrix by Venetian sculptor Antonio Canova (1757–1822), famous for his delicate renderings of nude flesh in neoclassical style (a return to classical forms after the excesses of the baroque). The seminude, reclining sculpture was commissioned by Pauline's second husband, Camillo Borghese, and was executed in Rome from 1805 to 1808, after Pauline's return from Haiti. In the novel, Soliman comes across the sculpture at the Borghese Palace shortly after the execution of Henri Christophe's heir in 1820; the sculpture, however, was not housed there until 1838.

The last two chapters of *The Kingdom of This World,* "The Surveyors" and "Agnus Dei," return us to Ti-Noël and his death after a lifetime of toil. The historical background to the chapters is President Jean-Pierre Boyer's Rural Code of 1826. Boyer (1776–1850), the first ruler of a united Haiti, was president from 1818 to 1843. In 1826 Boyer promulgated his famous code, which forced the peasantry to agricultural work, attaching them to the land and to a particular proprietor in a relationship akin to serfdom, a semifeudal *fermage* system. The surveyors Ti-Noël describes had as their task organizing a land distribution program that was to see the large plantations dismantled and the land parceled out among the peasants, who will, in turn, have to follow production quotas. The code failed; challenged by the peasantry, which had organized itself along a system of subsistence farming, the army was unable—and often unwilling—to enforce it.

The presence of the surveyors prompts a meditation on the nature of human toil and the cyclical nature of the patterns of oppression, revolt, and resistance that had characterized Ti-Noël's life and with which the novel closes. "The old man began to lose heart at this endless return of chains, the rebirth of shackles," Carpentier writes, "this proliferation of suffering, which the more resigned began to accept as proof of the uselessness of all revolt" (*Kingdom* 177–78). Ti-Noël's "supremely lucid" moment before he dies reveals the lessons he has learned through his proximity to the *lwa*-inspired heroes of the Haitian Revolution, that of "the possible germinations the future held" (*Kingdom* 186). "Man," he realizes, "never knows for whom he suffers and hopes" since his greatness "consists in the very fact of wanting to be better than he is" (*Kingdom* 185).

Chapter 4

Michelle Cliff's Abeng

Michelle Cliff was born in the then British colony of Jamaica on November 2, 1946. At the age of three, her parents moved to a Caribbean neighborhood of New York City, where they lived on and off until their permanent return to Jamaica in the late 1950s, just in time for their daughter to attend high school. Cliff returned to Jamaica at a time when the island was vying for its independence from Great Britain and establishing an identity as an African-diasporan nation. Cliff, a light-skinned Creole who traced her heritage to English immigrants and African slaves, became keenly interested in the construction of identity and self, thinking critically about the stereotypes and social norms of her surroundings. As a bisexual adolescent, her sexual identity clashed against traditional Jamaican expectations for women. The negative experiences of her childhood, with both racial and gender issues, would become central to her writing.

Cliff did not begin to address these issues in her literature until she was in her thirties, in part because her family had not been supportive of her writing efforts, considering that the concerns she was interested in addressing were thought to be taboo. Yet despite a somewhat belated introduction to writing as a career, she maintained a keen interest in observing the world around her, storing concepts and memories that would serve her in later literary work.

As a young woman, Cliff returned to New York City, where she attended Wagner College, graduating with a degree in European history in 1969. She left New York for London, where she received her PhD in comparative historical studies from the Warburg Institute of the University of London in 1974, writing her thesis on the Italian Renaissance. During and after her college years, Cliff worked as an editor for *Life* magazine in New York and London. She remembers the position fondly, recalling experiences researching a gamut of topics from the U.S. space program in Houston to returning Vietnam War soldiers in Northern Ireland. At this time, she also found a job teaching at the New School for Social Research (now the New School University) in New York, where she began to meet authors and members of the women's movement, with which she has been closely associated, such as Betty Friedan, Audre Lorde, and acclaimed poet and essayist Adrienne Rich, who has been Cliff's companion since 1976. It was in this environment that she began to nurture her writing career.

Cliff credits her entry into writing to a misinterpreted editorial she wrote for *Ms.* magazine. In response to what she considered a poorly written article about Jamaica, Cliff wrote a letter to the editor expressing her discontent, which was twisted by the magazine into an endorsement of the initial article. The experience prompted her to develop a more critical approach to writing, stylistically and historically.

Cliff's first major book project was *Claiming an Identity They Taught Me to Despise,* a collection of poetry and prose fiction published in 1980. Written while she was working full-time as an editor, the format of the piece mirrors the limited amount of time she could dedicate to her writing. Organized as a series of sketches, rather than a continuous story, it creates unity out of a diverse matrix of ideas and images. In *Claiming an Identity,* Cliff

focuses on the interracial prejudice, delineating how it feels to be urged to pass for white by one's own family members, acknowledging an awareness of both the advantages gained by being light-skinned in a colorist society and the ways in which light-skinned blacks are taught to collaborate with the masters to keep that dark-skinned down. ("Michelle Cliff," *Dictionary* 3)

In 1984 Cliff published her first novel, *Abeng.* Its young protagonist, Clare, is the daughter of a mother who traces her ancestry to the Jamaican Maroons who fought relentlessly for independence and a father proud of being the descendant of brutal plantation masters. Clare's desire to reconcile the two sides of her ancestry is the focal point of her search for identity in the text. It is woven in the novel with the myth of Nanny, the legendary Maroon and Obeahwoman "who could catch a bullet between her buttocks and render the bullet harmless" (14).

In 1985 Cliff published a collection of poetry and prose similar in format to *Claiming an Identity,* titled *The Land of Look Behind: Prose and Poetry.* It was followed in 1987 by her second novel, *No Telephone to Heaven,* in which Clare, the protagonist of *Abeng,* returns to Jamaica after spending time in England and the United States to reclaim the African portion of her heritage and engage, like Nanny, in a disastrous armed struggle against Jamaica's colonial oppressors.

In 1990, having lived for many years away from Jamaica in the United States, Cliff published a collection of short stories, *Bodies of Water,* that addresses her familiar topics of race relations, gender oppression, and imperialism through narratives set chiefly in the United States. It was followed in 1993 by her third novel, *Free Enterprise,* a fictionalized narrative about M.E.P., Mary Ellen Pleasant, the mysterious woman behind John Brown's raid on Harper Ferry in 1859. Her most recent book, a collection of short stories titled *The Store of a Million Items,* appeared in 1998.

Cliff has also published numerous influential essays, such as "History as Fiction, Fiction as History," in anthologies, journals, magazines, and newspapers such as *Ms.* and the *Village Voice.* She is the recipient of fellowships from the National Endowment for the Arts (1982 and 1989), MacDowell College (1982), the Massachusetts Artists Foundation (1984), and Yaddo (1984).

Cliff counts Toni Morrison, Samuel Becket, Ernest Hemmingway, William Faulkner, Nadine Gordimer, and James Baldwin as writers whose attention to colonialism, racism, and gender has had the greatest influence on her own work. In her writing, she has been particularly interested in the rewriting of flawed histories and the reclaiming of suppressed narratives and despised ancestries. She describes this process thus:

> To write a complete Caribbean woman, or man for that matter, demands of us retracing the African past of ourselves, reclaiming as our own, and as our subject, a history sunk under the sea, or scattered as potash in the canefields, or gone to bush, or trapped in a class system notable for its rigidity and absolute dependence on color stratification. Or a past bleached from our minds. It means finding the art forms of those of our ancestors and speaking in the patois forbidden us. It means realizing our knowledge will always be wanting. It means also, I think, mixing in the forms taught us by the oppressor, undermining his language and co-opting his style and turning it to our purpose. ("Michelle Cliff," *VG*)

Cliff has taught at a number of institutions, including the New School for Social Research; the Women Writers Center, Cazenovia College; the University of California, Santa Cruz; and Stanford University. She holds the position of Allan K. Smith Professor of English Language and Literature at Trinity College in Hartford. She also teaches in Santa Cruz, traveling regularly between Connecticut and the home she shares with Adrienne Rich in California.

Abeng

One of the most celebrated Caribbean bildungsroman of the independence period, *Abeng* has been praised for its exploration of the links between national and female independence in colonial societies. The novel, set in 1958, on the eve of Jamaican independence from Great Britain, follows a year in the life of 12-year-old Clare Savage, a light-skinned, middle-class Jamaican girl coming to terms with the complexities of race and class in her colonial society and with her budding (homo)sexuality in a homophobic society.

Abeng is dedicated to the memory of Jean Toomer (1894–1967) and Bessie Head (1937–1986). Toomer was an American poet of mixed racial ancestry whose novel in poetry and prose, *Cane* (1923), had a profound influence on Cliff, whose own *Claiming an Identity They Taught Me to Despise* explores her own struggles with her mixed racial heritage. Bessie Emery Head, considered by many to be Botswana's most important writer, was also of mixed racial heritage. Her novels, where the characters' dilemmas play against a highly detailed historical background, served as a model for *Abeng*. The novel's epigraph is drawn from *Jacob and the Angel and Other Poems* (1952) by Jamaican poet Basil McFarlane (1922–).

Abeng consists of 20 chapters divided into three parts. Part 1 (chapters 1–6), which opens with a traditional slave lament pleading the Lord to "carry me down to the burial ground," traces Clare's connection to the history of the plantation and to the slave revolts led by the legendary Maroon leader Nanny, with whom the character identifies. (The historical Nanny, believed to have been born in present-day Ghana around 1680, was known as a spiritual and military leader of the Jamaican Maroons between 1725 and 1740, the most intense period of their resistance against the British.) Part 1 concludes with the marriage of Clare's white father, Boy Savage, a descendant of Jamaican planters, to her mother, Kitty, a woman of mixed race and lower-middle-class origins. Part 2 (chapters 7–14), which opens with a traditional song about a young woman who holds on to her country ways despite being sent to the city, focuses on Clare's own ties to the country through her maternal grandmother, Miss Mattie. Part 3 (chapters 15–20) uses another traditional Jamaican song ("My Company Is Going Far and I Am Left Alone") to introduce the narrative of how Clare is sent away from Miss Mattie's home and ostracized from her family after she takes her grandmother's shotgun and kills her bull.

Clare's narrative of discovery and alienation is set against the pivotal events of 1958 in Jamaica, when the island had joined the West Indies Federation as a first step toward gaining independence from Great Britain. The federation, whose capital was in Port of Spain, Trinidad, brought together most of the British colonies in the Caribbean into a federated state, consisting of 10 self-governing provinces, whose avowed aim was to pave the way for independence from Great Britain. With a prime minister as head of state, the federation's parliament was formed by representatives from the various island nations, from which the prime minister (Grantley Adams of Barbados) selected a cabinet. The federation was inaugurated on January 3, 1958, but collapsed on May 31, 1963, as the result of growing internal conflicts centered primarily on issues of migration between the islands. Among the few lasting accomplishments of the federation was the creation of the University of the West Indies and the decolonization of the islands' educational system.

Chapter 1 of *Abeng* opens with references to the island's prehistory—which the text will show to be a particular interest of Clare's father, who thought of the islands of the West Indies as "the remains of Atlantis" (9)—and to the colonial history that followed, marked by the presence in Jamaica of Indians, Africans, and Europeans. A lyrical meditation on the many cultivars of the mango and their centrality to Jamaican life serves as the point of introduction to the Savage family and the people around them, as they prepare for church on a Sunday in 1958. Like the mango, which is not cultivated for exportation in Jamaica but which has developed dozens of different cultivars through grafting, Cliff presents the people and culture of Jamaica as full of variety and enriched by cross-fertilization and hybridity.

In this first chapter (and in the chapter that follows), Cliff is primarily concerned with establishing for the reader the historical background to Jamaica's cultural and racial hybridity. She does this primarily through her description of the two churches the Savages attend on Sundays: one the middle-class Presbyterian church, with its close ties to the colonial elite and the presence of the emerging American sector on the island, and the other the Tabernacle of the Almighty, with its black congregation and roots in Jamaica's revivalist religious traditions. The John Knox Memorial Church, Boy Savage's choice as a place of worship, sees as its function that of dampening its congregation's so-called natural tropical impetuosity; the school-teacher "advised the congregation to tone down their singing, to consider the nuances of harmony and quiet" (6). The Tabernacle Church, on the other hand, embraced the Myal-inspired revivalism through which English versions of Christianity were transculturated in Jamaica. Throughout the late eighteenth and early nineteenth centuries, "the Protestantism against which the slave population posited their [African-derived] dances and drumming was not the sedate Anglicanism of the Established Church of England, but the more exuberant Christianity of English Methodists, Moravians, and African American Baptists accustomed to enthusiastic manifestations of the Holy Spirit through music and trance" (Olmos and Paravisini-Gebert 146). Jamaican revivalism incorporated trances, such as those described by Cliff in *Abeng*, through which the Holy Spirit manifested itself to congregants, who "jump up and fall down moaning, or sway faster and faster back and forth, calling on God" to hear them (12).

The duality of these churches represents Clare's duality of backgrounds: her father's white colonial legacy and her mother's African-derived culture and religiosity. In *Abeng*, Clare's characterization is closely tied to the racial and cultural discrepancies that separate her parents. Both the plot of the novel and the development of Clare as a character will center on the impossibility of resolving the racial and class dichotomies her parents represent and which become an obstacle to Clare's personal development.

Clare's dilemma is that of finding a balance between her white and black heritages in a primarily black society that still suffers the consequences of slavery and white colonial rule and a text that increasingly privileges and validates black Jamaican culture and history. In chapter 1, Cliff signals the thematic centrality of the history of slavery and the plantation system in her novel. The focus of her description of the various churches in Kingston is the discovery in 1958, during renovations of the High Anglican Parish Church, of a heavy lead coffin of massive proportions that contained the remains of a hundred plague victims, many of them freshly arrived slaves from the Gold Coast, who had died in a holding pen in Kingston. This thematic focus is underscored in chapter 2 through the depiction of Clare's maternal grandmother as the leader of a revivalist church in the countryside and especially through the story of Nanny, the Obeahwoman who led the eighteenth-century Maroon wars against the planters and won her reputation as "the magician of this revolution" (14) and with whom Clare identifies.

Cliff's narrative strategy in the two opening chapters is to weave together past and present to show readers the links between historical events and conditions in Jamaica in the pivotal year 1958. In chapter 1, the discovery of the mass coffin brings the reality of slavery to life, as if to indicate that it is impossible to bury the legacy of the plantation, which will surface at crucial and unexpected moments. In chapter 2, Cliff skillfully intertwines the stories of her maternal great grandmother (who left her white family to live with one of their servants), of Nanny the Maroon leader, and of the congregation of the Tabernacle Church as they go about their lives of poverty and servitude. All colored island people, Cliff proposes, are linked by their common descent from Nanny the rebel or her sister Sekesu, who had chosen to remain a slave.

This link is reiterated at the beginning of chapter 3, when Cliff explains that although the members of the Tabernacle church were the descendants of slaves, they still did not know or understand their own history of exploitation. Underlying these early chapters is Cliff's own notion of the importance of an understanding of the colonial history of the Caribbean to the development of national and individual identities. In chapter 1, the narrator questioned Boy Savage's sui generis reading of history, which brought together disparate events and facts into a fanciful, if inaccurate, version of history. In chapter 3, Cliff uses the device of what "the people in the Tabernacle did not know" (19) to retrace the salient elements of the narrative of the Maroon wars in Jamaica, especially of the betrayal of Nanny by Cudjoe, leader of the Maroons of Accompong Town, who eventually signed a separate peace treaty with the British. Cliff's interpretation of Caribbean history leads her to see the infighting among various groups—the inability to strike a balance between conflicting interests and contending histories—as the primary obstacle to a unified Jamaica. Clare, as a mixed-race character who embodies these contradictions and must bridge them inwardly to emerge into adulthood with a sense of her own identity, stands as a symbol of the divided nation. Like the Maroons who failed in their bid for independence because of their inability to unite, Clare must struggle to reconcile her disparate heritages and eventually make a choice as to what kind of Jamaican she wishes to be. The Jamaican proverb that serves as an epigraph for chapter 3, "Do-fe-do mek guinea nigger come a Jamaica" (trouble led to African blacks coming to Jamaica), which refers to the seeds of New World slavery in the internecine wars among African kingdoms, sums up Cliff's meditation on history in this chapter.

In chapter 4, Cliff's rumination on history focuses on Clare's paternal family history and on a visit she and her father make to the family's former plantation at Runaway Bay. Runaway Bay, named so because it was a popular escape route for slaves, was the site of the first Spanish settlement on the island as well as the point of departure of the last Spanish troops after their defeat by the English in 1670. The bay is on Jamaica's north coast, just west of the well-known resort town of Ocho Rios. In 1958, when the novel was set, it had become popular with American and British ex-pats. British actor and composer Noel Coward lived (and is buried) in a villa in Runaway Bay called Firefly, while Ian Fleming (of James Bond fame) lived in a house named Goldeneye after one of his books. The area has since given way to fancy, all-inclusive resorts and offers restored former plantation homes like Seville Great House, Prospect Plantation, and Harmony Hall as tourist attractions. The great house at Paradise Plantation, Claire's family's house, had been left by the developers as a come-on, to persuade buyers "that they could buy into the past" (24).

For Clare, the stroll through the interior of the house, whose papered walls reflects her paternal heritage, links her to the history and trappings of Europe. An ancestor had once fought alongside William the Conqueror in 1066; the furnishings and ornaments abounded with Staffordshire, Wedgwood, and Waterford, fine oriental carpets, Carrara marble, and a portrait of a great grandmother painted by a disciple of Joshua Reynolds.

Cliff uses the occasion of the visit to Paradise Plantation to explore for the reader the nature of plantation life and the role of slavery and the cultivation of sugar in the plantation economy. Her walk through the geography of her family's former plantation reinforces her conviction that the institutions of slavery and the plantation live on in Jamaica's twentieth-century economy, where they continue to be responsible for the conditions of the island's poor population, which she describes in the novel's opening chapters. The "freedom which followed on abolition turned into veiled slavery, the model of the rest of the western world," she argues, as "all the forces which worked to keep these people slaves now worked to keep them poor" (28).

In chapter 4, Cliff explores—through her character's connection to the history of the plantation in Jamaica—the process through which history is transformed into romance in the Caribbean. From the notion of how prospective buyers of lots in the former plantation are invited to buy into a romanticized past to the ways in which the Savage family turns the most questionable aspects of their economic and racial history into a myth of Guatemalan ancestors and benevolent slaveholders, the text underscores the ways in which family history seeks to seduce Clare into assuming her place in a romantic fiction of belonging to a rich and powerful planter class. Clare's determination to understand the truth of her family and her island's history leads her to a review of how history was taught in the St. Catherine's School for Girls. The teaching of history by white and Creole schoolmistresses at the school mimicked the ways in which "a sense of history was lost in romance" (30) in the story of how the Savage family's large possessions took their "final downslide" (31).

In chapter 5, Cliff's focus turns to the half-Miskito Indian, half-Ashanti woman who had become her ancestor Justice Savage's mistress. Inez subsumes in her identity the legitimate sense of belonging of the native Caribbean population and the spirit of resistance of the Jamaican Maroons, to which her father belonged. Living in the liminal space between Jamaica's slave-owning society and the Maroons, Inez is drawn violently into white society when she is brought before the judge on a theft charge. The repeated rapes to which he subjects her work in the text as metaphors for the rape and exploitation of both the native and enslaved populations she embodies. Her escape from her violent predicament comes in the form of her association with an Obeahwoman, Mma Alli, who introduces her to the mysteries of ancient African magical practices and who embodies, with her stunted right breast, the spirit of the mythical Amazon warriors who lived in female-ruled societies. The reference to the Amazons allows Cliff to introduce the theme of homosexuality since Mma Alli "had never lain with a man" but instructed women "in the magic of passion" as a gift to her black brothers (34). Mma Alli uses her knowledge of herbs and roots and her hands and tongue in a rendering of lovemaking to help Inez expel the "mixed-up baby" she carried as a result of her multiple rapes by the judge since "a baby conceived in *buckra* rape would have so soul" (35). Their numerous nights of lovemaking after the abortion—which correspond to and invert the many nights of rape Inez underwent with the judge—heal Inez bodily and spiritually, until Inez is able to return to the great house "with a new-found power" (35).

The story of Inez's life in the great house—and of an escape from the life of enslavement and rape it represented, with the aid of the powers of Obeah and the self-discovery of lesbian love—forces Clare, as a young woman struggling to find the truth behind her family's complex history and to come to terms with her own equally complex sexuality, into a different awareness of the nature and history of those who lived in her family's former plantation house. She explores this awareness through the prism of Charles Dickens's *Great Expectations* (1860), a novel they were studying in school.

Cliff has Clare identify with Pip, Dickens's protagonist in *Great Expectations,* by establishing important connections between the two characters.

Like Pip, Clare's family history is shrouded in mysteries that she must eluci-
date to gain an autonomous sense of self. Like Pip, Clare has "great expectations" of life that she understands may require leaving her home island and
turning her back on what is nurturing and comforting in her childhood. Pip
and Clare are characters who find themselves suspended between worlds—
like Pip, Clare will, at the end of the novel, shift her original home for the
mausoleum-style home of her parents' old friend, into whose custody she is
turned after she kills her grandmother's bull in part 3 of the novel.

Part 2 (chapters 7–14) focuses on Clare's friendship with Zoe, whose
mother is a tenant of Clare's grandmother, Miss Mattie, in the Jamaican
countryside. This relationship is Clare's most important connection outside
of her family. All the complexities of Clare's personal, sexual, and historical
situation will play against her relationship with Zoe to devastating results.

Chapter 7 focuses on Kitty and her devotion to the country people of Jamaica. Through her mother's deep awareness of the traditions and spirit of
the descendants of slaves, which translates into a tenderness born of a deeply
set reverence for their history of survival, Clare imbues a desire to belong
to these people that clashes against her father's impulse toward separation.
Kitty's devotion to "the people" goes hand in hand with a reluctance to express her affection physically to her daughter that leaves Clare longing to be
breast-fed and to experience a close physical bond with her mother. Toward
the end of the book, Cliff writes that Kitty's "mistake in all of this was casting her people in the position of victim, so that her love of darkness became
a love conceived in grief" (128).

In chapter 8, Cliff links the feeling of exclusion she feels in her relationship to her mother to gender constraints that bar *gal pickneys* from certain
activities and secrets. Faced with her cousin's mysterious activity—the roast-
ing of a hog's testicles—she feels the true measure of her exclusion. Cliff will
use the chapter to set up the parameters of her protagonist's desire to break
the gender bounds; she is excluded from the world of the boys but feels no
connection to the more restricted world of the women, with their cooking,
crafts, and fear of male violence once they begin to "develop."

This sense of exclusion is underscored in chapter 9 by Cliff's exploration
of the homophobic undercurrents in Jamaican society. She does this through
the story of Mad Hannah and her dead son Clinton, left to drown in the
swimming hole in the river while the men and boys taunted him with cries of
"battyman, battyman," the pejorative term used for homosexuals. Hannah,
driven to madness by her grief and her exclusion from the community that
will not help her prepare her son for burial, seeks her son's restless *duppy,* or
"spirit," to perform the ritual that would finally allow him to rest.

Here Cliff uses the traditions of the folk so beloved of Clare's mother
and Miss Mattie to illustrate the profound loneliness brought about by what
many Jamaicans see as sexual deviation. Clinton's exclusion from the community as a gay man means that the preparations of the body for burial—as

described in the text—are not properly conducted. Neither does the community gather for the nine-nights Jamaican funerary tradition, an extended wake with roots in African practices, during which friends and family gather at the home of the dead person to share food, stories, and condolences. The underlying notion is that for a gay man—and for the mother who ends up in an asylum because of her grief—there is no community willing to take the necessary steps to ensure that the spirit moves in smoothly to the afterlife.

In chapter 10, Cliff expands her meditation on Clinton's death to those of Anne Frank and another 6 million Jews during World War II. Cliff's preoccupation is with the confluence of identity, exclusion, and death, as they manifest themselves at the local level in Clinton's case and become a political and human issue of great historical significance in the case of the exterminated Jews. Linking these thematically is the notion of adolescent death—Anne Frank's death in the Nazi camp, that of Claudia Lewis from leukemia, and the potential for Clare's own death if she is found out to be a battygal. Trying to understand why Anne Frank died becomes Clare's way of reaching "for an explanation of her own life" (72).

The notion of identity is central to this chapter, which begins with a brief meditation on Christopher Columbus's religious identity as a secret Jew, the presence of a black man (Pedro Alonso Niño) in his crew, and the survival of the much maligned Carib people, who gave their name to the region, reduced here to decorative figures framing the entrance to a cinema. Clare's identity is first gleaned in this chapter through her readings, those she chooses as important to her (the memoirs of Anne Frank) and those that have been give to her by her relatives (list of European classics like *Jane Eyre* and *Ivanhoe* and an earlier sensationalistic Jamaican novel about a murderous plantation mistress, Herbert De Lisser's *White Witch of Rosehall* [1928]). The most important to her, however, is the one "she had bought herself," Anne Frank's diary, through which she discovers the world's indifference to the plight of the Jews and concludes—when comparing their abandonment to the world's lack of concern for the exploitation of African slaves—that the Christian world saw both groups as "flawed in irreversible ways" (71). The meditation brings a crisis of faith, as she questions why God would let millions of his people die in such a way.

This meditation on the similarities between African diasporic peoples and the Jews who fell under the Nazis—which extends to chapter 11—is linked by Clare to the evils of colonialism, which brings her full circle back to Columbus and the books he carried to the New World, which described the peoples to be found outside of Europe as monstrous and therefore inhuman. (This connection between colonialism and the Nazis was central to one of the best known of anticolonial texts from the Caribbean, Aimé Césaire's *Discourse on Colonialism* [1950].) The circularity in the construction of chapters 10 and 11 is crucial in understanding Cliff's purpose—that of showing the roots of human exploitation and mass slaughter in the differences established by the colonial system (*"that* heart of darkness," in a reference to Joseph Conrad's famous 1902 anticolonial novella) between the non-Christian and colonized and "white and Christian Europeans" (79).

The two chapters are also framed by the tale of Clare's visit to the cinema to watch the film version of Anne Frank's story, which reveals the motive behind Clare's original interest in the young dead woman—a remoteness in Anne's relationship to her mother that had a counterpart in Clare's feelings of separation from her own. These are contrasted with the strength and dedication of another mother—that of Kitty Hart, another Holocaust survivor, whose endurance Clare attributes to her mother's deep engagement with her child. Clare had described her mother earlier in the text as holding herself back from her daughters, saving "all her ability to touch for the man she was married to" (51). Her mother's inability to understand Clare and her predicament will be one of Cliff's central themes as the character faces her most serious adolescent crisis.

Chapter 12 focuses on two interrelated themes: Clare's friendship with Zoe and the nature of colonial education. There is a significant class difference between the two girls, as Clare is a light-skinned member of the middle class, while Zoe is the daughter of a farmer and market woman, who rents her small plot of land from Clare's grandmother. In this chapter, Cliff sets the grandmother's land firmly in the margins of the historically significant Accompong Town, the Maroon settlement in the mountains of St. Elizabeth, in the western parishes of Trelawny and St. James. The liminal space of her grandmother's lands, where her ancestor's mistress Inez also lived, bordered a nation of runaway slaves living independently within the surrounding Jamaican state.

Black River, the small market town that was the commercial center of Miss Mattie's neighborhood, is a space uninhabited by whites and, most significantly, a female space where most of the labor and exchange is in the hands of black women. The story of Inez and Mma Alli, narrated earlier in the text, also makes this a space that allows freedom for varied expressions of women's sexuality. The vulnerability of these women to the forces of the global market is hinted at through the cannibalization of the traditional market woman's lament into a popular Harry Belafonte calypso. Clare's identity is fractured in this space, as her country-self enters into conflicts with the traits that, in the eyes of her father, make her a "true Savage."

Clare's transfer to Zoe's space offers Cliff the opportunity to reflect on the type of colonial education that her character's mother received in rural Jamaica. The West Indies Federation that formed the backdrop to the independence movements throughout the Caribbean made the Creolization of the education system in the region the cornerstone of their cultural policies in direct response to the colonial policies Cliff describes as underpinning Zoe's education. Guided by manuals shipped throughout the empire with little accommodation to local histories or circumstances, they served as a unifying force across Britain's vast worldwide empire. Cliff focuses here on the indignities of children being forced to memorize British romantic poet William Wordsworth's 1804 poem "Daffodils," about a flower they had no hope of seeing. Late in the text, the memorizing of this poem will be remembered by Kitty with similar misgivings. Her critique in *Abeng* made the poem a symbol of colonial education and would inspire bitter critiques from other writers, most notably Jamaica Kincaid, who, in her second novel, *Lucy* (1990), makes its compelled recitation the centerpiece of her anticolonial stance.

On the other hand, Zoe's teacher, Mr. Powell, shows the growing strength of black American culture, centered on the Harlem Renaissance (with its strong West Indian presence), as an emancipating counterdiscourse to colonial education. Having traveled to New York and lived on the margins of the Harlem Renaissance, Powell had come across, among others, Zora Neale Hurston, whom he had accompanied while doing her fieldwork on African-derived religiosities in Jamaica for her book *Tell My Horse* (1937). Imbued with Marcus Garvey's ideas for the modernization and betterment of diasporic peoples, and feeling that morally, "black people may have already surpassed white people" (87), Mr. Powell felt that Jamaicans "had to be taught to rise above their past and forget about all the nonsense of *obeah* or they would never amount to anything" (87).

Mr. Powell's association with the Universal Negro Improvement Association, founded by Marcus Garvey (1887–1940)—where he "found an excitement he never found again" (89)—prompted an approach to a decolonized education founded on Afrocentric, nationalistic principles. Garvey is remembered, among other things, as one of the most salient proponents of the Back-to-Africa movement, which called on descendants of African slaves to return to their ancestral nations to help decolonize Africa and which led to the development of the Nation of Islam and the Rastafari movement. Mr. Powell's approach to decolonization led him to place West Indian and African American writers in the same plane as English writers "because he wanted [his students] to know that there had been songs by Black men which were equal to any songs by Englishmen" (90). His end-of-the-year Jamaican tableau featured "Maroon Girl," a poem by Walter Adolphe Roberts (1886–1967), the historian, poet, and journalist who founded the Jamaican Progressive League. The audience's reaction to Zoe's recitation of this poem acknowledges the power of an autochthonous literary tradition in forging a national consciousness.

Chapter 13 discusses the development of the friendship between Clare and Zoe against the backdrop of a colonized society that makes such friendships impossible outside the narrow confines of the "wild countryside" bounded by "bush and river and mountain" of Miss Mattie's land in the country, "close to the earth, in a place where there were no electric lights, where water was sought from a natural source, where people walked barefoot more often than not" (95). Cliff is particularly concerned in this chapter with outlining the class and race obstacles that would have stood in the way of such a friendship outside these strict confines. Cliff underscores instead the rapport between the girls, based on "games of make-believe...entirely removed from what was real in the girls' lives" (95). Clare could pretend that she was an Aztec princess or the protagonist of *The Secret Garden*. Her friendship allows Clare to shed her constrained town identity and explore her mother's black world, where they can walk barefoot on the road, climb trees, and draw secret totems with a dye made from crushed flowers.

Among the girls' preoccupations during the months they spent together were the limits of their control over their own bodies, which Cliff explores in chapter 14. Their concerns are addressed through two stories they read in a newspaper and two conversations with their parents. The two stories—"the mythic disease and the mythic birth" (104)—relate an instance of a man suffering from a disease that will turn him into a woman and the story of a five-year-old girl from Peru who had given birth to a baby after a rape. Stemming from illness and violence, both stories appear to the girls as "caused by some mysterious force over which they had no control at all" (104). Comforting as is their realization that these things happened in the "world beyond Jamaica" (105), they are brought home to them in two separate conversations, one between Zoe and her mother, the other between Clare and Boy. In both, it is made clear to them that as girls in Jamaica, they are just as likely to feel victim to sexual attacks. Miss Ruthie warms Zoe that "de boys dem, 'specially de red boy and de buckra boy, can do all manners of wicked t'ing" (105), like they did when they raped a classmate of Zoe's. Boy cautions Clare that "boys are after only one thing" (106).

Part 3, which focuses on Clare's killing of Miss Mattie's bull and the ostracism from her family that is its result, opens with a traditional slave song that summarizes what will be her predicament at the end of the novel: "My company is going far/And I am left alone" (110).

Chapter 15 brings the narrative to its most dramatic point through the killing of Old Joe, Miss Mattie's old bull, with a shotgun Clare has borrowed without permission. "No punishment...would fit what she had done" was Clare's assessment of her act (113). The chapter focuses on the nature of transgression and the limits placed by gender, race, and class on what is permissible in Jamaican society. In taking the rifle and ammunition to hunt and kill Massa Cudjoe, the famous wild pig, Clare is aware of having "stepped far out of place" (115), prompted primarily by her desire have people know that "we is smaddy" (we are somebody), particularly when compared with Jacob, who, as a boy, does not have to prove any special qualities. Clare's desire for recognition, however, does not give her any insight into the ways in which she is already a "smaddy" as a light-skinned, middle-class girl from Kingston. The episode (whose consequences will be outlined in the next chapter) is presented here through the lens of how it shows the differences between the two girls that they had tried to erase through their friendship. As Zoe outlines the different consequences their act of hunting the wild pig would have for each of them, these differences come to the fore, underscoring the vulnerability of the bond they have established between them.

The greater transgression, ironically, comes after Zoe has talked Clare into giving up the chase for the pig, and it comes as an affirmation of Zoe's view of their relative circumstances. The moment encapsulates their vulnerability as two girls lying naked on a rock—the threat of sexual assault or accusations of homosexuality—and Clare lays claim to her class and race position in her demands that the man who has surprised them leave them alone: "She had dropped her patois—was speaking *buckra*—and relying on the privilege she said she did not have" (122).

Chapter 16 links the killing of the bull, with all its symbolic phallic content, to homosexuality as the unspoken taboo Clare has broken. The realization comes in two forms—through a hint of sexual desire, when Clare "had wanted to lean across Zoe's breasts and kiss her" (124) just before they were surprised by the cane cutter, and through the lengthy section that follows about Robert, a distant cousin Clare called uncle and who was a battyman, about whom everyone spoke in a "pitying tone" as if he were "hopelessly afflicted" (125, 126).

Through the story of Robert the battyman cousin, Cliff weaves Clare's exploration of her feelings for Zoe, "a dearest friend who was dark" (125), just like Robert's dearest friend had been. This is perhaps the best crafted of the chapters of *Abeng*, as Cliff seeks to delicately follow the tortuous path of Clare's meditation about her own incipient (homo)sexuality through the only parameters for exclusion and rejection she knows, those of class and race. Her meditation also encompasses issues of gender and marriage, thinking that marriage with someone darker would "place her firmly outside—'beyond the pale'" (127). Clare, who cherishes darkness like her mother, thinks of the barriers to her love for Zoe as stemming from skin color, while Cliff and the reader see in the weaving of the thematic strands of her thoughts a deeper obstacle in her society's homophobia.

The description of the flies covering Old Joe and the vultures circling over him and the girls that opens chapter 17 gives added poignancy to Zoe's thoughts, which focus on the fear that she would soon become known as "the pickney what killed Miss Mattie's bull" and that her mother would have to find a new place to live "because she had gotten too close to a *buckra* gal" (132). When they separate to each go home, Zoe knows this is good-bye, while Clare, less aware of the realities of life, does not.

The chapter, however, does not dwell on the consequences of Clare's action—other than her banishment from Miss Mattie's house now that she had proven to be a true Savage: "A beautiful pickney who was mean inside...A girl who seemed to think she was a boy. Or white" (134). Her parents will reach the same conclusion, that "she had stepped out of line, no matter what, in a society in which the lines were unerringly drawn" (150).

Clare's judgment on herself was perhaps the harshest of all, believing that she no longer deserved Anne Frank as a heroine, that "she had switched to the other side without meaning to" and suppressing that voice within her that still told her that she "had not been deliberately cruel, had had a right to the weapon" (146).

The chapter focuses, instead, on several episodes from Kitty's childhood, marked by disappointment and abandonment from a father who drank and had children with outside women, and a mother who left her to the care of a slow-witted neighbor while Kitty was in the hospital after an operation. The thread linking these stories is that of the story of the biblical Ruth, of "women left to fend for themselves" (142), as was Miss Mattie when working in the cane fields as a child and raising children with a womanizing and hard-drinking husband, as is Kitty, with a husband who spends every penny betting on horse races, as will be Clare, when banished to Mrs. Phillips's house as punishment for her transgression.

Chapter 18 introduces the extremely bigoted Mrs. Beatrice Phillips, with whom Clare will be sent to live indefinitely. An intolerant and narrow-minded old woman who believes that "'colored' people were not to be trusted" (142), she trains her dogs to attack any black person entering her yard. Marooned in her house, Clare will have to learn to live with a narrow-mindedness that Cliff ridicules through the story of Mrs. Phillips's ignorant reaction to the famous soprano Lily Pons's visit to Jamaica. Pons (1889–1976) was the principal soprano at the Metropolitan Opera House for 30 years. The coloratura that Mrs. Phillips mistakes for a racial category refers to a very high and light soprano voice able to add figuration or ornamentation to the music as written.

The chapter closes with a conversation between Kitty and Clare, in which Clare realizes that her mother, although conflicted by the decision, believes that her going to Mrs. Phillips will ultimately be good for her, that it will open almost limitless options for her and allow her to leave "this sad little island" (150). The conversation closes a thematic thread in the novel—that of Clare's perception that her mother (like Anne Frank's before her) is not her protector and will not challenge her father's decision, a realization that leaves Clare with a deep longing for something she thought she could find in her friendship with Zoe.

Chapter 20, which opens with the story of Lily Pons's visit to Jamaica, centers on Mrs. Phillips's sister, a woman who was "too ambitious for herself" (159). Like Clare, she "surrounded herself with books," had "some inflated notions about leaving Jamaica," and "did not want to marry" (159). A woman who "wouldn't be a woman" (159) and now lives her mad and unwashed existence in filthy clothes and no shoes, she startles Clare with a revelation of having had a child with a black man who was "done away" by her own father, who took the baby away in turn to be raised by nuns. Her story—"something which was vivid to her, something she had not made peace with" (163)—is meant to impress on Clare the importance of remaining true to herself, of not letting people "cross her up" (162). She is not "what I was meant to be," she tells Clare, "I was born to be somebody and I let that pass" (164). Like Clare, she has a clear sense of the links between her personal history and that of the island in which that history has unfolded, comparing the legacy of slavery to "the afterbirth...lodged in the woman's body" which will not be expelled. "All the waste of birth. Foul-smelling and past its use" (165).

The incident, on the eve of Clare's first menstruation, prompts a dream that returns Clare to her relationship with Zoe. In the dream, Clare hits Zoe under her eye, and "a trickle of blood ran down her friend's face and onto the rock where she sat," forming a pool (165). The incident echoes a pivotal scene in Jean Rhys's *Wide Sargasso Sea,* in which the white protagonist's black friend Tia hits her with a stone on the forehead, in a gesture of rejection because she is white and has been as poor as she is—a "white cockroach." The wound opens a gulf between the two friends, who had bonded in the countryside in a relationship much like that of Clare and Zoe's. The separation will haunt the protagonist, Antoinette, who will yearn for a return to the days spent with Tia in the ruined estate, running barefoot on the lanes and bathing in the river.

In *Abeng,* Cliff builds on the relationship between Rhys's characters, establishing a dialogue between her text and the earlier novel, published 18 years before. In *Wide Sargasso Sea,* Rhys worked with the notion of the two friends mirroring each other, one dark, one white, but both linked by similar experiences and, most particularly, by a gender identity that made them ripe for exploitation. In *Abeng,* Cliff explores the fundamental differences of class, race, and geography that made that earlier relation problematic and vulnerable—but also capable of some resolution, since Clare, being of mixed race and brought up with a dual consciousness, can embody both perspectives. As Cliff writes in her conclusion, although Clare is not ready to understand her dream, she would eventually come to realize "that everyone we dream about we are" (166).

Chapter 5

Maryse Condé's I, Tituba,
Black Witch of Salem

Maryse Condé was born Maryse Boucolon on February 11, 1937, in Pointe-a-Pitre, Guadeloupe, the eldest of eight children. Though born and raised in French/Creole-speaking Guadeloupe, Condé has spent much of her life living or traveling abroad. At the age of 16, she was sent by her parents to France, where she studied at the Lycée Fénélon and later at the Université de Paris III, Sorbonne, where she received a doctorate in comparative literature in 1976, with a dissertation on black stereotypes in West Indian literature. It is a subject that has had a profound influence on her subsequent work as a novelist and dramatist.

In 1958 Condé married Mamadou Condé, an African actor, with whom she moved to Africa, earning her living as a teacher. She worked as an instructor at the École Normale Supérieure in Conakry, Guinea, from 1960 to 1964. From 1966 to 1968, she taught at the Ghana Institute of Language in Accra and at the Lycée Charles de Gaulle in Saint Louis, Senegal.

Condé arrived in Africa during an important historical crossroad, as the countries moved from colonialism to independence, a process marked by violence and ethnic strife. Developments in the newly independent and turbulent African nations would inspire her first novel, *Hérémakhonon*, published in 1976. It tells the story of a young black West Indian woman, Veronica, seeking her cultural roots in an independent Africa filled with corrupt politicians, with one of whom she has a painful affair. Condé has denied that the book is autobiographical, although it owes its vividness to closely observed events and personalities.

Condé's years in Africa were tumultuous. She and her husband lived amid dissidents and moved frequently to avoid turmoil and government repression. Her four children were born during her sojourn in Africa. In 1968 Condé moved to London to work as program director for the British Broadcasting Corporation (BBC), a position she held for two years, until her return to France in 1970 to teach and pursue graduate studies. While in France, she taught at the Université de Paris in Jussieu and Nanterre and at the Sorbonne (1980–1985). During these years in France, she began her literary career, publishing *Hérémakhonon* in 1976 and writing and producing two dramas, *Dieu nous l'a donné* (1972) and *Mort d'Oluwémi d'Ajumako* (1973).

In 1981, after extended separations, Condé divorced Mamadou Condé. The following year, she married Richard Philcox, an Englishman who became the English translator of her numerous novels. Her new marriage marked the beginning of a period of great creativity and dedication to her writing, marked in 1981 by the publication of *Une Saison à Rihata*. Like her first novel, *A Season at Rihata* was inspired by Condé's experiences in Africa and follows African and Caribbean characters stranded amid corrupt politicians and turbulent social events in a newly independent African republic.

In 1984 Condé published the first installment of her two-part historical bestseller *Ségou: Les Murailles de terre*. It was followed in 1985 by its sequel, *Ségou: La Terre en miettes*. The novels, which explore the saga of the royal Traore family in Ségou, now part of Mali, brought Condé's writing to international critical attention and acclaim. In them, Condé boldly delves into issues of the slave trade, religion (chiefly the struggle between Islam and Christianity), and French colonialism (1797–1860), examining both their historical context and contemporary implications. It is in this novel that we see for the first time the solid research behind Condé's work, as the books include extensive ethnographical notes, maps, and genealogies.

In 1985 Condé received a Fulbright scholarship to teach at Occidental College in California for a year. Her time in the United States facilitated her return to Guadeloupe. For most of her remaining career, she has maintained homes in Guadeloupe and the United States, first in California, where she taught at Occidental and later at the University of California at Berkeley, and in New York, where Condé was a professor of French at Columbia University until her retirement.

During her Fulbright year in California, Condé wrote one of her most popular novels, *I, Tituba, Black Witch of Salem,* published in 1986 and winner of numerous awards, among them the Grand Prix Littéraire de la Femme in 1986. *Tituba* tells the tale of a Barbadian slave who was among the women tried as witches during the infamous witch hunt of 1692. She followed its success with *La Vie scélérate* (1987), winner of the highly coveted Prix de l'Académie Française 1988 (bronze medal); *La Colonie du nouveau monde* (1993), about a couple from Guadeloupe seeking to return to a precolonial space; *La Migration des coeurs (Windward Heights)* (1995), which brings the drama of Emily Brontë's *Wuthering Heights* to a Caribbean setting; and *Desiderada* (1997).

Throughout the 1980s and 1990s, Condé lectured extensively in her native Caribbean as well as in Europe, Africa, and the United States on topics as varied as "The Black Woman Writer and the Diaspora," "Politics and West Indian Literature," "The Woman Writer in the Caribbean," and "Pan-Africanism."

Condé is a professor emeritus of French at Columbia University.

I, Tituba, Black Witch of Salem

Condé's best known novel, *I, Tituba, Black Witch of Salem,* takes as its point of departure the historical events surrounding the famous witch trials of Salem, Massachusetts, in 1692. The historical Tituba—the first woman to be accused of witchcraft during the trials—was believed to be an Arawak-speaking Amerindian from British Guiana who had lived as a slave in Barbados. Purchased by Samuel Parris (1653–1720) in 1680, she and her husband, John Indian, were brought to Boston and subsequently to Salem Village around 1689, the year in which they married. Tituba and John Indian were believed to have had only one child, named Violet, who remained in the Parris household until Samuel Parris's death. Their owner, Parris, had been born in London, the second son of a wealthy cloth merchant whose sole inheritance was a small estate in Barbados that proved insufficient to support his family. He went to Salem as a Puritan minister—a rather rigid one by all accounts—accompanied by his wife, his daughter Betty, and his niece Abigail Williams. The latter two became the focus of the scandal that would lead to the Salem witch trials when, in February 1692, they accused Tituba of causing them to have unexplainable fits that led the doctor to conclude that they had been bewitched. Their symptoms included contortions, seizures, uncontrollable screaming, crawling under furniture, thrashing, and flailing. They would claim to see and hear the devil or would complain of being pricked and cut with pins and knives held by invisible beings.

The burden of the accusation of witchcraft fell almost naturally on Tituba, who was reported to have entertained the girls and their friends with stories of magic, witchcraft, Obeah practices, and West Indian lore. Sarah Good and Sarah Osborne, village women who had gained some notoriety for their refusal to attend church and for their nonconformist behavior (Osborne had married her indentured servant), were also accused and arrested on March 1, 1692. Other accusations followed in quick succession, until many neighbors, including four-year-old Dorcas Good and many who had been considered outstanding members of the community, found themselves in prison.

The historical Tituba confirmed the accusations against herself and others in an attempt to save her own life. Her confession substantiated growing fears of rampant Satan-inspired witchcraft in the community and intensified the zeal of the accusers and prosecutors. She became the leading prosecution witness against all the other accused in the early months of the scandal, although she later would recant her confession and other testimony. In all, at least 19 of those convicted on witchcraft were hanged for their alleged crimes. A handful of the accused died in prison. Tituba was bought out of prison for seven pounds in 1693, after 13 months of confinement, and disappeared from history.

The fictional Tituba of Condé's novel is not an Amerindian, but the daughter of an Ashanti slave raped by an English sailor aboard the ship that brings her to Barbados. Tituba was born "from this act of aggression" (3). In *I, Tituba, Black Witch of Salem,* as Angela Davis argues in her foreword to the novel, Condé lends Tituba the words needed to record the existence of an "individual, who was as much a part of the Salem witch trial as her codefendants of European descent" (ix).

I, Tituba, Black Witch of Salem offers the first-person account of Tituba's life from birth to her death after returning to Barbados following the Salem witch trials. The text is divided into two parts, followed by an epilogue. Part 1 consists of 12 chapters, which open with the rape of Tituba's mother before her arrival in Barbados and close with Tituba's appeal to her ancestors for help as she faces the first accusations of witchcraft in Salem. Part 2 opens with Tituba's first confrontation with her accusers and closes with Tituba's execution in Barbados for her leadership role in a slave insurrection. The epilogue is narrated by Tituba after she has "gone over to the invisible world" (164) and closes the narrative with a description of Tituba's continued role in fostering rebellion among the blacks of Barbados.

Chapter 1 (part 1) quickly sketches Tituba's life from her conception through rape to her young adulthood. She traces her ancestry to the Ashanti, a major ethnic group from central Ghana that had developed one of the most powerful empires in West Africa through trade in gold and slaves. Tituba's mother, Abena, arrives in Barbados and establishes two loving relationships: one with her young white mistress, with whom she shares a bond in their joint submission to a master and husband they despise, and the other with Yao, the enslaved warrior to whom she is given as an incentive to make him a productive and hardworking slave.

In chapter 1, Condé encapsulates the experience of West Indian slavery through a swift rendering of Abena and Yao misfortunes, which include—in addition to rape and repeated humiliations—brutal separations, backbreaking labor, longing for their lost homeland, and coercion through institutionalized violence. Her mother and adoptive father provide Tituba, nonetheless, a happy and protected childhood, during which Yao's unconditional love balances Abena's emotional coldness, the result of the memory of the rape through which Tituba was conceived. Her parents' early deaths are also emblematic of life on the plantation; Abena is hanged after attacking her master during a rape attempt, while Yao commits suicide after her death, unable to face a continuation of life as a slave.

Condé's purpose in chapter 1 (part 1) is to establish a firm connection between Tituba and African culture, particularly with the healing and spiritual practices of Obeah, the African-derived magicoreligious practices of the British West Indies. The connection to Africa is Condé's most important departure from the figure of the historical Tituba, believed to have been an Amerindian slave steeped in the beliefs and practices of her South American ancestors. African-derived culture and practices, however, are introduced in the text from its first pages through the narrator's allusions to the narratives that transmit the slaves' African cultural heritage and guide their beliefs and behaviors. Stories such as the tale of "the bird who laughed at the leaves of the palm tree" or "the monkey who wanted to be the king of animals" have survived in the Caribbean oral tradition as legends that embody lessons about ethics and moral behavior. In Cuban Santería, they are known as *patakís* and as such summarize the wisdom of the African ancestors and represent a direct link with their voices in divination ceremonies. In chapter 1 (part 1), they help Abena and Yao establish a cultural connection that they—and later Mama Yaya—will transmit to their daughter.

When Abena and Yao's early deaths leave Tituba forsaken and at the mercy of the larger community of slaves, she is adopted by Yetunde, or Mama Yaya, a practitioner of Obeah. Mama Yaya can communicate with the spirits of the ancestors (the "invisibles") and knows the secrets of herbs. As a skilled herbalist, as befits her traditional role as an Obeahwoman, Mama Yaya first prepares a healing/divinatory bath for Tituba, through which she senses the young girl's painful but ultimately triumphant future. Mama Yaya, as she initiates Tituba into the ways of her African ancestors, instills in the young girl a respect for nature and an understanding of the relative position of humans within the natural system as a foundation for her African-derived belief system.

Central to this belief system is the veneration of the ancestors. The dead, as Tituba explains, "live on if we cherish them and honor their memory" (10). The Obeahman's or Obeahwoman's ability to facilitate communication between humans and the spirits of the dead gives him or her a privileged position in African-Caribbean communities. Those born with this gift can use it to secure the ancestors' advice, guidance, and comfort for themselves and others. Tituba's ability to speak to her dead mother and hear her words of regret for the limits of her love while alive restores to Tituba the maternal love she had lost and signals her gift of communicating with the invisibles. It opens the path to her training as an Obeahwoman.

This training will have serious repercussions for Tituba in the text, as it will lead directly to her being charged with witchcraft in Salem. The training, as described in the novel, involves learning the words required to conjure the spirits (Obeahwomen are often known as conjurers or conjure-women), mastering the propitiatory gestures needed to appease the spirits when offended, becoming familiar with the rituals of sacrifice (predominantly with animal blood and milk), and gaining the ability to change bodily form and assume the form of various animals, which is believed to be a power granted only to the most skilled practitioners of Obeah.

Tituba, like many Obeah practitioners, lives isolated from her immediate community, which fears her powers. After Mama Yaya's death, she built a cabin on stilts on marshy soil—as a squatter on nonproductive plantation lands—and completed her training as an Obeahwoman under the tutelage of Mama Yaya's spirit. Both Mama Yaya and Abena will become Tituba's tutelary spirits, watching over her for the rest of her life. The completion of her education, which Tituba describes as "the happiest moments of my life" (11), is marked by the destruction of her cabin, which forces her away from her state of isolation and into direct and constant communication with the larger slave community and the white world. This is where Tituba's adventures begin properly, and her reception sums up the nature of her future relationships. The slaves are both respectful and terrified of her, and she feels their distrust as an injustice; she also discovers the limits of her powers, as they can heal and comfort but cannot undo the power of colonialism and the plantation.

Chapter 2 (part 1) narrates Tituba's discovery of love and sexuality. Here Condé seeks to present Tituba as she is seen by others, particularly by John Indian, who forces her to look at herself and explore her body. Very little is known about the historical John Indian, Tituba's husband; in her text, Condé gives him some of the ethnic attributes of the historical Tituba, describing him as the child of an Arawak and a Yoruba-speaking Nago woman (from a region now belonging to Nigeria). Condé uses Tituba's encounter with John Indian as the point of transition between the isolation of her world in her cabin and the social and racial complexity of Bridgetown, with its busy port, as an opening to the world at large. Acknowledged sexual desire ("Why can't women do without men?" [15]) functions as her impetus to face the contact with the white world she had avoided until that moment—a necessary displacement in the text as she must move her main character as quickly as textually possible toward departure from Barbados toward Salem, where the central plot of the novel will unfold.

Condé gives this encounter compelling cultural signposts that seek to anchor the events surrounding their initial romance in seventeenth-century Barbadian society: the growth of plantation society, the presence of remaining pockets of Amerindians, the growth of the port of Bridgetown. Barbados, which had been settled by the English in 1625, began developing sugar plantations as the foundation of its growing economy in the 1640s. The importation of African slaves increased exponentially after that date, and

Condé's depiction of Barbadian slaves as new arrivals is accurate. The island had become a British Crown possession in 1663, an event that formalized relationships with the European metropolis and afforded planters the presence and protection of the British army and navy, thus contributing to the growth and development of plantation society.

Condé links Tituba's pivotal encounter with John Indian to witchcraft by having the character resort to a spell to bind to her the man she desires. The scene in which Tituba gathers the drop of blood and handkerchief she needs to secure John Indian's love through Obeah is set during carnival celebrations. This setting is not historically accurate since Crop Over, as Barbados's carnival is known, traces its roots only as far back as the 1780s, about a century after the events narrated in the novel. The incident—during which John Indian calls her a "little witch"—allows the narrator to ponder the meaning of practicing witchcraft and the disapproval in which the practice is held.

The pivotal encounter with John Indian—and the sexual desire it awakens in Tituba—propels Tituba toward the world outside her isolated hut and toward her departure to Massachusetts since he will not return to the bush to live with her. He is also the path to her first encounter with Christianity since she does not know the prayers and finds the stories about the creation of the world and how Adam was turned out of paradise that John alludes to "strange." The allusions are not without their touch of irony since sexual desire is drawing her away from her own Garden of Eden.

Chapter 3 (part 1) introduces Tituba to her first mistress. By joining John Indian, a slave, and coming to him of her free will, she is joining a household where she is voluntarily accepting slavelike conditions. The introduction to the life of a slave is an unpleasant experience, as she is welcomed with a list of chores to be done and an expression of the deepest bigotry. To her, Tituba was reduced to being "a gawk of a girl with skin of a repulsive color" (26). Tituba discovers through her contact with the white slave-owning world that she has been written off "the map of human beings" (24).

The chapter focuses on the differences in the approaches to their situations between Tituba and John Indian, differences that will be responsible for the stresses in their life together and will have a determining impact on the ways their careers unfold. For John Indian, "the duty of a slave is to survive" (27), which he does by flattery and pandering to his mistress, while Tituba's chosen stance is that of unrelenting resistance. She refuses to repeat her religious lessons, for example, not willing to claim a faith she does not have to placate her new mistress, and challenges Endicott's faith and power, bowing that "one of us had to go and it wasn't going to be me" (28).

Thematically, the chapter introduces the notion of witchcraft and the differences in the ideas of what witchcraft represents among blacks and whites. The possibility of an accusation of witchcraft stands as a threat to Tituba, although she does not understand witchcraft in the Christian sense, which involves dealings with the devil—"Before setting foot inside this house," she tells John Indian, "I didn't know who Satan was!" (27).

The nature and essence of witchcraft and the Christian devil occupies Tituba in chapter 4, where she ponders her own training in herbalism and the African-derived practice of communion with the spirits. She does not associate these practices with what the Endicotts understand as witchcraft or the work of the devil. Her reputation as a dabbler in African-derived practices, however, leaves her open to accusations of witchcraft, which materialize when Susanna Endicott is afflicted with an illness that makes her skin yellow and that she claims was caused by one of Tituba's spells.

Condé, who builds the tensions between Susanna Endicott's and Tituba's worldviews chiefly through the deployment of irony, uses it to good effect when Tituba sees the man who will be her new master, Samuel Parris, for the first time: "Imagine greenish, cold eyes, scheming and wily, creating evil because they saw it everywhere" (34). A second level of irony surfaces through the juxtaposition of two weddings in the text: a mock ceremony conducted by drunken slaves, in which the so-called minister marries Tituba and John by pretending to open a book and chanting "a litany of obscenities" (32), and a second ceremony conducted by Samuel Parris, performed before "jeering sailors" on board the ship taking them to Boston and the fate that filled Tituba with "a horrible foreboding" (36). This juxtaposition of scenes is a technique that Condé deploys frequently in the novel since it allows her to offer simultaneously two differing worldviews and the misunderstandings that flourish in the interstices.

Condé builds her narrative along a series of dualities, through which she establishes the patterns of mistrust and contempt that weave the fabric of racism and cultural misunderstanding in slave societies. Above all, she is concerned with showing how Christian intolerance has led to the vilification of African-derived practices such as those practiced by Tituba. This is important thematically since it is Condé's contention that it is in the juxtaposition of Christian bigotry and the mysteries of African spirituality that the Salem witch hunt developed.

We see in chapter 6 an example of how Condé works with dualities, as here Condé narrates the friendship and mutual dependence that evolves in the relationship between Tituba and her new mistress Elizabeth Parris. The relationship works along parallel lines to that of her mother Abena and her mistress, both linked by the feminist notion of sisterhood along race and class lines against male oppression. Tituba and Elizabeth are thus linked by their dread of master and husband, respectively, a dread fostered by a too rigid adherence to matters of religious practice and a spirituality dependent on deprivation as the only path to heaven. Tituba finds, for example, that Betsey Parris and Abigail Williams had been "robbed of their childhood's natural store of lightheartedness and sweetness" (40), a persistent theme in the novel when children appear. It is in the context of this sisterhood in shared oppression that Tituba feels free to share with the women of the Parris household her culture and religion. She tells the girls stores of "Anancy the Spider, people who had made a pact with the devil, zombies, *soukoug-nans,* and the hag who rides along on her three-legged horse" (42). These stories, Tituba claims, were enjoyed by the girls precisely because they fitted in with the many superstitions about witchcraft and the devil that had come to them through Samuel Parris's belief in the devil and his familiar. It is here, also, that she feels free to "call on the supernatural" to help heal Elizabeth, an invalid whose life was made miserable by constant pain. This intervention would lead to the Salem events.

The family's move to Salem, which takes place in chapter 7, brings with it new thematic threads that will be more fully developed as the trial progresses. One of these is the intensification of the slave trade, as the events take place at a time in which the growing American economy, particularly in the South, required more labor than what was readily available. John Indian brings news of the enslavement of Native Americans, both from the United States and the Caribbean. There will be repeated allusions in the text to the spread of slavery throughout the Americas.

A second theme is that of Tituba's nationalistic feelings, her love of Barbados and of the plantation landmarks that constituted her world before her departure for the American colonies. It is a theme whose repercussions will not become clear until the last chapters of the novel. Later in the novel, she describes herself as placing a bowl of water near the window "so that I could look at it while I busied myself in the kitchen and imagine my Barbados" (62).

A third thematic strand finds Tituba witnessing the execution of Ann "Goody" Glover, the last woman to be executed as a witch in Boston. The event dates the move to Salem to have taken place in 1688. Glover, an Irish laundress, was accused of witchcraft by the Reverend Cotton Mather (1663–1728) after the children in the household where she worked fell mysteriously ill. The execution brings back the specter of her mother's death, and she asks plaintively about the nature of the world "that had taken her away from [her] own people" (49).

The last theme of importance in the chapter revolves around Tituba's termination of her pregnancy so as not to subject her unborn child to the life of a slave. A trope in slave narratives and in fiction about plantation life, Tituba outlines the various methods through which slaves procure "the expulsion of an innocent baby, who will have no chance to change its fate, into a world of slavery and abjection" (50). The abortion is accomplished through the help of Judah White, a Salem woman who claims to be a friend of Mama Yaya and who helps Tituba learn the medicinal qualities of New England plants, a training that leads to the hybridization of the herbal practices for which Tituba is known. Tituba, in her narrative, links the death of her unborn child to the execution of Goody Glover, claiming that she believes that "the cry uttered by Goody Glover setting off along the corridor of death came from the bowels of my child, tortured by the same society and sentenced by the same judges" (52). In the "Lament for My Lost Child," which she pens after the event, Tituba describes herself as "Sitting on a rock on the riverbank/I wept and lamented" (55).

Chapter 9 introduces the extensive cast of characters familiar to those acquainted with the history of the Salem trials. It also describes the foreboding atmosphere of the town, where Tituba feels she will undergo "terrible trials" and where "excruciatingly painful events would turn my hair white" (58). Condé here sets the stage for the beginning of the witch hunt by characterizing many of the girls in the village as inspired in their questions by a malevolent curiosity and a willingness to misrepresent Tituba's stories of African spirits and Obeah as related to the Puritan devil. The misguided Puritanism of Salem is described by Tituba thus: "I had not realized the full extent of the ravages that Samuel Parris's religion was causing nor even understood its real nature before coming to live in Salem" (65). Howard Mosher, in his review of the novel for the *New York Times,* summarizes the obsession with the devil of the citizens of Salem thus: "What a fanatical sect Ms. Condé's Puritans turn out to be: sadists and murderers, rabid misogynists and racists who hang and torture women, imprison tiny children, burn Jewish families out of their homes and regularly accuse black slaves of being in league with Satan."

Condé, in Tituba's narrative, will explore the notion of blackness as closely associated to the devil. Those surrounding Tituba in Salem are depicted as believing that her skin color is "indicative of [her] close connection to Satan" (65). Chapter 10 explores this notion in detail, an important thematic introduction to the first illnesses and fits observed in the children of the household. The argument Condé builds is twofold: Tituba struggles not to give in to her feelings of revenge, while all around her encourage her to use her powers to help them seek revenge on others. Her determination not to do evil reflects the blackness/goodness, whiteness/evil dichotomy that is the very opposite of the beliefs spread by the self-righteous Puritan leadership in the text. Condé will use chapters 11 and 12 of part 1 to build up to the arrest of Tituba and the other purported witches of Salem, following the historical record closely. She will do so against the backdrop of Tituba's growing strength—drawn not only from her sense of innocence, but from the support of her ancestors, particularly Abena and Mama Yaya (who assure her that she would be the only one to survive), and from her conviction of her eventual return to Barbados.

Chapter 1 of part 2 brings us back to the fundamental differences between John Indian and Tituba—between his philosophy of survival at all cost, which would require that Tituba testify against the other women in the village accused of witchcraft, and her desire for revenge, which she envisions as that of using her power to accuse to bring those who have tortured her to prison.

Chapter 2 (part 2) offers a somewhat anachronistic instance of intertextuality in the encounter it narrates between Tituba and Hester Prynne, the protagonist of Nathaniel Hawthorne's *The Scarlet Letter,* published in 1850 but set in Puritan New England in the seventeenth century. Hester, a young woman who has borne an illegitimate daughter, is forced by her community to wear a scarlet *A* on her clothing, branding her as an adulteress. Her story of grace and dignity in the face of her community's condemnation has some points of affinity with the story of Tituba as told by Condé, as Hester refuses to name her daughter's father and survives her humiliation to live a life of charitable works and redemption.

The juxtaposition of the two women in the same cell is not without its ironic humor, as Hester laments that she will never make a feminist of Tituba, but it works primarily as another parallel story, through which Condé can narrate the solidarity that exists among women when faced with a common oppressor. In this novel, the oppressor is the Puritan establishment that has forced women into restricted, joyless lives and that has learned to use the judicial system and the death penalty to force them into submission. As rebels against the Puritan cause, Hester and Tituba occupy parallel spaces in this struggle. Hester's wish would be for helping Tituba understand the gender dimensions of such a struggle by pointing out how she has come to this predicament by her dependence on John Indian, who betrays her, in any case, at this difficult moment in her life since he cannot survive and still continue their alliance. The question Tituba poses in the story-within-a-story she tells Hester—"Can't we even keep our daughters away from men?" (99)—echoes Hester's dreams of "a model society governed and run by women" (101).

Hester's ideal society, from her description, would resemble that proposed by radical feminist Shulamith Firestone (1945–) in *The Dialectics of Sex: A Case for a Feminist Revolution* (1970), a major text in second-wave feminism in the United States that argued against the gender oppression imposed on women through their biology. Firestone argued that their role in pregnancy, childbirth, and child rearing had placed women at physical, social, economic, and political disadvantage and argued that women should seize every possible opportunity—legal, economic, and technological—to escape their burden and place themselves at the center of political, social, and economic life. The brand of radical feminism that Hester embodies is beyond Tituba's comprehension since her own Utopia is not that of community living within a socialist-style system but of the world she had known in Barbados. The presentation of Hester's imagined community prompts a return in Tituba's imagination to her own lost community and prefigures her revolutionary role in Barbados that marks the end of the novel. She thinks of the beauty of her seemingly lost island—her *Paradise Lost*—but sees that "the men and women are suffering. . . . I have forgotten that our bondage is not over" (102). The theme of revenge, which runs throughout the novel, here moves its focus away from the people—particularly white women—who have persecuted her and toward political action as a source of redress.

Chapter 3 (part 2) is built on excerpts from the historical Tituba's deposition during the Salem trials, interspersed with commentary from the fictional Tituba. This pivotal chapter seeks to bridge Condé's intentions of presenting Tituba as a heroine and the historical testimony—which makes clear that she confessed to having harmed the girls and accused others of practicing witchcraft—as part of a strategy devised with Hester Prynne to effect her release and guarantee her survival. The fictional Tituba underscores the performative aspect of her testimony and claims that the only names she mentioned were those of guilty people (those against whom she wished to be revenged): "I did not have the heart to obey Samuel Parrish and give the names of innocent women" (106).

The chapter's importance derives from Condé's need to address the most damaging aspect of the historical record, which clearly records Tituba's confession and accusations. This chapter has drawn considerable and contradictory commentary from readers and critics. Some have accepted the explanation as a plausible one, with solid roots in the strategies for survival developed within slave culture. Others find the explanation—especially as linked to the intervention of Hester Prynne's radical feminism and hints of lesbian love—to be the weakest element in the text.

Tituba's narrative emphasizes the performative aspects involved in survival through the description in chapter 4 (part 2) of John Indian's own performance as a tormented soul to save his life. Condé, however, seeks to establish differences between the two performances by reverting to the differences between Tituba's resistant survival and John Indian's opportunistic self-protection, which in this case involves accusing innocent women, something Tituba claims to have refused to do. They differ also on their concern with each other's survival: Tituba is portrayed as worried that the increased talk about a "black man who forces his victims to write in his book" (108) may lead them to accuse John Indian, while he seems indifferent to seeing her chained in a barn, and she fears he would be capable of accusing her of witchcraft if it were necessary to his survival. After the meeting at the barn where she was held, she would never see him again.

Chapter 4 (part 2), which narrates a meeting between Tituba and her mistress, in which the latter asks Tituba's forgiveness, also addresses the historical erasure that Condé sought to tackle in her novel. This is accomplished chiefly through a passage in which Condé's own narrative voice—a voice cognizant of the future and of the omission of Tituba's name from most accounts of the Salem trials—speaks of the character's fears of historical oblivion. Tituba writes of "gradually being forgotten," of only being "mentioned in passing" in the accounts of trials "that would arouse the curiosity and pity of generations to come" (110).

We hear in Tituba, Condé's own voice articulating for the reader the process of historical reclamation at the bottom of her fictional project. The lament is anachronistic, as it shows the fictional Tituba as aware of events that would only transpire after her death and evidences aspects of the text's self-referentiality, as it addresses the motivations and potential impact of Condé's own work, which is designed to rescue Tituba from "this future injustice that seemed more cruel than death itself" (110). In an interview included in the text, Condé addresses this issue directly: "I felt that this eclipse of Tituba's life was completely unjust. I felt a strong solidarity with her, and I wanted to offer her revenge by inventing a life such as she might perhaps have wished it to be told" (199).

The chapter, with its emphasis on the injustice of Tituba's fading from historical memory, concludes, curiously, with Tituba's own temporary loss of memory, brought about by a mental breakdown on news of Heather's suicide in prison. She is examined by a Doctor Zerobabel, an allusion to Dr. Zerobabel Endicott (d. 1684), a Salem physician practicing during the time of the witchcraft trials who studied female maladies and left a manuscript with his remedies printed in *Every Day Life in the Massachusetts Bay Colony* by George Francis Dow (1967). Tituba gives here a sample of one of his prescribed remedies, which in and of itself is not different from the sort of potion that led to accusations of witchcraft to others. By the same token, as Tituba is being transferred to prison, she witnesses the flogging of some errant schoolboys, which signals the level of corporeal punishment on which the Puritans depended.

Chapters 5 and 6 allude to the spread of the accusations of witchcraft and their effect on a number of historical figures surrounding Tituba, from the child Dorcas Good to the arrest of George Burroughs. Condé moves quickly through these events, accelerating the narrative through the comparison of the wave of accusations, executions, and reprieves as a plague that spreads quickly throughout the region. The tale, which had lingered on the events as they affected Tituba and on her meditations on her relationship with Hester Prynne and John Indian's treachery, now moves to Tituba's freedom and her desire to return to Barbados, where the institution of slavery had consolidated its power through the richness derived from the sugar plantation and "the wretched herd of slaves continued to turn the wheel of misfortune" (121).

The freedom from prison that will allow for her return to Barbados, which come through Tituba being bought out of prison by a merchant Jew (Benjamin Cohen d'Azevedo), is experienced by Tituba as a new birth. This is, in turn, preceded by a dream in which Hester lays down with Tituba, intimating the possibility of a sexual relationship with "a body similar to your own . . . another kind of bodily pleasure" (122). The impossibility of Puritan tolerance for that sort of love introduces another level of Puritan intolerance—that against the Jews, represented here by Tituba's new master, whose house will be destroyed and his children burned in the process as an example of Puritan bigotry. The fate of the children underscores a sustained theme in the book, that of the harsh treatment of children in Puritan society, which seeks to stifle both self-expression and (as in this instance) life itself.

Chapters 8–11 of part 2, which Condé dedicates to Tituba's life with her Jewish master and lover, center on two main themes: the similarities in the histories of oppression and persecution that link Jews and African slaves and Tituba's power to conjure the dead to communicate with the living. This is the period of Tituba's most content domesticity, when she integrates herself into a household in which she is both worker and substitute mother of the only joyful and fulfilled children in the novel. Tituba describes her content-ment in this environment by explaining that "some men who have the virtue of being weak instill in us the desire to be a slave!" (140). This domesticity is punctuated by an increasing longing for Barbados, which she will only attain, tragically, when Benjamin blames the death of his children on his unwillingness to allow Tituba to return to her home island, a disinclination he attributes to his reluctance to give up the conversations with his dead wife that Tituba's powers as a conjurer made possible.

Tituba's return to Barbados is punctuated by a return of the three spirits who had served as her protectors, Mama Yaya, her mother, Abena, and her adoptive father, Yao. Her voyage, through the figure of Deodatus, like her grandmother "a Nago from the Gulf of Benin," is marked by a gradual return to the narratives and cadences of her childhood, brought back in the tales narrated by the black sailor. He also introduces her to one of the rare Maroon communities fighting for freedom in Barbados. (In Barbados, where much of the forests had been cleared for sugar cultivation, there were only a few Maroon camps.)

Tituba's first night in Barbados—when she hears the island murmuring that "she is back...and will never leave us again" (147), is marked by her narrative of her adventures in Salem to her new community, which opens the possibility of her skills being used for the good of the Maroon cause. Like Nanny in Jamaica, the legendary priestess and Maroon leader who was said to be able to protect men from bullets in battle, Tituba is asked to use her knowledge to make the Maroon leader, Christopher, invulnerable to the white man's bullets. Like Mama Yaya before her, however, she chooses to return to her hut at the edge of the plantation, coming full circle to the space of isolation from which she started.

Circumstances, however, will make that retreat impossible, pushing her toward the last refuge of the spirit world. The last chapters of the book, there-fore, will bring the thematic threads of the novel together, with an emphasis on this crossing to the spirit world. Her guardian spirits will remind her that her choice of men has always led her toward disaster, as proven here by her sexual links with the leaders of the Maroons—Christopher and Iphigene.

(The latter, a child of famed Maroon leader Ti-Noël, allows Condé to allude to the sustained history of resistance in the island.) Iphigene's failed revolt is meant to provide another link in that history, which prompts Mama Yaya to comment that "our memory will have to be covered in blood" since "there's no end to the misfortune of black folks" (165). Conscious of the ever expanding reach of the institution of slavery, which, a century later, will lead to the Haitian Revolution, Tituba meditates on the spread of colonialism on the backs of enslaved Africans. Resistance, Condé seems to imply, is the only option left, and Tituba, like Hester, will find herself condemned to die with her unborn child in resistence's name.

Sustained resistance is the focus of Condé's epilogue, in which Tituba's voice describes how her soul has remained among the living, bringing hope to the enslaved population and sustaining their spirit of resistance throughout the years.

Chapter 6

Raphael Confiänt's
Mamzelle Dragonfly

Raphael Confiänt is a figure of seminal importance in Caribbean culture, both as a writer and as one of the founders and leaders of the
Créolité movement in Martinique and Guadeloupe. Born in Lorrain,
Martinique, on January 25, 1951, Confiänt attended school in the capital
city of Fort-de-France. He left Martinique briefly to attend the University of
Provence (now the Institut d'Études Politiques d'Aix-en-Provence), where
he majored in political science and English, but returned to Martinique after
completing his studies.

Since the early 1970s, Confiänt has been a staunch defender of the use
of Creole, the French-derived language spoken by most Martinicans and
Guadeloupeans—derided by colonial officials and some metropolitan French
as an inferior dialect—as the basis for a national culture and literature. On
his return from France, then, he joined the efforts to establish a literature
in Creole, first as a contributor and avid supporter of *Grif an tè,* a journal
written entirely in Creole (1977–1981), and subsequently writing a number
of novels and collections of short stories in Creole (later translated into
French), among them *Jik dèyè do Bondyé* (short stories, 1979), *Jou Baré*
(poems, 1981), *Bitako-a* (novel, 1985), *Kôd Yanm* (novel, 1986), and *Mari-
sosé (Mamzelle Dragonfly)* (1987).

In the late 1980s, frustrated by publishers' reluctance to bring out books
in Creole due to their limited readership, Confiänt began to write in French.
His first book in French, *Eau de Café,* appeared in 1988 and was followed
by numerous other works published in French and translated into English,
German, Creole, and other languages. He publishes an average of two novels

per year and has accumulated an impressive list of titles to his credit. They include *L'Allée des soupirs* (1994), *La Vierge du grand retour* (1996), *Régisseur de rhum* (1998), *Brin d'amour* (2001), *Nuée ardente* (2002), *Le Barbare enchanté* (2003), and *La Lessive du diable* (2003). In 2004 Confiänt won the Prix des Amériques insulaires et de la Guyane for his novel *La panse du chacal*, where he narrates the experiences of *coulis*, as the nineteenth-century indentured servants from India were known. His most recent novel is *Adèle et la pacotilleuse* (2005), a fictionalized account of Victor Hugo's daughter Adèle and particularly of the woman who helps reunite her with her father.

Since 1979, Confiänt has been a professor of English and Creole at the University of the Antilles and French Guyana as well as the editor of *Antilla*, a weekly independent newspaper distributed in the Antilles and French Guyana since 1982. During the 1980s, Confiänt joined forces with other militant proponents of the use of Creole, chief among them Jean Bernabé and Patrick Chamoiseau, to form the Créolité movement. Confiänt is a member of the Groupe d'Etudes et de Recherches en Espace Créolophone, which supports the graphic system for the writing of Creole proposed by Bernabé in 1978. The three authors—Confiänt, Bernabé, and Chamoiseau—coauthored the seminal text of the Créolité movement, *Eloge de la créolité* (In Praise of Creoleness) (1989) and other widely influential theoretical texts, among them *Les Lettres créoles* (with Chamoiseau), a survey of Antillean literature from 1635 to 1975. The movement, developed in reaction to the Afrocentrality of fellow Martinican Aimé Césaire's Négritude movement, emphasizes the diversity of Caribbean ancestry and cultural heritage, which includes Amerindians, a variety of European groups, East Indians, and Chinese, among others. Himself a self-described *chabin*—a pale-skinned man with Negroid features—Confiänt embraces the range of cultural and racial differences he represents. He has dedicated his award-winning childhood memoirs *Ravines du devant-jour* to "all the little *chabins* of the world."

Confiänt's influential critical and theoretical work includes a controversial book on Aimé Césaire, *Aimé Césaire, une traversée paradoxale du siècle* (1993), *La Poésie antillaise d'expression créole de 1960 à nos jours* (with Maryse Romanos, 1998), the *Dictionnaire des néologismes créoles* (2000), and *La version créole* (2001). Confiänt is also militantly involved in Martinique's environmental struggle and is a founding member of the Martinican Association for Environmental Protection and of the Movement of Democrats and Ecologists for Sovereignty. He has been awarded numerous honors for his work, including the Casa de las Américas Prize and the Prix Jet Tours for his memoirs.

Mamzelle Dragonfly

Confiänt's novel, originally written in Creole, evokes the Creole lives of its protagonist, Adelise, and her family and neighbors during the postwar decades, the 1950s and the early years of the 1960s. When the novel was published, Confiänt praised it as "a great victory for Creole," declaring it "the most important event in his life" and inviting more Caribbean writers to work in their vernacular languages (Silenieks 854).

The novel is structured around 15 chapters, most of them narrated in the first person by the protagonist, Adelise; others are narrated by an omniscient narrator. They all focus on the central figure of Adelise, a native of Glotin, a small village on the Lézarde River in the central mountains of Martinique, northeast of the capital of Fort-de-France. Through the narrative of Adelise's travails as a poor, uneducated young woman in postwar Martinican society—when the island was struggling with crucial social and political decisions—Confiänt explores the tragedy of female lives caught between traditional patriarchal society and the demands of modernization in a postcolonial society.

The novel opens with a description of Adelise's life with her mother in the village, rendered poignant through the first-person description of her attachment to her tree and the foreshadowing of a tangled and difficult life. Adelise's relationship to her tree is rooted in African-derived practices common in the Caribbean countryside, where children were often born at home. Trees are often planted at the site of the burial of the placenta or of the umbilical cord, usually fruit-bearing trees like coconuts or breadfruits. The birth-tree becomes the property of the child, who is entrusted with its care as a way of teaching him or her responsibility. The practice is said to have reinforced a person's attachment to the birthplace and the family land. Adelise's tree, unnamed and fruitless, becomes her confidante, her "lover."

The mystery of the unnamed tree, whose white blossoms Adelise's mother calls "the devil's flowers" (3) and which the blacksmith described as useless, is used in chapter 1 to underscore the sexual vulnerability of Adelise as a young woman in Martinican society. Living on the edge of the cane fields "belonging to a Big Whiteman" (a Grand Beké) (4), where her mother works in almost slavelike conditions, Adelise's life seems suspended between the dangers posed by nature and the perils of the plantation fields.

Adelise's fear of the *bête-longues,* or fer-de-lances, the most dangerous snake in all of South America (pit vipers with deadly venomous bites), with their association with the loss of innocence in the Garden of Eden, prefigures her future life of sexual abuse. The chapter, indeed, underscores her vulnerability, the fragility that makes her appear, like her aunt Philomène, as a dragonfly "fluttering over waterlilies" (4). This fragility, which points toward tragedy to come in her life, is underscored in three episodes briefly narrated in the chapter: she has a dream in which she wanders around a city whose deserted streets "seemed to have stopped dead for ages" (6); she snaps the string of a kite she is asked to hold, letting the kite float away, while the young owner shouts at her that her life "will be zactly like that of the kite you just lost!" (7); and she tells her tree a secret whose origin she does not explain but that voices her conviction that she is fated to die at age 30.

In chapter 2, Confiänt moves the action to Morne (Mount) Pichevin, a marginal and crime-ridden area of densely packed shacks at the top of one of the steep hills surrounding the bay of Fort-de-France. Sent to the city by her mother in hopes of a better life than that offered by work in the cane fields and away from the sexual exploitation that accompanies it, Adelise's arrival is marked by the contrast between the rural-bound kindness of Mam Tidiane, a vegetable seller at the bus terminal at Croix-Mission (to the west of the center of the city and next to the vegetable and meat markets), and the sexual brutality of two young men she encounters as she climbs to Morne Pichevin.

In chapter 2, Confiänt introduces the reader to Aunt Philomène, her mother's younger sister, who makes a living as a prostitute. The character of Philomène is built in counterpoint to Adelise's innocence and her mother's premature aging in the cane fields. Characterized by her joyous nonchalance and sexual frankness, Philomène is the epitome of the stereotypical sensual *câpresse*, or light-skinned Afro-Creole quadroon. Her path to prostitution is tied to the lack of economic opportunity for Martinicans after their post-colonial integration into the French state. (Martinique became a French *département* on March 19, 1946.) "I didn't choose this trade," Philomène explains to Adelise. "I was dragged into it by poverty and bad luck" (24). She represents a sexually bound option for unskilled women in Martinique, presented ambiguously in the text, as her exploitation of her sexuality allows her to live in relative prosperity vis-à-vis her cane-cutting sister but leads to a loneliness that will drive her to an early death.

In chapter 3, Adelise narrates her path from "the Hell of the cane fields" (19) to the life of a prostitute. This transformation is accepted by the character as unavoidable, as part of the sexual exploitation that for her begins in multiple rapes by the plantations *commandeur*. When Adelise joins the "li'l gang" of children working on the plantation, she works in the appropriately named Savane-Zombi since her response to her repeated and brutal rapes is a disassociation of her body and soul—a transference of her capacity for feeling to her tree. "My body belongs completely to that tree," Adelise claims (20), as she schools herself to feel nothing as she is first raped and later submits to sex with anyone because her initial rapes have left her unable to refuse. This initial rape, and the assumption by the character of its inevitability, functions as a deeply set trauma from which the character struggles to recover throughout the novel. The true mystery of the narrative revolves around whether the character can transcend this trauma or will be haunted by it to her death.

Confiänt underscores the deep loss Adelise sustains because of her rape through her silent rejection by Téramène, a young, tall, and broad-shouldered man who was "lovesick" for her and represented the possibility of marriage and children. Unable to return his love, Adelise watches him turn away from her forever when he realizes that she is bleeding from a recent rape. He is paralyzed, like a duppy-ghost, another soul disassociated from its body, as if to accentuate the spreading loss stemming from one act of sexual violence.

Adelise's first act of prostitution comes after a year of multiple attempts at finding employment. The tale of her descent into prostitution is punctuated by both a brush with the Bureau de Migrations Interessant les Departements d'Outremer (Bureau for Migrations Affecting Overseas Departments, BUMIDOM) and a peek at the profound class differences that separate some Martinicans from others along racial lines. The BUMIDOM operated between 1963 and 1982 and encouraged migration from the new Overseas Departments of France into the metropolis. It was responsible for bringing thousands of workers, among them many unskilled workers who went on to work menial jobs, from the former colonies into France. Adelise's encounter with its bureaucracy emphasizes the racial dimensions of class in Martinique; the bureaucrat who so indifferently closes the office at the very moment in which Adelise's long wait is finally rewarded with an opportunity for a meeting is described as a *chabin-mulâtre,* a light-skinned, wavy-haired man of the type that usually held high places in the pigmentocracy of colonial Martinique. Confiänt underscores the nature of this pigmentocracy a few pages later, when, witnessing a group of rich Martinicans emerging from the cathedral after a christening, Adelise hears them speaking in French, the language of the upper classes, which, for Creole-speaking Adelise, was a "language that just never stopped wadding itself up into a ball in my throat" (28). When the time comes for her first experience as a prostitute, that ball in her throat seems about to burst forth as vomit when she realizes she is expected to bed an imbecile (30).

In chapter 4, Confiänt explores the world of the Martinican African-derived practice of *quimbois.* Here Confiänt addresses the spectrum of *quimbois* practices—from the belief that evil spirits roam the darkness awaiting victims and that spells can be cast for harming others to the healing practices drawn from an understanding of the medicinal qualities of plants and animals.

The chapter, however, opens and ends with Adelise's relationship to her tree, whose life is threatened by the negative forces unleashed on the young girl by rape. Interposed between Adelise and her tree—her "lover" and essence—are now evil spirits, or *soukougnans,* which can drive the life force out of both. The chapter is built on a mysterious illness akin to a nervous breakdown from which Adelise recovers but which kills her tree, severing her connection to the land. The illness, variously described as a sluggishness that prevents her from moving or a bewitching, leaves her with a deeply rooted sense of hopelessness that separates her from the simple country people who surround her. The loss of this hope leads to the death of her tree.

In chapter 5, Adelise describes the violence that arose out of the competition between gangs in the various Fort-de-France shantytowns in the 1950s. The description is part of a somewhat rambling narrative intended to convey not only the passage of time (the fact that Adelise has by now become an integral part of the close-knit neighborhood) but also the texture of life in Morne Pichevin. Although many of the narrative threads introduced in this chapter are not pursued later in the novel—Adelise, for example, sets out in search of her father but abandons her objective, never to resume it in the text—they help flesh out in the text how Adelise's spirit continues to grow "hard as iron" (52).

The most important narrative thread, since it explains an aspect of Adelise's hardness against men, is that of her father's abandonment of the family when she was a child of five. The abandonment is tied in the text to the father's passion for cockfighting, a quasi-addictive sports tradition in Martinique and indeed around the world, as its roots go back to the ancient Egyptians. (In the United States, it goes back to the Founding Fathers, and it is said that Abraham Lincoln "helped establish his 'honest Abe' reputation by deciding the winner of a disputed cockfight" [Moller].) The figure of the father is shrouded in an ambiguity that stems from his being for his daughter no more than a series of disconnected memories and overheard whispers: he was generous to his family but "too tight with his sous" (43) with others; he was not given to drink, nor was he believed to have a mistress, but Adelise suspected a connection between him and their neighbor Mam Anna; Adelise is surrounded by people who believe "the bugger doesn't deserve the name of father" (44), yet the mother praises him for never failing to send money for their daughter. This ambiguity enhances what is generally an approach to male characterization in the novel, marked by a wish to convey realistic portrayals of the varied types that people Martinican society.

This approach to nuanced characterization is shown in this chapter through the different ways in which Adelise presents herself: kind and caring— "a good-hearted girl!" (45)—to her neighbors in Morne Pichevin; calculating in her reasons for looking up her father; fearless and unfeeling in the way she approaches her sexual encounters with her rich clients; and "harder and harder" as a waitress at the Sailors' Daisies.

Thematically, however, Confiänt continues the thread that links Adelise's behavior to her rape by the *commandeur* and the trauma that stems from it as transferred to her dying or dead tree. Her contact with the women of Morne Pichevin reinforces the problematic gender issues built into the text through Adelise's rape and her father's abandonment. Confiänt characterizes Adelise as severed from her body as the tree born of her umbilical chord is severed from the land. Her disconnection from her body implies here a disconnection from emotions, and Adelise prefers to stay on her own, "dreaming about my countryside in Glotin and my tree" (51).

The trauma of rape impacts Adelise's characterization most directly in this chapter, where she is presented as possessing the fearlessness of those to whom the worst has already happened and have nothing left to fear from life. In Morne Pichevin, she is described as going through the motions of life, assuming a passivity that moves beyond her sexuality to matters of survival and finances, mocking her aunt's belief in the happiness that can stem from marriage and children. This is a posture that Confiänt will underscore throughout the novel, until she sheds her attitude of enforced submissiveness at the end of the novel, just as she begins to get ready to leave Martinique for Fort-de-France. In chapter 7, for example, she describes her mind as being "a thousand leagues away" (70) and finds herself, in the middle of the ceaseless chatter of the women, missing "the times when she and her mother would sit in front of their shanty, in the evening, waiting silently until darkness fell" (66).

In chapter 6, Adelise goes back in time to narrate the immediate reasons why her mother had sent her to Fort-de-France. Here—as Confiänt reaches the middle point in his novel—he slows the pace of the narrative, allowing the focus to shift away from the immediate events of Adelise's life and toward the fabric of life in the countryside (through this extensive flashback into Adelise's mother's failed efforts at securing her daughter an education) and toward the ways in which political tensions and the pressures of urbanization affect the inhabitants of Morne Pichevin.

The chapter, which narrates Adelise's brief experience in the house of two sisters "of the mixed-blood Chinese type" (56), builds on an eerily quasi-gothic atmosphere, where Adelise's ordinary, commonplace experiences working in the sugar fields and running a simple household with her mother are set against the midnight wanderings and melancholy ramblings of an old maid obsessed with the lover who betrayed her (comparable to those of Miss Havesham in Charles Dickens's *Great Expectations*). Adelise witnesses her temporary guardian's descent into love-inspired madness through the lens of her own feelings of abandonment, as she questions why her mother has left her in this strange house. Her feelings echo against the old woman's lament—"Ah, Romain, you betrayed me!" (59)—the two laments playing against each other as if stemming from the same source, that of women forsaken.

Witnessing this episode of heartbroken madness ends Adelise's brief window of opportunity for a better education than that offered in her rural school. Her mother had taken the sum of money sent every year by Adelise's father to purchase her an education in French and mathematics that would have opened some doors to better employment in an increasingly modern Martinique, where mastery of the French colonial language had become indispensable. Throughout the novel, Confiänt insists on presenting Adelise as a Creole speaker, but one who appreciates the cadences of the French language she could not speak herself but drank in "as if it were a prayer" (60). Later, when hearing Aimé Césaire speaking in French to the assembled masses at a political rally, Adelise reacts by letting herself "drift along on billows of sweetness" (108). The process of modernization that in Confiänt's opinion included a misguided effort to suppress the Creole language is here portrayed by the rural teacher's use of physical punishment to eradicate what is often to the rural population their only language.

In chapter 7, Confiänt continues his slow exploration of Creole life through his description of how the women of Morne Pichevin discover the place where the thieves of the neighborhood hide their cache of stolen goods. The chapter is notable for two things: it introduces the theme of how the growing urbanization of Fort-de-France (responsible for the growth of shantytowns like those of Morne Pichevin) is affecting the ways in which its inhabitants conceive of themselves as citizens, a theme Confiänt will develop more fully in subsequent chapters, and it prefigures Aunt Philomène's early death through the use of the local divination practice of reading the future in the forms glimpsed at the bottom of a bottle of water mixed with four fresh eggs. Lying to her aunt about the coffin she has glimpsed through the mixture, Adelise expresses for the first time her own hope of one day leaving for France. Her desire elicits from her aunt a view of the obstacles that confront the colonial subject wishing to join in the life of the metropolis, who must have plenty of money and a familiarity with polite behavior. Adelise's path through the rest of the novel is that of slowly becoming that very colonial subject who can leave her home island behind.

Chapter 8 narrates how Adelise finds in Homère—"a perfect country clod" (77)—a man that awakens her senses and whom she learns to love. The chapter, which is placed precisely at the center of the novel, following on Adelise's expression of her desire of going to France, finds in the character of Homère the expression of the essence of Martinique's rural culture, the manly equivalent of Adelise's tree. "Homère was a man with roots," Adelise explains, "planted firmly in the soil" (79). What she finds in him was the fundamental nature of rural life, the spirit of her village. The chapter is a pivotal one since, given its centrality, Adelise's fate in the novel is to depend on the outcome of her relationship with Homère. Confiänt's implied question here is whether Homère can revive Adelise's tree and reinforce her rural roots or prove those roots to be essentially dead, along with her rural self.

In chapter 9, Confiänt turns his attention to the Martinican carnival, a vibrant annual affair in the tradition of the great Caribbean carnival celebrations. Truman Capote, in "Music for Chameleons"—a story about a Martinican Grand Beké who proves to the American author that chameleons are attracted to music—described the Martinican carnival as "as spontaneous and vivid as an explosion in a fireworks factory" (qtd. in Lehmann-Haupt 13). Carnival in Martinique begins on the first Sunday after the Feast of the Epiphany (January 6, or 12th Night) and lasts until Ash Wednesday, the Day of the She-Devils (La Fête des Diablesses), when she-devils dressed in black and white—their faces painted white—gather to mourn the death of the carnival king, Vaval, and his alter ego, Bwa-Bwa, whose effigies are burned amid chants of "Vaval, pas quitte nous" (Vaval, don't leave us).

The chapter, which narrates events six years after Adelise's arrival in Fort-de-France (she is now 23), introduces the character of Féfé, Philomène's lover, a maker of carnival costumes who will introduce Homère to politics and Adelise to a rich lover, a jeweler whose wealth tempts Adelise, "its venom poisoning my feelings" (97). Féfé is introduced as a "Red Devil," a character who rules over Shrove Tuesday (Mardi Gras), the day of the most impressive parades of revelers. Red Devils, like Féfé, dress in "a red wooden devil's head covered with tiny mirrors, and a red bodysuit with a kind of black cape on the back" (85). His association with the Red Devil figure is ironically significant, as his "red" connections point to his status as an opportunistic Communist, while as a devil, he tempts Adelise into a relationship with a client that will have tragic repercussions. Féfé lives a life marginal to that of the community of Morne Pichevin, as he is believed to dabble in magic and consort with "devil-dealing *engagés*," practicing *quimbois* and participating in séances (87).

In chapter 10, Confiänt turns his attention to the famous riots in Martinique in 1959. Political tensions had grown on the island since it had become an Overseas Department of France in 1947. Disturbances in 1951 had claimed lives and injured scores of protesters, radicalizing the growing number of unemployed shantytown dwellers. Violence broke out again in 1959, stemming out of local tensions about the slow development of the urban infrastructure in Fort-de-France and generalized dissatisfaction with the lack of autonomy of the local government vis-à-vis France's central authority. The violence would lead to concessions, and in 1960, France granted the elected island councils a greater degree of control over local legislation and spending.

At the heart of these tensions were the enduring colonial economic and social structures that remained despite the island's neocolonial status as an overseas French *département*. Adelise and the inhabitants of Morne Pichevin lived lives circumscribed by continuing "forms of economic, monetary, and commercial domination that link metropolis and periphery, urban and rural areas of the global system" (Dawson 22). Pushed into urban centers by a collapsing plantation system, with little access to education and skills not suited to urban enterprises, they lived in the periphery of the main economy as squatters in marginalized spaces, with few services and limited access to steady employment. The novel historicizes here the conditions under which the shantytown dwellers of Fort-de-France paralyzed the city, as the inhabitants of Morne Pichevin, "brandishing stones, crowbars, cutlasses, *becs-de-mer*, and broken bottles" (93), confronted the police.

Since, as readers, we witness these events from Adelise's limited perspective, our point of view is restricted as to the reasons why the men in their community are rioting and violent: "the riots had been going on for three days," the narrator writes, "and the women in Morne Pichevin were still in the dark about everything" (94). On the other hand, the immediacy of her perspective allows Confiänt to describe the violent confrontations from within.

The narrative of Adelise's participation in the riots also includes a detailed description of the condition of the body of one of the dead youths from their shantytown. The confrontation with the dead prompts a flashback, through which the narrator seeks to bring to the realm of the reader's experience the dizzying quality of the events Adelise has witnessed. Likening them to a ride in a merry-go-round that becomes terrifying when Adelise perceives her mother looking vacantly at her, "as if she'd gone into a daydream" (99), the narrator conveys the startling nature of the violent events.

In chapter 11, the narrator delves deeper into the sociopolitical tensions behind the riots by having Homère become embroiled in political party maneuvers that lose him (and by extension Adelise) the trust of the Morne Pichevin neighbors and, most important, by allowing us to witness, through Adelise's presence, a rally in which the main speaker is Fort-de-France's mayor Aimé Césaire (1913–).

Césaire, a founding member of the Martinican Communist Party, had become mayor of Fort-de-France in 1945 at the tender age of 32, a position he would maintain for the next 56 years. The following year, he was elected as one of the Martinican representatives to the French National Assembly. He had been then a young professor at the Lycée Schoelcher in Fort-de-France, where he had Frantz Fanon among his students. Césaire, despite his inexperience, had won the crowds over with his eloquence in French, an eloquence that already signaled the masterful control of the French language that would make him, with the publication of *Cahiers d'un retour au pays natale* (1956), one of the best-known and most influential Francophone writers. Fanon would write in *Black Skins, White Masks* (1952) how a woman had fainted from emotion after hearing him speak—an incident Confiänt replicates through Adelise's reaction to Césaire's appearance at a rally in the text:

Adelise felt her throat go dry, and a deep tremor ran through her body. She couldn't hear anything more.... The people around her, especially the women, were all in the same daze. And when Césaire's voice, his warm and caressing voice, began to speak French, Adelise let herself drift along on billows of sweetness. (108)

Confiänt uses Césaire's speech to articulate the fundamental political issues behind the Martinican riots, something which, in the previous chapter, he could not accomplish since the narrative remained limited by Adelise's lack of understanding of the political issues at stake. Césaire, who had left the Communist Party in 1956 in protest against the Soviet invasion of Hungary, had founded a new party in 1957, the Martinican Progressive Party, committed to an autochthonous brand of communism more responsible to the needs of the people of the island. While a representative to the National Assembly, he had participated in the passing of the 1947 law that had turned the colonies of Martinique, Guadeloupe, French Guyana, and Réunion into French *départements,* a law he had supported as reparation for the burdens that colonialism had placed on these territories. (He would come under attack from proindependence activists for his involvement in the department-status debate.) By 1950, however, Césaire's anticolonial philosophy had become more fully developed, as attested by the publication in his journal *Présence Africaine* of his influential essay *Discours sur le colonialisme,* in which Césaire critiques European colonialism by finding in it the roots of the Nazi movement. The anticolonial ideas behind the *Discours* find their way into the Martinican Progressive Party's call for greater local autonomy, which Confiänt articulates in the novel. In this quest for autonomy, as Confiänt makes clear, the shantytown dwellers must fight against the old colonial structures, including the powerful Catholic Church.

In chapter 12, Confiänt returns the narrative to Adelise, returning also to the narrative of carnival—this time to the last few days of carnival, as before he had spoken about the opening days of the annual festival. The return of carnival also signals the return of the focus to Féfé, in his role as carnival mask maker and Red Devil/tempter. The chapter opens with a description of the elaborate mask Féfé has made for Adelise, that of Marianne La Po Fig, the presiding figure of the *Dimanche Gras* or Fat Sunday, known for the *nègres-gros-sirop,* who run through the crowd covered in coal tar and sugar-cane syrup. Marianne/Adelise, dressed in dry banana leaves (bananas, known locally as *figues,* succeeded cane sugar as Martinique's principal agricultural export), is meant to stand as a reminder of the fragility of the banana fruit.

The chapter underscores Adelise's growing feelings of entrapment in her relationship with Homère, from which she feels temporarily liberated while under the Marianne-la-Po-Fig mask. As the "black folks of Morne Pichevin," in true carnival fashion, forget "their crushing poverty" while under the carnival spell, Adelise's spirit "escaped off into the far away and [her] legs became oh-so-light" (117). The momentary freedom she experiences under the carnival costume—abruptly ended when she catches sight of Homère—is threatened both by the relationship with a local jeweler into which Féfé has lured her and by a pregnancy that seems to tie her to Homère just as she is beginning to outgrow their relationship and search for something beyond her life in Morne Pichevin.

Her dilemma is played out through two narratives—a dream in which Adelise sees the tantalizing figure of her father offering and then withdrawing love, and a second narrative of the Br'er Rabbit stories in the text, which shows how Rabbit manages to save his skin through trickery. The first of these narratives is that of a dream she has shortly after learning that she is pregnant, in which a multiplicity of symbols all points toward the inadvisability of her pregnancy and the poor prospects of her relationship with Homère, which has deteriorated since they have been living together. Her father, dressed in a carnival costume, is as empty as the sacks of suste-nance (flour) that make up his clothing. The howling dog points to death and mourning as Adelise passes through a threshold (a bridge in a color she does not recognize) into bitterness. The passage speaks of silence and misunderstanding—of things that cannot be articulated and a father's rejection of his child.

The second narrative is told by Richard, who suggests a *veillé de vivants,* a wake for the living, rather than a *veillé de mort,* since the intention is to celebrate the coming birth of Adelise and Homère's child (although the wake prefigures the death of the unborn child). This is the second Br'er Rabbit story told in the text. The first one, in chapter 4, is told by Mam Anna and refers to the futility of a wife finding her husband's secrets. The stories of Br'er Rabbit, like those of Anansi the Spider (which are often identical), trace back to the trickster storytelling traditions of western and central Africa, where the character depends on its wits to overcome obstacles or seek revenge against enemies. Richard's story, introduced by the traditional announcement of *Krik!* and the audience's echoing *Krak!,* offers veiled allusions to his understanding of the trickery and deceit in which Homère, Adelise, and Féfé are embroiled and hints at the trickery Adelise will need to keep her situation secret from Homère. The chapter ends with Adelise once again going with Féfé, unbeknownst to Homère, to meet her wealthy jeweler client.

Chapter 13 narrates an odd episode in which Adelise seduces/is seduced by a young mulatto with whom she dances at a local club. The incident, played against women's dreams of social mobility through marriage with someone of higher position and lighter skin, focuses on Adelise's sexual desire for this young man, which she displays before Homère and her friends with complete indifference to its consequences. The incident, which would seem to add a gratuitous erotic interlude not directly related to the plot of the novel, foreshadows the end of Adelise's relationship with Homère and her desire to separate herself from her neighbors and seek an independent future. It is marked by the introduction of a secondary character—that of Jesus Christ, "a white Creole who lived like a tramp" (136)—driven mad by the heartbreak of not being allowed to marry the woman he loved because "white-Creoles mustn't marry coloreds" (137).

Chapter 14 brings the narrative to a close by returning in its opening paragraph to the figure of Ma Titiane, the market woman Adelise had met on the morning of her arrival in Fort-de-France some seven years before. The focus of the chapter is to narrate in quite vivid detail Adelise's miscarriage and the resulting end of her relationship to Homère, who abandons her during her crisis, only to return later to insist on Adelise moving with him to Trénelle, another growing shantytown in Fort-de-France. Confiänt, not given to great introspection in the development of his characters, describes the changes in Homère that prompt the break outwardly—"He didn't smell the same anymore, hadn't the same voice, or the same bearing" (151). Above all, it is his peremptory command that she follow him to Trénelle that finally elicits Adelise's rebellion, and she flees from him, returning to Morne Pichevin and her life with her aunt. Having lost her child, recognized the error of her relationship with Homère, and assessed the personal cost of her sexual relationships with rich mulattoes, she is now ready to make a decision about her future.

In chapter 15, Confiänt ties up the loose ends of his narrative, as he leads his heroine toward a departure for France with the BUMIDOM. He concentrates on three thematic threads: the death of her aunt Philomène, linked here to significant changes in Morne Pichevin as part of a process of urban renewal in Fort-de-France in the early 1960s; the identification of Adelise's tree by Homère; and the preparations for Adelise's departure for France.

The chapter opens with a narrative of Philomène's ill health, three years after Adelise's loss of her baby. Confiänt establishes the passage of time by an allusion to Féfé having been jailed for that length of time after a charge of embezzlement of an investment fund. Shaken by Féfé's marriage to a secretary from another neighborhood, and "unhinged" by the process of urban renewal that was the result of the riots of a few years before, Philomène takes "to her bed to await her death" (155). This death is necessary textually since it is part of the lessons the text imposes on Adelise as motivation for a change in her life that requires leaving her previous life behind to start anew elsewhere. Philomène had established a path for her life as well as for Adelise's, and this early death points to a new beginning, a rupture with a path not her own. Philomène, moreover, makes it possible for Adelise to realize her plan to go to France by establishing a contact for her in the metropolis and revealing that, despite Adelise's misgivings, she had indeed been saving her niece's earnings, making it possible for her to have the funds required for her departure.

Adelise's meditation on her failed relationship with Homère focuses on two aspects: the changes in his emotional state prompted by the changes being planned for Morne Pichevin (his reaction is as "unhinged" as Philomène's and contributes ultimately to his suicide) and the reasons behind the bond he established with Adelise (he was "the first to reveal to me the name of my tree" [156]). The tree, we finally learn, was a jastram, the name used in Martinique for a crape myrtle, whose botanical name is *Lagerstroemia indica*. A deciduous tree, it is among the longest-blooming trees in nature, with flowers that sprout in big, colorful clusters in white or many shades of pink, purple, or red. Its inedible fruit releases disk-shaped seeds. Although not common in Martinique, it is widely used in the United States as an ornamental tree.

As Adelise prepares for her aunt Philomène's death, which will mark also her departure for France, she returns to two themes that bring the text full circle. One is her love for her tree, which she had mistakenly transferred to Homère, with tragic consequences. The other is the lingering impact of her rape by the *commandeur*, which had made the offering of her body an act of little significance afterward. It is the offering of her body, ironically, that has made it possible for her to plan her departure for France, where "jobs are growing like trees" (158).

Judy Lightfoot, in her review of the novel for the *Seattle Weekly*, wrote that "*Mamzelle Dragonfly* flutters along, touching down in gritty neighborhoods then flying off again, making the life within it feel both fragile and tough, heavy and light." It is an apt description for a text whose structure does not seek to offer full explanations for the character's actions and thoughts, but rather aims for a cumulative feeling of how a young woman can assume control of her life despite rape, poverty, prostitution, and social unrest. Adelise's path through the nine years in which we follow her life is followed against a rich historical and social background that paints for the reader the hard realities of life in Martinique in the early years of its *département* status.

Chapter 7

Edwidge Danticat's
The Farming of Bones

Edwidge Danticat was born near Port-au-Prince, Haiti, on January 19, 1969. When she was still a young child, her parents migrated to a predominantly Haitian neighborhood of Brooklyn, New York, while she and her younger brother remained in Haiti with their uncle Joseph, a Baptist minister, and his wife, both of whom Danticat deeply loved. The separation was a painful one for Danticat, who felt she and her brother had been "discarded," especially after two additional children were born to their parents in the United States. Her uncle's house was filled with the children of those who had left Haiti to work in the United States, Canada, the Dominican Republic, or France. He was a kind man, a strict disciplinarian who encouraged her love of writing and of books.

Childhood during the late years of the Papa Doc Duvalier's regime—and later under Baby Doc, whom Danticat once glimpsed tossing newly minted coins out of the window of his motorcade—could be difficult, even for those who, like Danticat, were supported by remittances from abroad. She attended a small private school, paid for with money sent by her parents, where she was punished if she spoke Haitian Kréyòl instead of French. But she cherished her role as her uncle's assistant, writing letters for illiterate adults on a typewriter her father had sent, and later being his mouthpiece after a laryngectomy to treat throat cancer.

Writing was an early vocation, and Danticat wrote her first short story, a tale about a girl who is visited by a clan of women at night, while still living in Haiti. She has said that the Haitian tradition of gathering to tell oral stories—which remains viable because of a high level of illiteracy—had a profound influence on the way she approaches her writing. She has fond memories of summer holidays in Léogane, during which her aunt's mother would tell stories. The stories, announced by the storyteller's *Krik*, were welcome by the audience's cries of *Krak!* "I loved the vibrant interaction between teller and listener," she has explained (Jaggi).

A speaker of French and Haitian Kréyòl, Danticat did not learn to speak English, the language in which she writes, until she was reunited with her parents at the age of 12. It was a difficult reunion; she had been reluctant to leave her uncle and felt all the difficulties inherent in joining her family again after such a long separation. She arrived in the United States, moreover, at the height of the so-called boat people crisis, when Haitians were struggling against their rejection by immigration authorities and accused of having brought the AIDS epidemic into the United States.

Danticat embraced English as a "neutral" tongue, "a place of safety and privacy" (Jaggi), and as a source of inspirational reading. The first book she read in English was Maya Angelou's *I Know Why the Caged Bird Sings* (1970), whose honesty and autobiographical foundation had a significant impact on her as a budding writer; she would later discover Haitian works like Marie Chauvet's *Amour, Colère et Folie,* Jacques Roumain's *Masters of the Dew* (1944), and the novels of Jacques-Stephen Alexis, whose *In the Flicker of an Eyelid* (1957) she later cotranslated into English. Despite feeling shy and self-conscious about her accent and cultural differences—which made her seek refuge in reading—she mastered English quickly enough to publish a newspaper article about her immigration experience within two years of her arrival. It would be the inspiration for her first novel, *Breath, Eyes, Memory* (1994), a tale of the struggles of four generations of Haitian women against poverty, abuse, and violence, in which she tried to recreate the gradual increase in the command of the English language that she experienced as a young immigrant.

Danticat had initially planned on training to be a nurse, but she attended Barnard College instead, where she majored in French literature. She went on to work on a master of fine arts degree from Brown University, where her thesis became the manuscript of her first novel, published in 1994 to immediate acclaim. It put to rest her parents' fears that writing was not a secure occupation and won her the 1994 Fiction Award from the *Caribbean Writer,* the 1996 Granta Best Young American Novelists Award, and a significant readership when, in 1998, it was chosen as a reading selection for the influential Oprah Club.

After graduating from college, Danticat worked as an intern for film director Jonathan Demme, whose documentaries on Haiti have been among the most eloquent renditions of Haiti's political and economic plight. She worked with Demme on his documentary on Jean Bertrand Aristide's return to Haiti after the 1991 coup and on his recent film, *The Agronomist* (2001), about slain radio journalist Jean Dominique. (She had a small part in Demme's 1998 film of Toni Morrison's *Beloved*.) She has also worked as associate producer on Patricia Benoît's film *Courage and Pain* (1996), which gathered testimony from those of Aristide's supporters who had survived torture.

Danticat followed the publication of *Breath, Eyes, Memory* with a collection of short stories that had an even more auspicious reception, titled *Krik? Krak!* (1995). The book, which gathered stories about Haitians and Haitian Americans, among them boat people and others struggling for freedom and democracy, was a finalist for the National Book Award in 1995 and won the Pushcart Short Story Prize. It has also been translated into Haitian Kréyòl for broadcast on Haitian radio. Following the success of *Krik? Krak!*, she received a Lila-Wallace-Reader's Digest Grant for the writing of her next book, *The Farming of Bones*, her fictionalized account of the 1937 massacre of thousands of Haitian cane workers by the army of Dominican dictator Rafael Leonidas Trujillo. The book, published when Danticat was not yet 30, won the 1999 American Book Award and the International Flaiano Prize and led to Danticat's selection by the *New Yorker* as one of the 20 examples of American fiction of the future in 1999.

Danticat followed her success with *The Farming of Bones* with two anthologies of literary texts she edited, *The Beacon Best of 2000: Great Writing by Women and Men of All Colors and Cultures* (2002) and *The Butterfly's Way: Voices from the Haitian Dyaspora* (2001). In 2002 she published a travelogue on her visit to the coastal city of Jacmel during carnival, titled *After the Dance: A Walk through Carnival in Jacmel*, and a book for young adults based on her autobiographical experiences as a young Haitian immigrant, titled *Behind the Mountains*. A second book for young adults, *Anacaona: Golden Flower of Haiti, 1490*, a retelling of the story of the Taíno princess who led the struggle against the Spanish in the early years after the Columbian encounter, appeared in 2005. Her most recent novel, *Dew Breaker*, came out in 2004. It tells the haunting story of a daughter who discovers that the father who has joined her in New York, whom she believes escaped from prison, is in fact a former prison guard and henchman for the Duvalier regime, a so-called dew breaker who came at dawn to arrest his victims or burn their homes, and still a haunting presence to his many victims.

In 2002 Danticat married Faidherbe Boyer, a Haitian New Yorker, owner of a translation services agency, whom she met while he was guiding a school group on a visit to Haiti. Their first child was born in 2004, the same year in which she lost her uncle Joseph in ironic and tragic circumstances. Danticat, whose passionate commitment to Haiti and to Haitians in the diaspora has been in evidence through her writing and activism, has long been a critic of the U.S. immigration policies toward Haitians. Her uncle had been forced to flee his church and school after it was ransacked by armed gangs of youths, some of whom he had helped throughout the years. At age 81, he arrived at the Miami airport seeking political asylum and was detained by the Immigration and Naturalization Service without being allowed to see Danticat or any other member of his family. He died in custody five days later, in her words, a "casualty of both the conflict in Haiti and an inhumane and discriminatory US immigration system" (Jaggi).

The Farming of Bones

The historical background to *The Farming of Bones* is the infamous massacre of Haitians unleashed by Dominican dictator Rafael Leonidas Trujillo in October 1937. Trujillo (1891–1961) gained power in 1930 after organizing a coup against then president Horacio Vázquez and would rule the Dominican Republic continuously from 1930 to his assassination in 1961. His regime, known for the torture, disappearance, and assassination of opponents, saw its most infamous moment when he ordered the massacre of Haitians living along the border between Haiti and the Dominican Republic. Ironically, the border between the two countries is marked by the Massacre River, named, not for the events of 1937, but for a slaughter of French pirates in the seventeenth century. The massacre came at a time of worsening economic conditions in the Dominican Republic and growing resentment against Haitians seeking to escape the abject poverty facing them in their homeland by crossing into the Dominican Republic to cut cane or work as domestic servants. What precisely prompted Trujillo to issue the order to attack Haitians has never been precisely determined. Some claim that the attack order was issued in retaliation for the alleged betrayal and execution by the Haitian government of a Dominican covert agent working in Port-au-Prince. Others claim that the attack came as a result of border tensions following the failure of a treaty between the two countries to stop the flow of Haitians across the border. The mixed Dominican-Haitian population of the border, which made a living primarily out of trade and contraband, had created a zone that functioned beyond national allegiances and had fallen out of the control of either the Dominican or Haitian governments. One of Trujillo's goals, it has been argued, was to fix the borders and secure sovereignty over contested areas. Historians have also advanced the theory that Trujillo ordered the massacre under the influence of Adolf Hitler's rapidly spreading racist notions, which supported Trujillo's goal of *blanquismo,* or the whitening of the Dominican population. Contributing to the massacre was the enmity that has existed between the two countries since the newly independent Haiti repeatedly invaded and plundered the Dominican Republic in the early nineteenth century. As economic and political conditions worsened in Haiti in the late nineteenth and early twentieth centuries, Dominicans came to regard Haitians as backward, African, and uncivilized, inferior racially and culturally to the Hispanic and more Europeanized Dominican Republic.

Although the exact number of those killed will never be known, it has been estimated that between 15,000 and 26,000 Haitians—defenseless men, women, and children living in the border region, portions of Santiago and Samaná, and the western portion of El Cibao—were slaughtered by machete blows. The massacre, known in the Dominican Republic as El Corte (the Cut), was carried out by machetes and clubs so as to cover the Dominican Army's role in the killings. (The intention was to leave the impression that Dominican peasants, responding to local tensions, had attacked the Haitians using machetes, whereas the army would have used bullets.) International outrage forced Trujillo to offer indemnity to those wounded in the attack and to the families of those killed. However, the amount negotiated through the United States ($750,000, later reduced to $525,000), although ludicrous in view of the numbers of dead and wounded, was the only sanction he faced for the massacre.

Danticat uses as a leitmotif in her novel the use of the *perejil* shibboleth as the means of testing whether a potential victim was indeed a Haitian. The word *shibboleth* originates from Hebrew and means "an ear of corn." It appears in the biblical story of how, after the army of Gilead inflicted defeat on the tribe of Ephraim, the Ephraimites who had crossed into Gilead to escape retribution were put to the test of pronouncing *shibboleth* correctly or facing death. Forty-two thousand Ephraimites are said to have been killed at the River Jordan for failure to do so. Danticat uses a quotation from Judges 12:4–6 as an epigraph for *The Farming of Bones*. It is claimed that Haitians, unable to pronounce the trilled r in the Spanish pronunciation of *perejil*, were identified and killed at the Massacre River. It is not known to what extent the use of the *perejil* shibboleth contributed to the identification and death of Haitians during the 1937 massacre, but the story has come to encapsulate the horrors of the massacre amid the impossibility of truly determining by race or language (particularly in the border area) who was indeed a Haitian.

The book is organized into 41 chapters, narrated in the first person by the novel's protagonist, Amabelle Désir, who, as a young woman, survived the 1937 massacre. There are two types of chapters, identified easily by different typesetting: the chapters in bold type, interspersed between chapters set in roman type (in one case inserted into a roman chapter), tell the story of Amabelle's dreams and, through her dreams, of her dead, chiefly her parents, who died crossing the Massacre River when Amabelle was a child, and her lover Sebastien, killed during the massacre.

The novel is dedicated (in the name of the narrator) to Yemayá, the Mother of the Waters in Haitian Vodou. Yemayá, initially a river spirit or *lwa* of Yoruban origin, was the source of all the rivers of western Africa, particularly the River Ogoun. Her name derives from the Yoruba words for "Mother of the Fish," from which she draws her motherly, protective role for all creatures. In the islands of the New World, however, she is most often associated with the sea.

The specific setting of the story is a sugar plantation in the fictional town of Alegría, in the province of Dajabón, on the northern border between the Dominican Republic and Haiti. The novel opens on August 30, 1937, the day of the birth of the twin children of Señora Valencia, daughter of the owner of the Alegría sugar plantation, Don Ignacio (Papi), a Spanish immigrant from Valencia who, throughout the novel, follows with growing distress the progress of the Spanish civil war, where the progress of Francisco Franco's forces seems to parallel Trujillo's path toward the massacre of Haitians. Amabelle Désir, the novel's narrator, is the servant and companion of Señora Valencia, who is married to Señor Pico Duarte, an ambitious officer in Rafael Trujillo's army. He is perhaps the least successfully drawn of the novel's characters and remains throughout the novel a character more often described than fleshed out.

Chapter 1 introduces Amabelle's lover, Sebastien Onius, a cane cutter in a neighboring plantation. He is introduced as being the only one capable of putting an end to Amabelle's nightmares, during which she relives the death of her parents, who drowned while attempting to cross the Massacre River into the Dominican Republic as Amabelle watched. The line between dream and living—and between realities and shadows—is one that Sebastien marks for Amabelle in the beginning stages of the book, where he provides an alternative notion of home to that of the plantation house where she works. Sebastien, like Amabelle, seeks a home and a love that will heal him from the great tragedy of his past, the death of his father during the devastating hurricane of September 3, 1930, which left more than 8,000 people dead in the Dominican Republic and Haiti and forced Sebastien into the life of a cane worker in the Dominican Republic. The storm, a category 4 hurricane and one of the deadliest of the twentieth century, is known in the Dominican Republic as Huracán San Zenón. The bond between Amabelle and Sebastien, drawn from shared pain and hopes, gives the novel its poetic resonance. It is to Amabelle like the life of the spirits, the repository of hope: "[Juana] asked me if I believed in anything," Amabelle explains, "and all I could think to say was Sebastien" (65).

The date of the commencement of the action, however, suggests that this alternative home and happiness of Amabelle's will be of short duration, as the beginning of El Corte is just a few weeks away. The brief chapter suggests, then, that Amabelle will be plunged into her nightmares and shadows by events to come.

Amabelle's narrative of her love for Sebastien incorporates her memories of her parents and of her life in Haiti before their deaths left her stranded in the Dominican Republic. Part of the comfort offered by their relationship is that of sharing their memories of Haiti and of their respective parents—of Amabelle's mother, whose words "were direct and precise"; of her father, always looking for "some new way to heal others"; and of Sebastien as "a boy carrying his dead father from the road, wobbling, swaying, stumbling under the weight" (34). Amabelle's memories include those of playing in Henri Christophe's Citadelle, one of the most impressive fortresses in the New World—built to protect the new Republic of Haiti against a possible return of the French colonizers and now a UNESCO World Heritage site. The Citadelle is perched on top of the Bonnet L'Eveque, overlooking the Plaine du Nord in northern Haiti, near Cap Haïtien and the ruins of the Sans Souci Palace.

Chapter 2 introduces the household of Don Ignacio as his daughter Valencia goes into labor with only Amabelle's help. Amabelle and Doña Valencia, friends despite their different race and class status, have been companions since the latter and her father found the young girl weeping by the river that had just swept away her parents. It is left to Amabelle, then, with only the help of the memory of her herbalist parents' steps in such a predicament, to safely birth the twin children—a girl and a boy.

The ultimately inauspicious birth (the boy will die within a few days of his birth) is marked by two ambiguous omens: the umbilical cord is tied around the girl's neck, and she is born with a caul over her face. These are developments that the señora interprets as a curse on her daughter (although events will determine that the appearance of the caul, as in its medieval interpretation, was a sign of good luck). The daughter, moreover, has skin the color of deep bronze, "between the colors of tan Brazil nut shells and black salsify" (11).

The daughter's unwelcome color, which would seem to indicate a certain degree of African ancestry, is described by the local doctor in chapter 4 as "a little charcoal behind the ears," prompting Don Ignacio to respond to the "very impolite assertion" by asserting that both he and his wife were of pure Spanish blood and could trace their descent to the conquistadores (12). The African ancestry, therefore, can only be attributed to Señora Valencia's husband, whose poverty early in life would make his social and racial provenance suspect. Here Danticat alludes to the complexities of social hierarchies in the Dominican Republic, where the typical Caribbean social pyramid has whites at the top echelons of society, mulattoes (or those of mixed race) in the middle classes, and predominantly blacks (those formerly enslaved) in the working classes. As peoples of mixed race were usually the offspring of liaisons between blacks and former slaves, dark skin and Negroid features also carried the social stigma of illegitimacy. It has been the latter who have borne the burden of "the farming of bones," as working in the cane fields has come to be known—a reference to the backbreaking labor of cutting sugarcane amid leaves as sharp as razor blades that cut to the bone.

Señora Valencia seeks to link her dark-skinned daughter to Anacaona (1474–1503), the Taíno (Amerindian) queen of one of the chiefdoms of what is now the Dominican Republic, executed by Spanish conquistador Nicolás de Ovando. It reflects a tendency in the Dominican Republic, begun with the publication of Manuel de Jesús Galván's novel of the epic deed of the Taínos in their struggle against the Spaniards, *Enriquillo* (1882), to seek

the ethnic roots of the Dominican race and culture in the indigenous inhabitants, rather than in the enslaved Africans, whose culture was denigrated as
belonging more properly to Haiti.

Later in the text, Señor Pico, after the death of the boy, whom Señor Pico
had insisted on naming Rafael after the Generalissimo, develops a marked
aversion for his daughter. The text is ambiguous on whether the avoidance of
his daughter grows out of resentment that the child of the wrong gender has
survived or out of feelings of revulsion because of her skin color. However,
his actions after his wife, following their son's burial, invites the cane workers
in for a cup of coffee—he takes the imported orchid-patterned tea set with
which they were served and shatters the cups and saucers against the cement
walls of the house latrines—would indicate that race, rather than gender,
may be behind his feelings toward his daughter.

Chapter 8, which marks the arrival of Señor Pico to meet his new children,
introduces two important plot elements into the narrative. He brings with
him news of a new border operation under his command that will ensure
Trujillo's safety when he comes to celebrate a grand ball at the frontier, and
in his rush to get home to his new children, he runs over and kills a cane
worker returning home.

His arrival complicates the novel's political context, as it depicts the family that employs Amabelle as deeply connected to the Generalissimo, whom
Pico seeks to emulate and whose portrait Doña Valencia has painted at her
husband's request. (Her painting showed him in full military regalia.) Within
the parameters of the plot, it aligns the family Amabelle works for with the
repressive forces that will soon murder many of those working on the plantation. Only Papi seems concerned about the identity and the condition of
the man Pico's car has struck—Joël, only son of Old Kongo—and the lack
of concern on the latter's part stands here for the indifference of the regime
for the Haitian cane cutters it is about to slaughter. The careless accident—
and the subsequent lack of concern—will bring tensions to the relationship
between Amabelle and Sebastien, as it opens a rift between the Haitian workers and the Dominican planter family for whom she works.

The relationship between Sebastien and Amabelle—which will shortly
be formalized into an engagement—is an important gauge for the tensions
expected at the border during this period that precedes the massacre. Félice,
Joël's fiancée, speaking of the impossibility of starting a war on a land not
their own to avenge one of their dead, still hopes that something could
be done "to teach them that our lives are precious too" (66). Sebastien
and Amabelle—he by his leadership role in the community and friendship
with Joël, she by her closeness with Señora Valencia, who is to her like her
own kin—are in a position to understand best the breach that has opened
between Haitian workers and their masters by the unacknowledged and un-
avenged death. Irritated by her unwillingness to acknowledge her employers'
culpability, Sebastien asks Amabelle, "Who are these people to you?...Do

you think they're your family?" (110). And when he sends Old Kongo to Amabelle to ask for her promise of marriage, it is to the incident at the ravine, to Joël's death, that Old Kongo alludes as the reason for Sebastien not wanting "to waste more time" (122). The lovers' last meeting, when the massacre has already been unleashed and they are planning their flight, brings to the fore the accumulated tensions that followed Joël's death. Sebastien, in a brief moment of anger, reproaches Amabelle for her lasting trust: "You never believed those people could injure you" (143). It prompts an immediate apology from Amabelle, who understands that she had trusted too much and too long.

Chapter 9, which speaks of Amabelle's memory of a childhood illness, incorporates the world of the Haitian spirits into the narrative. Here, while very seriously ill, Amabelle has visions of a doll her mother had made for her, and of her singing comforting songs to her. Dolls are frequently used in healing practices in Vodou and Santería, the African-derived Caribbean religions, and can embody beneficial spirits. Here the spirit embodied in the doll promises Amabelle a long life since she has "come so close to death while young" (58).

Chapter 14 speaks to the plight of Haitian immigrants in the Dominican Republic, many of whom, like Amabelle and Sebastien, have lived most of their lives in Alegría or have had children born there. The cane cutters as well as those whose skills, trades, or ownership of land should make them feel they had "their destinies in hand" (68) speak of the rumors circulating about expelling all Haitians as part of the injustices they have faced throughout their history. The chapter also speaks to the efforts the Haitian community in the Dominican Republic had made not to become completely assimilated into their new surroundings and to keep their culture alive. Like Father Roumain, they have maintained those things which "reminded everyone of common ties" (73).

The other side of this discourse—that of the propaganda for Trujillo's regime—is incorporated into the novel in chapter 18, where Danticat introduces portions of actual speeches of Trujillo as part of a radio broadcast, to which some of the characters listen. It is the one place in the text where Danticat seeks to explain to the readers the regime's justification for the massacre to come. Since Danticat maintains the narrative within the limited perspective of Amabelle—and to a certain extent of Sebastien—there is little access to the political discourses addressed to the masses of Dominicans. Here Danticat has Trujillo himself speak to the Dominican people about how "tradition shows as a fatal flaw . . . that under the protection of rivers, the enemies of peace, who are also the enemies of work and prosperity, found an ambush in which they might do their work, keeping the nation in fear and menacing stability" (97).

Chapter 20, in which the burial of little Rafi takes place, introduces the *perejil* shibboleth into the narrative, as the cane workers, hearing of Señora

Valencia's invitation to coffee, distrustfully wonder if they are going to be poisoned. It gives occasion to a sharing of rumors of actual and impending violence, among them that of Trujillo having issued an order to have all Haitians in the Dominican Republic killed.

In chapter 24, with Señor Pico's imminent departure for the border, we move into the historical events of El Corte, the preparations for which seem to his wife "like we are at war" (137). From here to the end of chapter 29, the novel will follow the violent and at times despairing efforts of Amabelle and her companions to make it across the Massacre River to Haiti, a reversal of her crossing as a child, during which her parents died. It will be to her another rebirth, but one into pain and frequent despair. Amabelle must wonder, first of all, whether the señora to whom she has been so close has the strength to protect her from the violence that seems to be flowing their way like a gigantic wave. Her confrontation with Sebastien, and the feeling that her "chest was cramping with a kind of fear [she] had known only once before, when [her] parents were drowning" (143), alert her to the realities of the dangers she is facing. Commending themselves to the Vodou *lwa,* or spirits, through Old Kongo's drawing of a *vévé,* or ritualistic sign, on the floor with cornmeal (a ritual gesture associated with Vodou ceremonies), Sebastien goes in search of his sister, and they agree to meet at the chapel to flee together.

Danticat uses the figure of Señor Pico to frame the beginning and ending of Amabelle's path to the river and, eventually, to Haiti. He is present at the two scenes that usher in and close this phantasmagoric trip across the mountains to the city of Dajabón, past a village remembered for the stench of "blood sizzling, of flesh melting to the last bone" (181), in the company of strangers she is not sure to trust and through physical trials that will leave her scarred for the rest of her life. He is at the head of the soldiers who stop the cane cutters from the plantation from fleeing. "The soldiers were using whips, tree branches, and sticks, flogging the fleeing people" (157) in an attempt to avoid the use of the telltale bullets that would offer evidence of government involvement. For Señor Pico, as Amabelle describes, the flogging and whipping of the cane workers, most of who are taken away in trucks to their death, "seemed to have been regular work" (158). Her mistress's husband thus becomes linked to the soldiers and trucks that take her lover Sebastien away to an unknown fate. She will never see him again and will have to wait years for a final word on his death.

Amabelle meets Señor Pico again in Dajabón, during the desperate hours when she is at her most vulnerable to capture and when she receives the beating that marks her for life. The atmosphere of carnivalesque revelry of Dajabón, where the Generalissimo is attending Mass at the cathedral and the streets are decorated with fringed color papers and murals of Trujillo's face, contrasts sharply with the scenes of violence and desecration they had traveled past on their way there. The crowds eagerly await Trujillo's exit from church, "as though his presence were a sacred incident, something that might transform the rest of their lives" (190).

Danticat captures in her description of events in Dajabón on that fateful night the complexities in the feelings of the Dominican population toward the persecuted Haitians, which ranged from pity to repeating the worst of rumors about Haitians, among them that they ate babies, cats, and dogs. The brutal attacks against her and her friend Yves—who, of all her friends from Alegría, has made it this far with her—have as a central motif the *perejil* shibboleth: "Our jaws were pried open and parsley stuffed into our mouths.…I told myself that eating the parsley would keep me alive" (193). Their beating is accompanied by the strain of Luis Alberti's 1936 merengue "Compare Pedro Juan," the most famous of all Dominican merengues, a sort of secondary national anthem. The playing of a merengue is appropriate since the music, of African origin and characterized by sometimes lewd lyrics, had not been accepted by all Dominicans as representative of the nation until Trujillo had used a merengue band during his presidential campaigns. Amabelle and Yves are saved, ironically, by Trujillo's exit from the cathedral, which draws the crowd away and allows them to retreat toward safety and, eventually, the river. The music shifts to the official Dominican national anthem, "Quisqueyanos Valientes" (Valiant People of Quizqueya, the Amerindian name for the island), adopted in 1934. Its lyrics refer to the country's determination to fight against all types of slavery, in what is widely believed to be a reference to the struggle against the Haitian invasions of the nineteenth century.

Amabelle's dramatic and painful escape from the massacre ends with the scene of Odette's death, a rather melodramatic scene that revolves around her uttering, "with her parting breath," the world for "parsley" in Kréyòl (the French-derived Creole language of Haiti) as "a provocation, a challenge, a dare," à la Scarlet O'Hara in the 1939 film version of *Gone with the Wind* (203). This is by far not the only cinematic reference in the text that introduces what in criticism is called intertextuality, the quotation or incorporation of scenes that provides echoes of other narratives. Among these are the reference to *The Great Gatsby* (1974) in Pico's car accident and the birthing of Señora Valencia's babies, which again refers to *Gone with the Wind.*

Chapter 30 describes the scenes of pain and despair in the makeshift hospital on the Haitian side of the border where wounded Haitians (and some black Dominicans mistaken for Haitians) seek help after crossing the river. Since Amabelle finds herself between life and death, Danticat incorporates one of her dreamlike reminiscences of her dead parents (usually inserted as separate chapters in bold type) within this chapter. In this section, she sees her mother rising above the river where she drowned, like a river spirit, wearing "a dress of glass, fashioned out of the hardened clarity of the river" (208). Her words of comfort to her daughter acknowledge the seriousness of her situation now—comparing it to her childhood sickness, when the doll was sufficient for a cure—and speak to Amabelle of the constant presence of her mother's spirit as a source of protection. The scene becomes the pivotal moment in Amabelle's path to physical recovery and is linked to the belief in Haitian Vodou that the spirits of the ancestors serve as guiding spirits for the living. Her recovery, however, leaves her open to the narratives of horror of her fellow refugees, who give testimony of the many atrocities committed during El Corte: the 700 people shot in the back in Santiago; the 200 they forced off the pier in Monte Cristi; the vultures eating the flesh of the many dead lying in fields.

During their escape through the mountains, Yves had questioned why the Haitian government and its people had not gone to war in response to the killings in the Dominican Republic. In chapter 20, Danticat returns to Haiti's lack of response to the massacre, having Yves question what had happened to the Haitian creed of "L'union fait la force" (Union makes strength). Haitian president Sténio Vincent, ruling a country over which Haitians had regained control only three years before with the departure of the American marines, had acknowledged the lack of power of his army to enter into an open war with Trujillo's army, which outnumbered his by almost 10 to 1. "We are a China pot against an iron pot," Vincent is said to have responded to questions about his lack of response. In the novel, the survivors lament the absence of leaders like Jean-Jacques Dessalines (1758–1806), Haiti's first chief of state, Toussaint L'Ouverture (1743–1803), considered the father of the Haitian nation, and Henri Christophe (1767–1820), who proclaimed himself King of Haiti in 1811 and built the Citadel in which Amabelle played as a child. The survivors, feeling forsaken by their former leaders, again allude to the role played by ancestral spirits in Haitian Vodou; within Vodou, the spirits of their former leaders should still be looking after their people, especially Dessalines, who in some parts of Haiti is venerated as a *lwa*, or consecrated spirit.

Chapter 31 chronicles Amabelle's return to the city of Cap Haïtien with Yves, who is helping her search for news of Sebastien and his sister Mimi. The return to the Cap also marks the return to the topic of Henri Christophe and the Citadel, which looms in the distance, visible from the city, with its links to the plantation society against which Dessalines, Christophe, and Toussaint waged their revolution. In Amabelle's imagination, the Cap is a city of ghosts; from the shadows of the grand planter houses that Henri Christophe burned to the ground to the souls of their slaves haunting the space, it seems an ideal background for her own search for the ghost of Sebastien, who while alive had kept other ghosts at bay. It is ironic, then, that the merchants and shopkeepers that watch them walking back see her and Yves as revenants, as the "nearly dead" who "had escaped from the other side of the river" (220).

The chapter, however, is centered on Amabelle's physical healing, a necessary step before she comes to term with Sebastien's disappearance and the emotional pain it will convey. Her physical ordeal has left her helpless as a child, unable to walk without pain, her mouth too bruised to be able to eat solid foods. Her need for mothering finds an echo on two women: one hands her an orange to burn in an open fire and rub onto her flesh so her "bone aching will stop"; the other, Yves's mother, feeds her pumpkin soup "with a tiny spoon as though [she] were a sick, bedridden child" (223, 225).

In chapter 32, Amabelle addresses the notion of the body as a witness, of scars as a testament to history. Amabelle's body, transformed beyond recognition by the ordeal of "the slaughter," is no longer a body Sebastien would recognize. It is now "simply a map of scars and bruises, a marred testament" (227). The scars, bruises, and disfigurement bear testimony to the violence of El Corte and can be read as signifiers of a historical event that Danticat (and through her, Amabelle) knew had been willed into erasure by the official history of both countries. In chapter 33, Danticat addresses the controversial issue of the compensation the Dominican Republic was forced to pay to victims of the massacre. The visit to the justice of the peace to request compensation becomes a ritual of testimony, an opportunity to add the names of the dead and wounded to the record: "He writes your name in the book and he says he will take your story to President Sténio Vincent...then he lets you talk and he lets you cry and he asks if you have papers to show that all these people died" (234). Without the papers, the ritual becomes an empty exercise, so that only the body's scars are left as evidence of a slaughter that cannot be permanently recorded on paper. As the crowd erupts in violence after the justice of the peace announces that no further testimonies will be taken, they burn President Vincent's photograph, one in which he proudly displays the Grand Cross of the Juan Pablo Duarte Order of Merit, given to him by the Generalissimo as proof of the friendship existing between the two countries. In chapter 34, Yves brings Amabelle the gift of news that the priests at the Cap Haïtien cathedral have begun to listen to and record testimonials, offering another venue for her much needed testifying to the massacre. Later on in the text (chapter 40), she will return to the notion of scars as testimony, writing that "this past is more like flesh than air; our stories testimonials like the ones never heard by the justice of the peace or the Generalissimo himself" (281).

The presence of the justice of the peace in Cap Haïtien has one practical outcome, as it brings Sebastien's mother, Man Denise, out to stand with the others seeking to give testimony of their loss. Amabelle's encounter with Man Denise forces her to confront the reality of Sebastien's death through his mother's knowledge that before her children died, they had sent a stranger to bear testimony of their death to her. Stranger after stranger has since come to tell her that her children had died still wearing the bracelets she had given them as tokens of her love. The knowledge brings Amabelle full circle to her arrival at the Cap, and she goes back to strolling "like a ghost through the waking life of the Cap" (243).

The relationship between Amabelle and Yves is explored in chapter 34, a chapter of confessions, in which each seeks to share his or her guilt for having survived, while Sebastien, Mimi, and the others died. The element of chance, of having been delayed the precious minutes necessary to have avoided their fate, haunts them both, and here culminates in a perfunctory lovemaking that fails to fill the void they each feel in their souls. Looming ahead for them is the need to find employment and to make a living in a meaningless life after their transforming experiences during the slaughter. For Yves, as for Amabelle, the past has become his emotional prison: "He detested the smell of sugarcane...and loathed the taste of parsley; he could not swim in rivers; the sound of Spanish being spoken...made his eyes widen, his breath quicken, his face cloud with terror, his lips unable to part one from the other and speak" (273). He has, however, maintained his faith in the Vodou *lwa*, as indicated by his gesture of spilling some of his costly rum on the ground before drinking, as an offering to the spirits, known in Haiti as the "untouchables," *les invisibles*.

Amabelle's path to emotional recovery involves the tracking down of those people she knew from Alegría who, like her, survived the massacre. Although accepting that her body and her purpose are her testimony, she seeks comfort in knowing that part of her former world remains with her, that she and Yves are not the sole survivors of a world that witnessed her happiness with Sebastien, hence her joy at hearing that Father Romain and Father Vargas lived despite their sufferings in prison—and her pain at realizing that Father Romain's memory has been replaced by the empty slogans of a corrupt Dominican regime. Her dreams, however, continue to focus on the need to tell her story. "My dreams are now only visitations of my words for the absent justice of the peace, for the Generalissimo himself," she writes (265).

Chapter 38 moves the action to May 1961, when Trujillo was assassinated by a hail of bullets while he was being driven in his car, unleashing a joyous celebration in the Cap. Amabelle has grown old living with Yves in a passionless version of love, earning a living as a seamstress and finding comfort in the company of Yves's mother and the women of the courtyard, their *lakou*, or homestead. They have, as Amabelle explains, "chosen a life of work to console us after the slaughter" (274). The assassination sets in motion a series of events that will lead Amabelle to return to visit Alegría and Señora Valencia. The first of these is Man Rapadou's (Yves's mother's) confession that she had poisoned her husband after she had learned that he had agreed to spy for the Yankees during the American occupation since her love for her country had been greater than her love for her man. The second is a visit to the Citadel, where Amabelle follows a guide explaining the history of the fortress to a group of tourists. The guide's allusion to the absence of graves and the silence of the dead brings back to her earlier anxieties about giving testimony of the most salient event of her life—the slaughter of Haitians that left so many nameless dead. In her dreams, the absence that is

Sebastien returns, like her shadow, his breath offering substance. And since she imagines his spirit "inside the waterfall cave at the source of the stream where the cane workers bathe" (283), she embarks on her return voyage to meet him again.

Chapter 41, the last chapter, narrates Amabelle's return to Alegría and her anticlimactic visit to Señora Valencia, who, unlike Amabelle, had settled into a complacent existence, not asking too many questions of those around her and feeling that the effort to help others in a halfhearted way atones for her vicarious guilt through her husband in the slaughter of so many. The presence of Sylvie, a young servant now working for Señora Valencia, speaks to Amabelle of the vanishing quality of historical memory, as she asks, "Why parsley?," seeking a connection to a history that seems so remote. The voyage takes her full circle back to the Massacre River, where a portion of her life ended when it took her parents, and to which she now returns to join them, since she did not find Sebastien's spirit in the waterfall. The water, which has been so central an element in Amabelle's life, becomes the place where she will slip quietly into death, "into Sebastien's cave, [her] father's laughter, and [her] mother's eternity" (310).

Chapter 8

Zee Edgell's Beka Lamb

Zee (Zelma) Edgell was born on October 21, 1940, in Belize City, the capital of Belize, formerly British Honduras. She dates her ambition to become a writer to the age of 11, when an essay she wrote about wanting to be an author was so well received that she was asked to read it to all her classmates, with very encouraging results. She remembers the nuns at her Catholic school as enthusiastically supporting her ambition from primary to secondary school, as did her mother, herself an avid reader. Her father had his doubts about a literary career but encouraged her to pursue a career in journalism.

Her literary models were first and foremost the patriotic songs and poems written by Belizean writers during the struggle for independence in the 1940s and 1950s, a period that coincided with Edgell's adolescence. She also enjoyed the *Tata Duhende* and Annancy folktales narrated for her by relatives. Edgell has always stressed her identification with the birth of the Nationalist movement in 1949, a trait she gave the heroine of her autobiographical first novel, *Beka Lamb*, who, like the young writer-to-be, would immerse herself in the political meetings and family discussions that shaped the transformation of British Honduras into the nation of Belize. She has talked in interviews about how her love for her country came naturally, through visits up the Shibun River to visit her grandmother's house in the bush and holidays spent on Belize's offshore islands or in Mérida and Chetumal, in what is now Mexico's Riviera Maya. She came to believe that she lived in "the most beautiful country in the world" (Evaristo 55). These experiences account in part for the keen nationalism and concern for environmental issues in Edgell's writings.

Edgell grew up with an acute understanding of the complicated ethnic, social, and racial categories that marked her society. Belize's population is a complex mixture of Creoles (Afro-Belizeans); the Garifuna (dark-skinned Belizeans of part-Carib descent); the native Maya; the Panias (mestizos of mixed Spanish, Native American, and Portuguese descent); the Bakras, or whites; the mestizos; the coolies (descendants of East Indian indentured servants); the Chinese; the Mennonites; and others. The resulting hierarchy of color and ethnicity has been one of the major obstacles to national integration since independence and becomes a central element in Edgell's fiction.

Edgell was also keenly aware of the work of Belizean writers like Raymond Barrow, Leo Bradley, James S. Martinez, S. A. Haynes, Hugh Fuller, and George B. Singh, among other names that remain unknown outside the country. She was also imbued with the notion of living in a territory that had been a vital part of the Maya culture and that, through the Maya, Belize has had "a five-hundred-year literary heritage" (Evaristo 56). Of her early readings of European and American literature, she particularly remembers Mark Twain's *Tom Sawyer* since the discovery that an author could write "about ordinary everyday chores like whitewashing a fence" was "a very liberating discovery for a young girl whose greatest ambition was to be a writer" (Evaristo 56). Other favorites were Shakespeare, particularly *The Merchant of Venice,* and Charles Dickens's *David Copperfield* "because Dickens, too, wrote about ordinary people" (Evaristo 55).

Edgell left home around the age of 19 to pursue journalism studies at the Central London Polytechnic. She furthered her education at the University of the West Indies in Mona, after which she remained in Jamaica as a journalism intern with Kingston's *Daily Gleaner,* for which she worked from 1959 to 1962. She returned to Belize as editor of the monthly newspaper the *Reporter* and taught at the St. Catherine's Academy in Belize City from 1966 to 1968. After her marriage in 1969 and the birth of her two children, a boy and a girl, Edgell and her husband worked with the Peace Corps and various other development projects in Nigeria, Afghanistan, the United States, and Bangladesh. It was during these years that she worked on *Beka Lamb,* her first novel, which from idea to publication took her 10 years to complete. It appeared in 1982, fittingly enough, the year after Belize gained its independence, becoming the first major literary work of the new nation. It won Britain's Fawcett Society Book Prize, a prize awarded for books contributing to the understanding of women's lives. It was the first international award bestowed on a work of Belizean literature.

Edgell followed the success of *Beka Lamb* with a second novel, *In Times Like These,* published in 1991 and considered by many a sequel to her first novel. Also set during the transition from colony to independence in Belize, it looks at the corruption that Belize's first independent government has inherited from its colonial masters through the eyes of a woman with limited power and influence. In her third novel, *Festival of San Joaquin,* published in 1997, Edgell moves away from her personal experience, writing in the first person from the perspective of a woman of a different ethnic group, Luz Marina, a mestizo woman struggling to regain custody of her children from her powerful mother-in-law after she has been acquitted of the murder of her abusive husband, whom she killed in self-defense. It reflects her goal of writing fiction true to all the cultures and ethnic groups that form the nation of Belize. Her work in progress, *Cobbo Nathaniel Jones, a.k.a. Rain-drops,* about a young woman struggling to free herself from forest slavery in the early nineteenth century, has as its protagonist an underprivileged black Creole boy. In 1999 Edgell won the Canute Broadherst Prize for her short story "Uncle Theophilus."

Edgell has combined her development work in Belize and Africa with writing and teaching positions in universities in Belize and the United States. From 1978 to 1980, years when she was primarily a mother, she was a secretary to the governing board for Concerned Women for Family Planning. In 1981 she was appointed as the director of the Women's Bureau, and from 1988 to 1989, she was director for women's affairs in the government of Belize. While in Nigeria, she had been vice president of the YWCA in Enugui. From 1984 to 1985, she served as a United Nations Children's Fund consultant to the Somali Women's Democratic Organization. From 1988 to 1989, she lectured at the University College in Belize. In the spring of 1993, Edgell served as a visiting-writer-in-residence at Old Dominion University in Norfolk, Virginia. Since 1993, she has been a professor of English at Kent State University in Ohio.

Beka Lamb

Beka Lamb is a bildungsroman, or novel of development, presented as the central character's elegy to her young friend Toycie. The intertwined stories of Beka Lamb and Toycie Qualo are built against the background of Belize's struggle to gain its independence from Great Britain. Belize (formerly British Honduras), the only English-speaking country in Latin America, achieved self-governing status in 1964 and gained its full independence in 1981. Renamed Belize in 1973, it is now a member of the British Commonwealth of Nations. It continues to be embroiled in territorial disputes with neighboring Guatemala, which claims part of the Belizean territory as its own.

The novel is divided into 26 chapters and is told by an omniscient narrator who follows Beka's perspective from beginning to end. We experience the events narrated through the character's eyes, and although the narrator's scope reaches at times beyond what Beka can witness, his perceptions are most often circumscribed by the limitations of Beka's understanding. The story of Beka's maturation and of the events that led to Toycie's death are told mostly through flashbacks that explain Beka's transformation from an unpromising young girl who had failed first form (ninth grade) to the award-winning student we meet in the first three chapters of the book.

Beka's transformation from a "flat-rate Belize creole" into a young woman of "high mind" (1) is closely associated in the novel with Belize's own development as a nation after securing self-government. Indeed, Beka's success in school—her very presence in a convent school—would not have been possible "befo' time," in the climate of racial and social discrimination that had prevailed in Belize's colonial society. Beka's grandmother (Miss Ivy or Gran) articulates eloquently throughout the text the limits that would have been imposed on a child like Beka before the changes brought about by self-government. As an early member of the People's Independence Party (which stands for the People's United Party [PUP], founded in 1949, nearly two years before the events of the novel begin to unfold), Miss Ivy is able to systematically address the political dimensions of Beka's newfound success at school:

The author clearly encourages the association [between Beka's development and that of the nation of Belize] by pointing out on both the first and last pages that Beka Lamb won the essay contest on the very day that Gadsden and Pritchard were imprisoned for sedition by the British colonial government. Both Beka's personal action and Gadsden and Pritchard's national action were turning points in corresponding drives for self-realization and independence. And both were of an equivalent degree— not final achievements but first steps leading toward fulfillment. Since history proves that the sedition of the 1950s led to Belize's attaining actual independence in 1981, we feel assured that Beka Lamb, too, will attain the mature self-possession that the end of the novel implies for her. (Beck 1)

The fictional political events of the novel mirror closely Belize's political history in the 1950s. Miss Ivy's People's Independence Party is modeled on the PUP, which evolved out of the Workers and Tradesmen's Union in the later 1940s and early 1950s. Like the PUP, the fictional People's Independence Party advocated the end of colonialism and better labor conditions for the working masses. In 1951, in an incident Edgell fictionalizes in the novel, PUP leaders Leigh Richardson and Phillip Goldson (Pritchad and Gladsen in the novel) were jailed for an article in which they defended the legitimacy of revolution against arbitrary colonial rule.

The distress of political events—the novel opens on the day Pritchad and Gladsen have been found guilty—parallels Beka's mourning for her friend Toycie Qualo, dead four months when Beka wins her school prize. Beka's postponed mourning will take the form of a recreation through memory of her close friendship with the older Toycie (17 to Beka's 14), a victim as much of the hurricane during which she was struck by a tree as of the conditions for women "befo' time." The hurricane that led to Toycie's death was most likely based on Hurricane Janet, the most powerful hurricane of the 1955 season and the 10th strongest on record, which devastated portions of Belize and caused 681 deaths in the Yucatán peninsula. Since the community had not gathered for the prescribed nine nights of mourning necessary to help the soul of the deceased leave this world—Toycie's grandmother, Miss Eila, had been too poor for the nine nights of hospitality—Beka promises at the end of chapter 1 "to keep a wake for her" now that her school struggles are over and she has obtained the sort of success that had been Toycie's when alive (6).

Chapters 1–3 establish the formal and thematic parameters of the novel, underscoring Beka's development in the months that had elapsed since she failed first form, the months to which the narrator will return through flashbacks to explain to the reader both the events leading to Toycie's death and the impact that her death has on Beka. The family's pride in Beka's achievement will be seen against their earlier disappointment at Beka's failure and at the pointless lie through which she tries to cover her failure. Faced with the possibility of not being able to return to school and with the shock of the discovery of Toycie's pregnancy and subsequent nervous breakdown, Beka is forced to confront the realities of life as a girl in a society in which, without an education, she would have been limited to domestic work and low-level employment.

Beka's fears of failure are punctuated by a dream narrated at the opening of chapter 2, in which she sees herself falling into the waters and excrement of Haulover Creek as she tries to cross to the other side before the bridge swings to the middle of the creek to allow vessels to cross into open waters. Her fears are juxtaposed against the threat which Guatemala, with its claims to Belizean land, poses to the burgeoning nation. Beka's father's cautious approach to politics—an approach more conservative than her anticolonial mother's—is here displayed in his lukewarm defense of British colonialism and willingness to engage with Guatemala (at least through trade). A reference to an argument he had had with Miss Ivy on the subject of the People's Independence Party, which had been accused of receiving monetary aid from Guatemala (an accusation that had also been raised against the nonfictional PUP), reveals the nature of Beka's father's political allegiances. His views echo those of the National Party, founded in 1951 in response to the growth of the PUP. The National Party drew its support from the middle and merchant classes and advocated a more restrained approach to the possibility of independence, arguing that given that development along all ranks of Belizean society was uneven, any thoughts of political and economic independence were premature. Bill Lamb's assertion that "the British brand of colonialism isn't the worst we could have" reflects the ideology of the National Party (7), as befits an employee of a major import/export corporation and aspirant to the middle class. The presence in one household of representatives of the two major Belizean political parties allows Edgell to address the national debate through the domestic space of the Lambs' household.

In chapter 3, Edgell addresses the racial complexities of Belizean society. The country's population of about 300,000 people is divided among a multiplicity of ethnic groups. Belize, in fact, has one of the most diverse populations in the Americas, incorporating Maya Indians (Yucatecs from Yucatán, the indigenous Mopans, and the Kekchi, who fled slavery in Guatemala), Belizean Kriols (African slaves who have intermarried with other ethnic groups), English and Scottish settlers, the Garifuna (of African and Carib descent), and smaller immigrant groups from China, India, Syria, and Lebanon as well as Mennonite German farmers. Overt racial tensions are uncommon, despite the variety of races and ethnicities, and Edgell describes Belize City as "a relatively tolerant town where at least six races with their roots in other districts of the country, in Africa, the West Indies, Central America, Europe, North America, Asia, and other places, lived in a kind of harmony" (11).

Edgell's subtle exploration of the racial and ethnic differences among the various groups is part of the appeal of the novel, as she shows the delicate nuances that filter into relationships across race and class. On the description of Beka and Toycie's regular Sunday walk, for example, the narrator speaks of the segregation evident in the men's clubs, "one for Creoles, local black people, and the other one for bakras, local white people and expatriates...the pania club for Spanish-speaking people overlooked the creek in the center or town" (15). Later, as one of many episodes she relates that alludes to veiled ethnic tensions, she tells of a masked man who covered his face, hands, and arms because he had been obeahed (made the victim of a spell). A black man, he had compromised the daughter of a Carib man, a girl he could not marry "without losing face in the creole community, whose members seldom married among the Caribs" (31).

Chapter 3 also introduces the figure of Baron Bliss, to whose grave the girls liked to walk. The ersatz baron, Henry Edward Ernest Victor Bliss (1869–1926), a British-born traveler, had willed his fortune (approximately 2 million dollars, a considerable fortune in the first decades of the twentieth century) in trust for the benefit of the people of Belize. The bequeath, which came from the baron's speculation in petroleum shares, supports the Bliss Institute, the Bliss Lighthouse (where his grave is located), and the Bliss School of Nursing, among other institutions. Such is his continued popularity that Belize celebrates Baron Bliss Day on March 9 of every year. The recollection of their walks to Baron Bliss's tomb is the starting point of Beka's conscious decision to recall "everything that had passed to her from April past, when she had failed first form, until today," a process she intends as the only way she "can continue [her] wake for [Toycie]" (16). The next chapter (chapter 4) will begin the chronicle of the difficult period that marked Beka's "change."

This "elegy" to Beka's dear friend Toycie takes us through a leisurely narrative of everyday life in Belize during the 1950s, allowing Edgell to lovingly—sometimes poignantly—recall the cadences of a simple life punctuated here and there by political strife and personal pain. Edgell draws on her own experience growing up in Belize during this period to recreate Beka's experiences during those crucial months of her adolescence. The rich and detailed background sharpens our understanding of the character's dilemma and gives texture and verisimilitude to her tale.

In chapter Four, when Beka arrives home after having failed the form and lies to her parents about it, the futility of her lie is made more affecting by her minute recollection of her father's previous lashing after a similar offense and of their discussions about straightening her hair or wearing lipstick—both of which her father opposed, as he feared it would make her "ashamed of herself and her people" (20). Subtly, circuitously, Edgell brings the reader's attention to what is really at stake for Beka—whether she will be allowed to return to school to repeat the form or whether this has marked the end of her formal education, a decision that will determine the kind of woman she will be allowed to become.

Beka's failure is presented here in the context of her family's aspirations to move into the solid middle class of Belize, an aspiration made possible in the new political climate, as political as well as economic power moves into the hands of the local upper and middle classes. The family's upward mobility has made it possible for Beka to have advantages she, as a black girl, would not have had "befo' time," and the continuation of these advantages is now at stake. Held in her mother's arms as she cries tears "coming out in ugly gulps," Beka needs to start her process of "change" by giving up her lies. "For most of her life," Beka reflects, "the members of her family had surrounded her tightly, like sepals around a pod. But today that security had fallen away, and for a while she felt lonely" (27). Underpinning these feelings of abandonment are her family's modest social and economic aspirations, exemplified by Bill Lamb's struggle "to progress in the business world of the town" and their position as one of the "few black families on Cashew Street that had much of anything at all" (21, 20). Beka's school failure could lead "to the washing bowl underneath the house bottom" and the end of any dream of a life in politics since "how could she be a politician if she had to stand around a bowl and barrel all day long?" (21).

Chapters 5 and 7 look at Beka's punishment for her failure and transgression through three brief episodes that are framed by an allusion to the drafting of a new constitution for Belize, once again linking Beka's growth to that of the Belizean nation. In the most significant of these, one that establishes a theme that Edgell will follow throughout the novel, Bill Lamb cuts down Beka's tree, a bougainvillea vine that was breaking down the fence and which had already prompted complaints from their neighbor. The destruction of her tree by her father is a metaphoric severing from her family that Beka feels profoundly. Personal trees are usually planted at the spot where a child's umbilical chord or afterbirth is buried; this one, however, is described as the first thing that Beka had planted that had taken root. Beka interprets the cutting down of the tree, correctly, as a sign that in his anger her father has, at least temporarily, cut her off. The loss of the bougainvillea vine will be associated later with the death of two of Beka's siblings in childhood and will prefigure Toycie's death. The rebirth of the bush will signal the resolution of Beka's dilemmas at the end of the novel.

The second episode finds Beka cleaning the attic "with feverish energy" as a way to "show her family that she could be different" (26). This self-imposed penance, an offering to her family, is both a way to try to erase the "puzzled disappointment" she saw in her relatives' eyes and to reinsert herself into the routine of a house from which the "'spunks' had gone out," a change she blamed on herself (27). It also mimics the very fate that would be hers if her father does not allow her to return to school, that of endless domestic work.

The third episode has Beka refusing a bar of chocolate offered to her by Mr. Gordillo, the local grocer, as consolation for her having failed the form. His comment that he had offered "a special mass at the Cathedral, and every night for a week, the beads" so she would pass brings home all the renewed guilt she felt because of her failure (39). It also signals the public dimension of her failure, bringing it from the domestic sphere to the outer social space and making it more difficult for Beka to hide her disappointment and shame.

Chapters 5 and 6 are also notable for their presentation of perspectives on Belizean history that span three generations. Miss Ivy focuses on the injustices of the colonial past, when British neglect had left control of the colony in the hands of investors and speculators: "The Boss of the British Lumber Company was living in Government House, and all the big merchants and so on were mostly foreign, and paid bad wages and were in league" (28). Her sense of the injustices of the past fuels her dedication to the anticolonial, pro-independence cause. Her son, on the other hand, counsels caution, suggesting that in an increasingly globalized postcolonial world, merely achieving independence is no guarantee of an improvement in the lot of the majority of the population.

Their perspectives also contrast with the hopefulness of Beka and Toycie's approach to the future, which, fueled by the optimism of decolonization, sees economic, political, and gender possibilities as limitless. Beka envisions a career in politics, while Toycie looks ahead to the end of another school year, after which she can get a job and perhaps the "insane ambition" of saving "enough money to buy a property near Baron Bliss Lighthouse" (34). The girls act out their dreams in a game they play while on holiday at St. George's Caye, in which they mimic the political meetings they have witnessed in the capital: Beka attempts to give a speech in imitation of the ones she has heard at Battlefield Park, while Toycie sings "Land of the Gods," a parody of the Belizean national anthem, "Land of the Free" (44–45).

Chapter 8, which finds the girls with Beka's family during their annual vacation at the Caye, focuses on Toycie's relationship with Emilio Villanueva, a relationship that will ultimately lead to her death. Here Edgell builds this pivotal moment on their relationship—the summer when Toycie will become pregnant—against the history of the Caye, an island occupied by the country's earliest settlers as an escape from "the insect life, disease, heat and swamps of the mainland" (45). The site had been the stage for a 1789 battle between the British slave masters and a fleet of Spanish man-o-wars—"one of the few things attempted in this country that had not broken down" (45).

The historical setting, with its links to the questionable beginnings of the colony, is an apt setting for the expression of Beka's misgivings about her friend's relationship with a Pania boy, a descendant of Spaniards and Maya Indians. Aware that Toycie had been slipping out of the house at night when she thought everyone was asleep, Beka warns her friend with an allusion to the ethnic divisions that characterize Belizean society. "Panias scarcely ever marry creole like we, Toycie," Beka tells her, aware that Toycie, the brightest student in her school, could "wind up with a baby instead of a diploma" (47). Beka's race-based concerns are supported by Edgell's description of Emilio as prouder of his Spanish blood than of his Maya complexion. Edgell also underscores the class divisions between Toycie and Emilio; the former is a poor Creole hoping at best for work as a typist when she finishes school, while the latter is a middle-class Pania with plans of going to the United States for a university education.

Chapter 9 looks in greater detail at the idiosyncrasies of the middle and upper classes in Belize, underscoring the obstacles to the marriage between Toycie and Emilio that Toycie envisions as a possibility. Despite sharing a house with the Blanco family (her father's employer), the children were divided by "wealth, class, colour, and mutual shyness" (51). The Hartleys, a Creole family whose children attended boarding school abroad and who were invited to functions at Government House, "had more in common with civil servants from England" than with the likes of Beka and Toycie (53). Granny Ivy recalls how badly she was treated by the white women for whom she cooked and cleaned. These incidents, following so closely on Beka's expressed concerns about Emilio's intentions, sets the stage for Toycie's coming disappointment. By placing race and class at the very center of Toycie's tragic story, Edgell underscores the difficulties such tensions pose for the development of Belize as a potentially independent nation.

The possibilities open to the nation of Belize include that of joining the West Indies Federation. Discussions between the various British colonies in the Caribbean about the option of achieving independence as a federated single state—similar to the Australian Federation or the Canadian Confederation— began in the early 1950s. The federation, inaugurated in January 1958, was to last only until May 1962, when Jamaica voted to withdraw and was followed by Trinidad. Among the lasting legacies of the brief federated state was the Eastern Caribbean currency, the University of the West Indies, and CARICOM. Belize never joined the federation.

Chapters 10 and 11, which narrate the events surrounding the funeral of Beka's great grandmother, Granny Straker, offer Edgell the opportunity to give the readers a comparative picture of contending cultural traditions among various ethnic groups in Belize and of how these traditions are threatened by the impulse toward modernity. The description of the funeral procession, which Edgell describes as "a small lesson in community history" (60), is followed by a discussion among the family as to whether the traditional nine nights of mourning should be observed. Bill Lamb's contention that "the old ways will poison the new" crystallizes his feelings that Granny Straker was "trying to progress" and would not have wanted to return to the Obeah-inspired ways of her youth, which the family associates with the Caribs (62, 63).

The discussion of the Caribs shows the deeply set prejudices harbored by modernity-bound Creoles such as the Lambs. Beka, whose understanding of Carib culture is deeper than that of her family—since it is informed by the explanations offered by her Carib teacher—is slapped by her mother when she screams at her Granny Ivy that she will marry a Carib when she grows up, a scene whose ambiguity hides the truth of whether she has been slapped for her sassiness to her grandmother or for the expression of such a scandalous aspiration. Her mother's apology comes in the form of a tale about her relationship with her formerly estranged father and her resentment for not being allowed to return to complete her education at a school where she felt inferior given her poverty and race. At the center of her tale is the role of education in driving Belizeans toward a modernity that requires the relinquishing of time-tested traditions. "In the old days," Lilla explains, "the more you left behind the old ways, the more acceptable you were to the powerful people in the government and the churches who had the power to change a black person's life" (70). Edgell returns to this topic later in her portrait of Father Nunez, a Belizean priest who is described as "hypocritical" because he adopted "the mannerisms, language, and style of living of his foreign counterparts" (89).

Lilla's critique of this position implies a definition of the new independent nation that can incorporate modernity without relinquishing old cultural practices—a new definition of the nation that fosters pride in old traditions. As one of the neighbors asserts, "Course nowadays everybody so genteel with all this education...that they shame to do the old things" (76). Lilla's gift to Beka of a new fountain pen and an exercise book constitutes an invitation to write down things about her life and traditions she has observed, so as to have a record to share with her own children and thus preserve the national culture.

The old ways come to life in chapter 12, when the community holds the traditional wake for Granny Straker to which Bill Lamb had objected. The wake functions as a repository of culture, where an uncle tells the stories of Brer Anancy, the Spider, where traditional food is prepared and shared, and neighbors and relatives call for the spirit of Granny Straker to come reside within and guide Beka. The community's singing of "Rock of Ages" makes Beka feel as if "it could lift the floor boards right up, and her with it" (77). The drumming at the wake leads to spirit possession, a characteristic feature of African-derived religiosities in the Caribbean basin. Juxtaposed against this scene, as an affirmation of the power of the wake to bring about positive resolutions, Bill Lamb announces to Beka that she will be returning to school for one term and will remain in school afterward if she passes.

Beka's return to school is introduced by a reference to the devaluation of the British Honduras dollar, which took place on December 31, 1949, as a response to an earlier devaluation of the British pound in September of that year. The decision to devaluate the dollar had been taken unilaterally by the colonial governor in defiance of the local Legislative Council and enraged Belizeans in general, but most particularly organized labor, which saw in the decision a move to protect the interests of multinational corporations operating in Belize such as the Belize Estate and Produce Company. The immediate response to the devaluation, which had led to a rapid worsening of the workers' condition, had been the formation of the People's Committee (the precursor of the PUP) and the growth of the anticolonial movement.

In the novel, the subject of devaluation is introduced through the changes it produces in the businesses frequented by the Lambs, which seem to be "breaking down." From her limited understanding, Beka personalizes the impact of devaluation, as "she scrambled around in her mind trying to fix on a way to prevent her own life from breaking down" (82). The discussion serves as a preamble to the breaking down of Toycie's life, as she shows the first signs of the pregnancy that will have her expelled from school. Having seen her vomit in church before all the schoolgirls and nuns, Beka realizes her friend is in trouble since vomiting "was something to be observed with the utmost suspicion" (86). In counterpoint to Toycie's "breaking down," the next chapter will introduce the essay contest on the subject of "The Sisters of Charity in Belize," which will provide the opportunity for Beka to rise above her former failure. (The Sisters of Charity of Nazareth is a Catholic religious order founded in 1812 in Kentucky. They have served in Belize, particularly through their education ministry, since the late nineteenth century.)

Beginning with chapter 15, Toycie's pregnancy becomes the focus of the novel, following her acknowledgment of her condition to Beka and her request that her friend accompany her to break the news to Emilio. The economic and political context of the relationship between Toycie and Emilio is underscored in the opening pages of the chapter, where Bill Lamb and Granny Ivy resume their discussion about Guatemala's intentions toward a potentially independent Belize, rumored to be behind Guatemalan assistance to the fictional People's Independence Party (and the nonfictional PUP). The British government had aided the Creoles by helping them "gain a monopoly in the civil service," while the Panias (the group to which Emilio and his family belong) could be seen as favoring Guatemalan interests in "trying to make one big Keatolic nation" (95, 103).

Toycie's tragedy will continue to play against the background of Belizean politics throughout the novel. In chapter 16, Edgell offers a detailed description of a political rally at Battlefield Park, where the People's Independence Party presents its anticolonial, pro-independence positions, based on Belizeans presenting a united front against the world. They "must show…that a poor, suffering, homeless, undernourished people can stand together until our not unjust demands are met" (108). In this context, the fragmentation of Toycie's dreams of marriage—Emilio cannot marry her "because he has to finish school and go to university in Mexico" (108)—is blamed on the obstacles to the national unity pursued by the People's Independence Party. Beka will articulate the impact of the uncertainty—both political and personal—brought about by the juxtaposition of the country's and Toycie's woes to Sister Gabriela thus: "Sometimes I feel bruk down just like my own country, Sister. I start all right but then I can't seem to continue. Something gets in the way and then I drift for the longest while" (115).

Beka's fears of breaking down prefigure Toycie's psychological collapse, described in chapters 19 and 20. Ironically, this collapse brings about the unity politicians are striving for, as all, including Emilio Villanueva and his family, rally around Toycie. In fact, as a symbolic victim of the class and ethnic stresses of Belizean society, Toycie's increasingly violent state exemplifies the potential consequences of a failure to achieve unity among the various groups constituting a potentially independent Belizean nation. Edgell offers the reader two versions of Toycie: the image of her "ear-shattering screams" and aggressive convulsions, and that of Beka's reminiscences of the time they spent in Sibun, innocently working the land in a deep connection to a former slave settlement that marked the beginnings of the Belizean nation.

The news of Toycie's death during a storm comes close on the celebration of National Day, and despite its tragedy, it belongs to a period of regeneration. The message of national unity of the politicians at Battlefield Park has taken root, as Lilla counsels Bill, "We'll have to get used to it, Bill. Don't you hear what the politicians are saying in Battlefield Park? We must unite to build a nation" (150). Beka's bougainvillea bush has sprouted new shoots as a symbol of rebirth within tragedy.

It is through Beka's winning of the essay contest, however, that Edgell underscores the profound changes about to take place in Belize, pointing to the social and economic transformation that will be the result of national unity. The novel, by making the anticolonial, nation-building message of the PUP its own, gives us Beka as the symbol of the new Belize, a young woman and budding writer whose independent life need not break down.

Chapter 9

Magali García Ramis's
Happy Days, Uncle Sergio

Puerto Rican writer Magali García Ramis was born in Santurce, a thriving sector of the San Juan metropolitan area, in 1946. She came from a middle-class family, prosperous by island standards, with cultural and racial roots in the urban sector of nineteenth-century Spanish Creole society. Like most children of the Puerto Rican middle class, she and her brother Gerardo were educated in local Catholic schools. Their childhood transpired in a multigenerational, predominantly female household that included her mother, aunts, and grandmother, and a large extended family of numerous aunts, uncles, and cousins. García Ramis pays tribute to the vital role played by her female relatives in her life in a work in progress, *El libro de las tías* (The Book of the Aunts), a biography of the Ramis sisters—her mother and six maternal aunts.

García Ramis was an avid reader from early childhood; reading and writing were her most ardent pursuits. She drew her early inspiration from family anecdotes and from the stories told to her by her friends at school, which became the foundation of a fictional world based on tales of family interaction and characterized by humor, light irony, and a delicate touch with the Puerto Rican vernacular. In interviews she has said that even at that early age, her writing was marked by the light sense of humor that is a salient characteristic of all her work. During her high school years, she wrote for the school newspaper, which she edited in her senior year, an experience that was instrumental in her choosing journalism as a career.

García Ramis attended the University of Puerto Rico, where she majored in history. Shortly after completing her degree, she began writing for the San

Juan newspaper *El Mundo*. In 1968 she left for New York to attend Columbia University's School of Journalism, from which she would receive a master's degree. The sojourn in New York represented a cultural epiphany for the budding writer. Having grown up with the notion fostered by her family and teachers that she was an American, she felt herself to be, culturally and linguistically, in alien territory. Her first short story, "Todos los domingos" (Every Sunday), dates from this period. It won the short story contest sponsored by the Ateneo Puertorriqueño, Puerto Rico's most important short fiction prize.

Back in Puerto Rico, in 1971, García Ramis started writing for local newspapers like *El Imparcial, Claridad,* and *La Hora* and for the magazine *Avance*. While working at *El Imparcial*, García Ramis met the Pérez Otero family, whose commitment to Puerto Rico's political independence profoundly influenced her. Feeling "strange and isolated" (Esteves, "Literature/ Journalism" 863) in her own support of independence while working amid colleagues who supported the pro-statehood or pro-commonwealth political options, she found a refuge in the Pérez Oteros as an adoptive family. Her closeness to the family became her "first encounter with a completely Puerto Rican world, a discovery of a Puerto Rican reality in contrast with the world of my family which is so Spanish" ("Literature/Journalism" 863). It was following her connection to them that she began working on the stories that would form her first collection of tales, *La familia de todos nosotros.* In 1973 she submitted four of the short stories to the Casa de las Américas literary contest in Havana. The jury determined that they did not yet constitute a book, but her story "La viudad de Chencho el Loco" (The Widow of Chencho the Madman) received an honorary mention and was published in 1974. In this same year, she left for Mexico with the Pérez Otero's daughter Maritza to work toward a doctorate in literature at the Universidad Autónoma de México, but her stay in Mexico was brief, and she returned to Puerto Rico without completing her degree.

Back in San Juan, in 1977, García Ramis joined the faculty of the School of Communications at the University of Puerto Rico, where she still teaches. Since then, she has been a frequent contributor to Puerto Rican newspapers, among them *El Mundo, El Imparcial, Claridad,* and *La Hora*. A collection of her best journalistic essays, *La ciudad que me habita,* appeared in 1993, when it won the Puerto Rico Pen Club nonfiction award. During this period, García Ramis collaborated with her brother Gerardo, a professional translator, on various artistic projects, producing prints and serigraphs for book illustration or for sale in local art galleries.

She began to write fiction in earnest shortly after her return from Mexico, publishing *La familia de todos nosotros* in 1976. The six tales in this collection are narrated by female voices that range from the upper-middle-class young girl of "Todos los domingos" and "La familia de todos nosotros" to the proletarian voice of "La viudad de Chencho el Loco." Centered on the urban culture of the Santurce sector of San Juan, where the author grew up, the stories chronicle the changes brought about by industrialization and the sprawl of suburbs around the capital from the point of view of their impact on women.

Between 1977 and 1985, García Ramis worked on a novel she had begun in 1972, *Felices días, tío Sergio,* which was published in 1986 and translated into English in 1995. It won the Puerto Rico Pen Club Award for fiction. Her second collection of short stories, *Las noches del Riel de oro,* appeared in 1991. Her second novel, *Las horas del sur,* written with the help of a Guggenheim Fellowship she received in 1988 and a Rockefeller Foundation fellowship in Bellagio, Italy, was finally published in 2005 to mixed reviews.

García Ramis has also written a number of film and documentary scripts. These include *La flor de piel* (1989), a film sponsored by the Commission for the Status of Women and produced by Zaga Films. She wrote the script for a mini-series about Bartolomé de las Casas (1991) and for a half-hour documentary titled *The Spanish Revival in Puerto Rican Architecture* (1994). She has also published two titles for children, *Doña Felisa Rincón de Gautier, alcaldesa de San Juan* (1995), a biography of the first woman to become mayor of San Juan, and *De cómo Genaro se hizo hombre y otros cuentos* (How Genaro Became a Man and Other Stories) (2002). She has been a visiting professor at the Escuela de Artes Plásticas in Puerto Rico and at Yale and other universities in the United States.

Happy Days, Uncle Sergio

Felices días, tío Sergio (Happy Days, Uncle Sergio), the island's best known bildungsroman, or novel of development, has been unquestionably the most widely read literary text in Puerto Rico in the last 20 years. The novel's popularity rests on the authenticity of its narrative voice—that of a young girl narrating the changes that come into her life when her mysterious young uncle returns home after a long exile—as well as on the detailed account of the changes undergone by Puerto Rican society in the late 1950s and early 1960s.

The novel is set in the early years of Puerto Rico's Estado Libre Asociado, or commonwealth, which articulated the political association between the island and the United States and was approved in 1952. The agreement was linked to Operation Bootstrap, an ambitious program for economic revitalization that began in 1948, following the collapse of the sugar industry during World War II. The program called for the distribution of lands formerly owned by sugar producers to the displaced peasantry and for the speedy industrialization of the island to provide employment in the rapidly growing urban areas. The program encouraged U.S. companies to establish factories on the island by offering a skilled labor force at wages below those of the mainland and ready access to U.S. markets, without import duties and with exemptions from federal taxes.

The project, which involved the building of extensive facilities for tourism, was accompanied by a broad program of infrastructure development that included extensive highway construction, the building of water reservoirs and hydroelectric plants, and the modernization of sewage systems. During the 1960s, the manufacturing sector would shift from clothing, tobacco, leather goods, and apparel to capital-intensive industries such as oil refineries, pharmaceuticals, and electronics. These are changes recorded by the young protagonist of the novel—whose uncle Roberto works for the government-run Puerto Rico Development Corporation—as a background to the tale of the changes brought to her family by her uncle's arrival.

Operation Bootstrap also brought major changes to the city that provide the backdrop to Lidia's story. With the advent of industrialization and tourism came massive migration from the countryside to San Juan. The old city was surrounded by suburban developments that transformed the urban landscape. The text chronicles the violent deforestation and digging into the blood red mud of the fertile valley surrounding the *area metropolitana* to build a modern San Juan in the 1960s. The book is perhaps the most eloquent revelation of the destruction of natural landscapes necessary for the expansion of metropolitan San Juan. Everywhere around the characters, people are digging into the land to build a new airport, to carve out a new water reservoir, or to build housing developments, factories, and highways.

Happy Days, Uncle Sergio chronicles its protagonist's cultural, political, and intellectual development through the crucial period of her adolescence, during which her uncle Sergio lives with her family. Lidia's autobiographical narrative tells of how she is trapped in her family's identification with colonial cultures—be it the traditions of Spanish culture or the modernity of North American mores—and how she finds in her uncle a startlingly new articulation of Puerto Rican culture that transforms her interpretation of the society in which she lives.

The novel is set in Santurce, a thriving sector of San Juan that includes a variety of neighborhoods housing working-class as well as middle- and upper-middle-class families. Santurce is linked to Old San Juan, the colonial capital, by two bridges dating back to the early twentieth century (Old San Juan stands on an islet of its own). Lidia, the novel's narrator, lives near the Puente Dos Hermanos (the Two Brothers' Bridge), within walking distance of the ruins of the old Spanish fort of San Gerónimo and the beaches of the fashionable Condado Area, San Juan's central tourist section. Santurce's nerve center is the Avenida Ponce de León, which joins Old San Juan to the university district of Río Piedras, crossing Santurce and the business district of Hato Rey. The bus stops along the avenue are numbered, and the numbers serve as points of reference for residents of San Juan as well as for the narrator, who uses them to locate spaces in the novel for the readers.

The novel is divided into six sections of varying length. The first four describe the events that transpire during Uncle Sergio's stay with Lidia's family. Part 5 consists of a letter Lidia writes to her uncle in her freshman year at the University of Puerto Rico, years after the events narrated in parts 1–4. Part 6 offers a coda that tells of the death of Uncle Sergio in New York and of Lidia's devastation.

Part 1 of the novel, which comprises about 40 percent of the text, opens with the description of the narrator, Lidia, as she walks on the beach near the old San Gerónimo fortress with her mother and brother. The opening image is of the three of them standing on one leg, like storks, challenging "the world, good manners, and the family" (13). Although living in the same household with her late father's female relatives, the narrator wants to set aside her immediate family (mother and brother) as a subset of the larger concept of family. The stork imagery allows her to depict the three of them as examples of challenge and balance, as a group that is a part of the larger family but still recognizable as a separable unit that does not necessarily follow the rules of the larger group. The graceful stork beginning is followed immediately with the historical and political background—"It was in the times of Muñoz Marín" (14)—and the geographical setting, that of "Santurce in the fifties," a 20-square-block area that was the city's central middle-class enclave (25).

The narrative proper begins on the day before the unexpected and unannounced arrival of her uncle Sergio, who has been living in the United States and whom Lidia has not met before. The narrative centers on an example of childhood transgression, as Lidia, her brother Andrés, and their cousin Quique greet a neighbor, Margara, as she walks past their house, breaking the interdiction against communication with this beautiful young woman of lower class, reported loose morals, and associations with the Nationalist Party. Uncle Sergio's arrival will help open Lidia's eyes to the family's prejudices that lead to the repudiation of people like Margara.

In many pro-American, middle-class Puerto Rican families like Lidia's, the Nationalist Party was anathema, as they advocated a continued struggle against U.S. colonialism through means that included political violence. In 1950 they had led an island-wide revolt that was quickly overcome and had attempted to assassinate President Harry Truman. In 1954 they had carried out an armed attack against members of Congress. *Happy Days, Uncle Sergio* assumes the reader's familiarity with Puerto Rico's political struggles concerning the island's status. Since the transfer of control of the island from Spain to the United States after the Spanish-American War of 1898, Puerto Rican politics have been focused on the status question—whether Puerto Rico should become a state of the United States, secure its political independence, or (since 1952) remain a free associated state, or commonwealth. Lidia's family, from evidence offered throughout the text, is torn between the statehood and commonwealth options. The family's rants against the independence option had left the protagonist fearful "that something evil called independence was going to arrive through the veranda door" (38). Nationalists, in the text, are linked with communism and with violence of the sort produced by the Mau Mau uprising, the bloody insurgency by Kenyan rebels against British colonialism (1952–1960). Uncle Sergio's arrival is thus associated with transgression, with "fleeing from the punishment for the rules I went on breaking" and with "growing up in fear" (18), and with the disappearance of her cat Daruel, which Lidia interprets as punishment for her transgression and whose funeral in absentia Uncle Sergio helps her organize, thereby cementing their relationship.

Sergio's arrival from New York offers the narrator an opportunity to introduce her extended family. Sergio, who will remain a man of mystery throughout the narrative, is described as a tall, thin man of ambivalent sexuality with "enormous eyes with long, feminine eyelashes" (20) whose association with the Nationalists has forced him into a life of exile in New York, where he sold encyclopedias house to house. The children are warned not to ask him questions about his past, and they suspect he has also been forbidden, as a condition of his welcome to the family house, from talking to the children about Puerto Rican history or politics.

The rest of the household, except for Lidia's brother Andrés and their cousin Quique, who spends the afternoons with them after leaving school, consists of female relatives. Mamá Sara, the matriarch, draws her power from her connection to her late husband, Papá Fernando, paradoxically ruling over a female household while upholding male authority, keeping the chair opposite hers at the dining table empty to be occupied by whatever male adult was in attendance. Her unmarried daughters Aunt Ele (a doctor) and Sara Fernanda (a secretary who works for the Department of Health) live in her house, together with Lidia's widowed mother (María Angélica, married to Mamá Sara's son Gustavo, who had died in World War II), Cousin Nati (a medical technician brought up by Mamá Sara), and their maid Micaela. As Lidia comments in reference to her predominantly female household, "in our daily lives there had never been a man who would establish his masculine rhythm and way of life in our world" (25). The extended family includes Auntie Meri (a childless daughter of Mamá Sara, married to Uncle Vicente); Auntie Clara (married to Uncle Roberto), who has three sons, Quique, Germán Andrés, and Robertito; and Cousin Germámico, married to Aunt Rosa, who has three very proper daughters, Rosi, Angelita, and Monsi. The family's genealogy, as described in part 1, is solidly rooted in white Spanish immigrants of professional standing, with a grandmother "from the French islands" whose clear green eyes signal her unquestionable whiteness. Their whiteness represents their most evident claim to belonging to the middle and upper middle classes in an island whose social structure has been described as a pigmentocracy, in which the masses are black or of mixed African, European, and indigenous ancestry and the whites or very light skinned occupy the upper echelons of society.

Following the introduction of the family, Lidia's narrative concentrates on a description of how Puerto Rico's political options (statehood, commonwealth, or independence) are linked to cultural choices. Lidia's family, because of its Spanish roots, land-owning background, and geographical location (in the established neighborhood of Santurce, with its closeness to the old Spanish enclave in Old San Juan), identifies with Spanish culture and mores. They have also, however, embraced U.S. popular culture and technical prowess. The children, for example, are avid readers of American comics like the adventures of Tarzan, Black Hawk, Wonder Woman, the Fox and the Crow, *Exemplary Lives,* and *Legends from America,* while Mamá Sara is enthralled by *Gunsmoke, The Untouchables,* and similar programming about American law enforcement. They have adopted American-style celebrations like Easter egg hunts, Santa Claus, and Thanksgiving and are great admirers of American household appliances.

Their focus on European and American cultures as models to be emulated leaves very little room for the recognition of Puerto Rican culture. There is a denial of the value of Puerto Rican culture that goes hand in hand with their conviction that Puerto Rico does not possess a culture mature enough to warrant the status of an independent nation. Uncle Sergio's efforts at teaching the children about styles in art bring the cultural issue to the fore. As Andrés asserts, mimicking family dictums, "There are no famous Puerto Rican artists because Puerto Rico doesn't have much culture and this island is too small. Only now as part of the U.S., as a Commonwealth, has Puerto Rico begun to progress" (34).

Part 1 offers two family discussions about gender issues that will be central to subsequent parts of the novel. They are preceded by Lidia's list of the family's standard of "Good and Evil." The Good includes Catholicism, the United States, and all refined Europeans, but also includes Francisco Franco—the infamous authoritarian leader of Spain (from 1936 to 1975), who saw himself as the Leader of the Last Crusade and defender of Hispanism and who had outlawed homosexuality and prostitution. The Evil includes Communists, atheists, Nazis, young African nations, Puerto Ricans favoring independence, mambo, Dominican strongman Rafael Leonidas Trujillo (who ruled the Dominican Republic from 1930 to 1961), and Cuban dictator Fulgencio Batista (who ruled Cuba from 1933, until he was ousted by Fidel Castro in 1959).

The Evil list, which includes the notorious Mexican actress María Félix, allows García Ramis to discuss the family's acceptance of the Catholic notion of the essential sinful nature of women. Sara Fernanda asserts that "women who misbehave are evil" (42), while men transgress because they cannot help themselves. This notion of womanhood, against which Lidia must carve her own identity as a rebellious young girl, is followed by a detailed discussion of exile to the United States as a family's means of ridding itself of the embarrassing inconvenience of having a gay man in its midst. The theme will surface again in the novel through veiled references to their mysterious cousin Andrés, "the most handsome man in our family" (43), who for unexplained reasons rarely visits, and to intimations of Uncle Sergio's own homosexuality.

Two incidents narrated in part 1 are significant to the development of the overall themes of the novel. One involves the family's attendance at the inauguration of the new water reservoir, which brings them together with a young American family whose habits and mores offer a point of comparison to Puerto Rican middle-class mores, while allowing the family to satirize the assimilation of Puerto Rican immigrants to the United States. The visiting American executive, Arnold Killey, is described as having changed his name from José Arnaldo Quiles to succeed in the United States. His American wife and daughters, whom Lidia sees as free in their sandals and casual clothing, while she is uncomfortably dressed in her Sunday best, are depicted by the family as "untidy women." American wives, in their eyes, "don't iron their husbands' handkerchiefs" (54). American versions of womanhood, with whose freedom Lidia identifies, are repudiated by the family as lacking refinement and sophistication.

The second episode revolves around a coming hurricane that prompts Uncle Sergio to climb the fence that separates the family from Margara's house to help Don Gabriel Tristani, her father, secure their house. This infraction of the family rules mirrors Lidia's infraction at the beginning of the chapter, when she greets Margara as she walks past their house. The Tristanis' house recreates the rural dwellings that have become symbolic of Puerto Rican nationhood. The small house, painted yellow, has a garden planted in pigeon peas (an important ingredient in Puerto Rican cuisine), two or three caged fighting roosters (the national pastime), and a tattered Puerto Rican flag on a pole. Since any approach to this family of Nationalists is considered dangerous by the aunts, it is significant that Lidia finds "clemency" toward Uncle Sergio in her mother, "a very brief and clear gesture of tolerance and compassion towards those people" that supports her daughter's rebellion against the family's intolerance (70). It becomes one more example of the mother's sanctioning of Lidia's questioning of the family's strict injunctions, which are confirmed in the final episode of part 1: passing a school named after Segundo Ruiz Belvis (1829–1867), one of Puerto Rico's most ardent abolitionists and pro-independence leaders, Cousin Nati refers to him as "one of those shitheads...sort of national hero" (71). Her stern reaction to Sergio's explanation that he had "helped the cause of justice" and had been "against oppression" convinces Lidia that he had been cautioned not to speak to the children about his views on Puerto Rican history (72). Sergio's sympathies with the Nationalist movement and his knowledge of the island's history of anticolonial, pro-independence struggle, however, become a key element in Lidia's understanding of those aspects of her life and society from which the family appears intent on separating her.

Part 2 of the novel focuses on Lidia's adolescent crisis following her first menstruation and her guilt-ridden introspection as her interest in sexual matters clashes against the Catholic Church's notions of sexuality as sinful. The narrative balances Lidia's greater exposure to the world outside her family and her growing empathy with her Uncle Sergio against her frustration with her family's narrow-mindedness and prejudices. The section opens with Aunt Ele's ecstatic description of having seen Eva Perón twice while visiting Spain. Her admiration of the famous Evita (1919–1952), the charismatic and controversial first lady of Argentina, is linked here to her equal admiration for Franco. Both evidence Aunt Ele's and the family's political naïveté and blindness to the realities of political life beyond surface appearances. Evita is described as "the only woman I've ever seen with peach-color skin," while Franco's Moorish Guard is described as "wearing matching uniforms" and mounted on horses whose "hooves were polished and painted" (73). Neither depiction goes beneath the surface in an attempt at understanding the political complexities and negative aspects of Perón's government and Franco's dictatorship. One of the indications in the text of Lidia's growing understanding of the limitations of the information provided by the family is her comment that she and her brother were to learn as adults about the Moorish Guard's "atrocities during the [Civil] war" (95). Aunt Ele's description of her trip to Spain also allows her the opportunity to disparage the notion of traveling to South America, which she describes as "a very sad region" peopled only by "poor, hungry, very dirty Indians" (74).

Lidia's greater exposure to the world outside her family is exemplified in this part of the text by her work in her Cousin Nati's lab (which brings her in contact with her first quasi-romantic interest, Manuel), the people she meets during her outings with her mother (which include a woman "from the islands" and a beggar), the books about sex that she and Andrés procure behind the family's back, her awareness of the tensions surrounding the migration to Puerto Rico of Cubans fleeing the Castro regime, and her encounter with the bullying and inherent violence of adolescent life at her school. Each one of these encounters brings Lidia to a better understanding of the contradictions inherent in her family's conservative notions and closer to the perspective represented by Uncle Sergio.

The contradictory nature of the family's position is exemplified by the first of Lidia's rebellions against family practices in this section of the narrative, this once concerning what Aunt Ele calls Lidia's tendency to be "provincial about food," a tendency she must remedy if she is to travel with the family in the future. This is an important episode since it prefigures the family's refusal to take her and Andrés on a highly anticipated vacation at the end of Part 2 as a punishment for having been involved in a fight at school. The family's usual denigration of Puerto Rican traditions does not usually apply to food, as local produce and recipes are used in the house, especially those associated with holiday celebrations. Lidia's refusal to eat *yautías* and *lerenes,* and her preference for fried steaks, hot dogs, and French fries (and other U.S. diet staples such as Coke and grilled cheese sandwiches), is derided by the family as a sign of her lack of sophistication and stubbornness. Lidia's response is to point out the class and culture contradictions of the family's position: "That's the food country bumpkins like.Why do you tell us that we have to eat everything to be sophisticated and then try to get us to eat the junk that hicks eat?" (75). Having internalized the message that autochthonous culture is inherently inferior and everything American superior by definition, she confronts Aunt Ele with the contradictions in their position as relating to local food. The reference to *jíbaros,* or "peasants" ("country bumpkins" in the English translation), also alludes to the family's frequent disparaging of the habits and customs of the Puerto Rican poor from their middle-class-bound perspective. Later in part 2, there is a lengthy description of food connected to Christmas Eve celebrations, which includes a broad selection of imported foods (predominantly from Spain), but where the main dishes are traditional Puerto Rican recipes. The Puerto Rican dishes, interestingly enough, are prepared by "two elderly black women who had brought up my family" (81), a direct allusion to the family's roots in plantation society.

Lidia's outings with her mother expose her to the gaze of others, and she begins to internalize the pressures of conforming to the expectations of family and outsiders. From Nati's ridicule of Lidia's unmanicured hands to the comments of the friends they meet on the street, Lidia's self-image must confront the multiplicity of gazes that seek to leave their imprint on her developing identity. Her mother's openness to others (particularly the tiny black woman from the islands whose English patois only her mother can understand and the former lawyer whose madness has forced him into living in the streets) offers a lesson in understanding the humanity and value of those around her, which runs counter to the family's "unsociable [approach] towards anyone who was not part of the immediate family" (78).

In part 2, the mystery of Uncle Sergio's situation takes center stage. The receipt of a letter, purportedly from New York, appears to shatter him emotionally, and the family resorts to espionage and conspiracy. Their approach to Uncle Sergio's presence is that of a contaminating agent that threatens to infect the family, particularly the children. They piece together what they can of his letter, learning that there is danger in his return to New York. They despair of his being able to secure a job, given his past activities. They complain of his grooming and suspect he is drinking. They move the children to a different school to increase their homework and reduce the idle time that they normally spend with their uncle. They go as far as to separate his laundry from that of the rest of the family, as he was a man and "his humors, his perspiration, are different" (96). Lidia explains how these efforts only succeed in intensifying her fascination with her uncle: "children, even the very young, sense and recognize themselves in a forbidden person, especially if it is in their nature to become one" (92).

Lidia explores her potential to become "a forbidden person" as she "involuntarily entered puberty" (97) and sought to actively separate herself from her family. The path to separation is twofold; Lidia and Andrés seek their own identities through their identification with Uncle Sergio and through their efforts at satisfying their "morbid curiosity about sex" (99). For Lidia, the exploration of sexuality—since it can only be done primarily through Church-produced materials and through notions derived from Catholicism—leads to feelings of worthlessness associated with the Church's notions of women's innate sinfulness. She is a "vicious woman," she concludes: "I was a lost evil woman, I wasn't in God's grace" (101).

Lidia's choice of a rebellious identity finds its best expression in her decision to take a stand against the bullies that are harassing Andrés at school. The homophobic nature of the taunting and abuse infuriates Lidia, who indulges in fantasies of revenge, feeling herself "ready to become an assassin" and knowing she could kill them "in cold blood" (105). She retaliates by coming to Andrés's defense when the group finally attacks him, taunting them herself with accusations of being queer—"the worst possible insult" (106)—and physically attacking them, forcing them eventually to run away. The fight has profound repercussions since it leads the family to exclude her and Andrés from a much anticipated vacation to El Yunque rainforest and the thermal springs at Coamo, and leads Lidia to conclude that she could no longer be a part of the family. Their flaw as a family, she realizes, is that "the only thing that mattered was what other people thought of us" (109). In this, the most crucial moment in her adolescent trajectory, she finds comfort in Uncle Sergio's embrace and in his promise to one day take her to the rainforest and the thermal springs.

Part 3 of the narrative represents the happy days of the title, *Felices días* in the original. The phrase is the title of a Puerto Rican *danza* by composer Juan Morel Campos (1857–1896), with lyrics by Sicila Arce. The *danza* is a nineteenth-century Puerto Rican dance form, similar to the habanera and incorporating the European *contradanza* and African-derived rhythms. The lyrics of "Felices días" express nostalgia for former joyous days that cannot return to comfort us. This section of the narrative is framed by two lengthy absences of the family—it opens when the family has left on their vacation, leaving Lidia and Andrés with only their mother and Uncle Sergio, and closes with Uncle Sergio and Mamá Sara dancing "Felices días," while Aunt Ele and Cousin Nati are traveling through Europe. During a brief period of time, the children are alone with Uncle Sergio and experience a few days of perfect freedom and transgression. The events narrated here thus become the happy days of the title.

There are four main themes in part 3: the freedom experienced by Lidia in the absence of her aunts; human life unfolding in historical time (births, deaths, and burials); the aunts' deeply rooted racism; and a return to the theme of woman's innate sinfulness, a notion that Lidia is now ready to challenge. The tone of the narrative has changed perceptibly, moreover, as Lidia abandons the angst that characterized her perception of herself as a lost woman in part 2 and gives herself to the enjoyment of her burst of freedom from her oppressive aunts. The reference to the Russian invasion on Hungary dates the events in this portion of the text as taking place in 1956.

Lidia's meditations on death and burial—on her own part in the continuum of life and history—is an apt introduction to both the birth of Margara's son and the death of her baby cousin. It also prefigures the loss of Uncle Sergio when he returns to New York in part 4 and the news of his death in part 5. The theme is deftly deployed through references to Lidia's reading of *The Floating Cemetery,* a book about Chinese immigrants to the United States who send their dead to China for burial. It allows Uncle Sergio to make his wish to be buried in Puerto Rico after his death known to Lidia. But in part 3, these losses are still in the future, and the sequence of events narrated in this section are examples of the liberating possibilities of living outside of the limiting influences of the aunts. The constraints represented earlier by religion are ridiculed here through stories revealing the absurdities of the life of Blessed Contardo Ferrini, marching to sainthood on the strength of never having looked at a woman. Lidia and her immediate family live idyllic moments playing Parcheesi until midnight and watching TV until late. The highlight of their freedom, however, is their involvement, "like members of a secret brotherhood" (90), in the birth of Margara's baby and in the acquisition of the baby's clothes and bottles, an action in which Lidia's mother once again becomes their accomplice.

Lidia's estrangement from the aunts and the cultural notions they uphold is established convincingly in this section through García Ramis's unveiling of their deeply entrenched, class-based racial prejudices. Spurred by fear that their cousin's soon-to-be Cuban wife may have black ancestry, the aunts display a range of profoundly racist notions that are characteristic of their class in Puerto Rican society. Stressing that they "don't have anything against blacks," they nonetheless offer a summary of the most denigrating racial notions imaginable in Puerto Rican culture: "the children of black and white parents can never be happy," you couldn't caress the head of a child with kinky hair "because your hand could get entangled in its hair," blacks are not as healthy as white people "because the blood of white people is different from the blood of blacks," it's not a good idea to have a transracial transfusion because there is not "homogeneity in the blood" (124–125). These racist notions, supported by pseudo-science by a doctor and a medical lab technician, are shown here as evidence of the aunts' faulty understanding of race, history, and modernity.

The section ends with a bittersweet scene that prefigures the disillusionment and pain of the last three brief sections, when Lidia feels betrayed and abandoned by Uncle Sergio. Here Uncle Sergio and his mother dance to the tune of the *danza* of the title, whose lyrics underscore the impossibility of returning to the days of past happiness. She will return in later sections to the happy days when Uncle Sergio lived with them, with nostalgia for a happiness she felt she had squandered. They are represented by the parallel images of Uncle Sergio dancing with his mother, on one side, and of Lidia refusing his invitation to teach her how to dance, on the other.

Part 4 of the narrative opens in the middle months of 1960, as established by the references to the Soviet Sputnik unmanned rocket program (1957–1960), especially to the rocket that carried animals on board, that of August 1960. The section tells of Uncle Sergio's departure and the mysterious reason behind it. It opens with a brief catalog of the authors he reads over and over again, which include Scandinavian authors Paar Lagerkvist (Sweden, 1891–1974), winner of the Nobel Prize in 1951, and Sigrid Undset (Norway, 1882–1949), winner of the Nobel Prize in 1928. Both were expressionist authors who shared a growing concern with totalitarianism. He also reads Spanish poet Miguel Hernández (1910–1942), whose poetry has become a symbol of the Republican struggle against Franco during the Spanish civil war, and Luis Palés Matos (1898–1959), whose poetry celebrating the African roots of Puerto Rican culture would have been anathema to the aunts.

At the very center of part 4, García Ramis inserts a discussion of two new elements in Puerto Rican society, placed here to indicate the changes in social hierarchies brought about by Muñoz Marín's development projects: the emergence of a new social club, the upstart Casino de Puerto Rico, to challenge the hegemony of the Spain-centered Casa de España, and the appearance of exclusive, upper-middle-class housing developments west of the city of San Juan (particularly Santa María and San Francisco), which displace the center of fashionable living away from the Condado and Miramar areas (Lidia's family lives in the latter) to the new luxurious suburbs, now gated communities. Both developments (club and suburbs) aim to open a social space for families who had gained wealth through the government's new development ventures but had found themselves blocked from the fashionable district for lack of space and from the Casa de España because of questionable family backgrounds or obvious African ancestry. The narrator describes their group posing for photographs at the Casa de España Halloween party as being "memorialized as Spaniards for future generations of Solises, white, respectable members of the Casa de España" (135). Linked to these developments is the notion that money—not ancestry or race—has become the measure of class, and that the social standards that had allowed relatively impoverished families like Lidia's to maintain their social hegemony have been radically altered. The family, however, eager to maintain its hold, will join in the new mercantilistic efforts by importing German figurines and Christmas ornaments for sale.

The discussion of the "new and expensive suburbs" that redefine the concentration of wealthy families (with extensive repercussions as new private schools, businesses, and clubs shift to the suburbs to serve that new population) offers an opportunity to enter into a discussion of the class and

economic instability that they believe will result out of Muñoz Marín's policies. Citing the unfairness of building housing projects for the poor (and
dark skinned) "next to the suburbs of the well-to-do" (137), they accuse the
governor of being a Neo-Malthusian, of creating the favorable conditions
that could lead to a population explosion among the poor, which in turn
could result in the total collapse of the Puerto Rican economy.

The second half of part 4 narrates Lidia's feelings of emotional and
sexual betrayal as she faces Uncle Sergio's return to the United States. The
calls from a mysterious friend in New York hint at the possibility of his
homosexuality—of an emotional connection that transcends the link he has
established with Lidia and her brother. The aborted attempt at lovemaking
with their servant Micaela—which Lidia witnesses—is both a shock to Lidia
(partly because of Micaela's class status and partly because of her smell of
cheap lilac water) and a confirmation of Uncle Sergio's inability to sustain a
sexual relationship with a woman. Lidia's statement later in this part of the
novel, that Sergio had been "the only man I had ever learned to love" (146),
has been cited by a number of critics as evidence that homosexuality was a
burden Lidia and her uncle had shared, a link that would explain their deep
understanding of each other.

Lidia's grief over what she sees as her uncle's abandonment of her and betrayal, despite his promises to remain, is on one hand inscribed in adolescent
despair and, on the other, presented as a crisis from which Lidia is never to
recover. The lasting grief caused by the separation is hinted at through the
name of the boat on which Uncle Sergio sails away, "the white ship Bohéme,"
with its allusion to Giacomo Puccini's opera of the same title. *La Bohéme*
(1896), about lovers ultimately separated by death, ends with a famous duet,
in which Mimi and Rodolfo sing about their past happiness before she takes
her last breath.

Part 5 of the narrative consists of a letter written by Lidia to Uncle Sergio years after his departure, during her freshman year at the University of
Puerto Rico. In it she narrates the immersion in Anglo-American culture
and literature that was the result of his departure and details her recovery
from her alienating Americanism. Without his openness to Puerto Rican
culture and the alternative he presented to profound Americanization, Lidia
describes her descent into colonial deculturation. English becomes her "true
language," and she learns to "think and feel in English" (149). The cultural
loss is expressed in images of her world narrowing around her: she becomes
jaded and distrustful, sees her classmates as dishonest, fails to excel academi-
cally, and becomes a censor of the *Paris Match* magazines used for French
class. For all this, she blames her uncle's abandonment:

*Did you feel free of guilt? Didn't you know you also had a responsibility to give continu-
ity to what you had begun, our complicity, our awakening, our attempt to fight for our
identity?* (152)

Lidia's plea to her uncle is that of validating an island and a culture that is outside history books and has no heroes celebrated in poetry or prose. Her description of the Spanish colonial capital of Old San Juan in the early 1960s as "dirty" and "peeling" evokes the period before this section of the capital, with its buildings dating back to the 1520s, was renovated to its present ready-for-tourist splendor. It leads her to conclude that *"we're nothing. We don't exist. We are shit,* I thought, *and I don't want to belong to this country!"* (153). She travels through Europe with Sara Fernanda, finding in the splendors of its monuments and architecture further confirmation of the insignificance of her home island.

Ironically, it is an unwanted kiss from a boy she was not attracted to while dancing a bolero that reawakens her to her suppressed feelings for her uncle and sets her back on the course of recovery of Puerto Rican culture. The bolero, described by Ed Morales as the "most popular lyric tradition in Latin America" (120), is a slow-paced, romantic ballad, whose lyrics speak of passionate and often unrequited love. The one cited by Lidia as ushering in her epiphany is "Nuestro juramento" (Our Pledge), a famous composition by Ecuadorian singer and composer Julio Jaramillo (1936–1978). Its introduction into the text serves a purpose equal to that of two other compositions that play prominent roles in the novel, the *danza* of the title and Puccini's *La Bohéme.*

Lidia's recovery of her Puerto Rican heritage is narrated primarily through descriptions of her alienation from her Americanized and shallow classmates and her insistence on her right to proclaim her Puerto Rican identity through the discovery of music her aunts consider only fit for maids: boleros, *plenas* (an important genre of Puerto Rican folk music, a precursor of the popular salsa), and Christmas songs (traditional tunes as the year's Christmas hits, usually humorous, sometimes bawdy songs composed for each year's holiday season). It is not surprising, then, that the section ends with Lidia picking up her pen to start her own composition, the letter-bolero (and finally, the text we are reading) that becomes her declaration of love for her uncle.

This declaration of love is stylistically similar to Lidia's symbolic self-flagellations when assessing the nature of her sinfulness in previous chapters. Here a declaration of a love that is passionate and romantic would appear inappropriate, incestuous, in a letter directed from niece to uncle. In the context of the rhetoric of the bolero, which serves as inspiration for the letter and the book itself, it mirrors her adolescent passion, her will to "draw [him] in a book, to paint [him] with words" (155).

The brief final section, or coda, of the book is set years after Lidia's letter and narrates two parallel tales: that of the consolidation of Lidia's identity as a Puerto Rican and that of Uncle Sergio's lonely death in New York. There are two threads symbolically connecting the two narratives: Lidia's painful recovery of her proper space as a Puerto Rican (a process begun under Uncle Sergio's tutelage) and the Puerto Rican flag that appears prominently in her establishing of her identity and that replaces the crucifix in Uncle Sergio's hands after his death. The novel ends with a summary of Uncle Sergio's painful progress as a patriot persecuted for his opposition to American domination over the island and with an ambiguous confirmation of a homosexuality that made him a double pariah. García Ramis's bildungsroman is ultimately the story of how Lidia achieves a personal identity linked to a colonized nation, with no claim to a protagonist's role in world culture or politics.

Chapter 10

Jamaica Kincaid's Annie John

Jamaica Kincaid was born Elaine Cynthia Potter Richardson in St. John's, the capital of Antigua, on May 25, 1949. She came from a moderately prosperous family, part of the island's lower middle class. Her mother, Annie Drew, was a homemaker, and the man she regarded as her father, David Drew, was a skilled carpenter who had married her mother shortly after Kincaid's birth. She did not come to know her biological father, Frederick Potter, until she was an adult. Her feelings about his neglect of his illegitimate children are at the heart of her unsparing dissection of his life in *Mr. Potter,* an autobiographical novel she published in 2002.

Kincaid, precocious and gifted as a child, did very well in school. Around the age of 13, however, she was taken out of school because she was needed at home to help with her siblings. She reacted to relinquishing her education with a bitter resentment of her half-siblings. She had been emotionally shattered when her brother Joseph was born in 1958. Feeling "cast out of paradise," she had suffered "a sort of nervous breakdown" ("Airtalk"). Two other brothers—Dalma and Devon—had followed Joseph's birth.

During adolescence, Kincaid began to withdraw into the world of books, reading favorites like Charlotte Brontë's *Jane Eyre* repeatedly. Books offered a refuge from her limited prospects and growing alienation from her mother. Despite her enjoyment of English literature, however, she rebelled against British colonialism in Antigua, which did not gain independence until 1981. She felt that the island's transformation into a tourist destination had degraded island culture. It was one of the factors that reconciled her to her parents' decision to send her as an au pair to the United States in 1965.

In New York City, Kincaid worked for *New Yorker* writer Michael Arlen and his family. She obtained her high school diploma and studied photography at the New School University. She attended Franconia College in New Hampshire on a scholarship, but her college experience was "a dismal failure" (Kenney), and she returned to New York City without completing her degree. In the early 1970s, Kincaid began to work as a freelance writer, writing for *Ms., Ingenue,* and the *Village Voice.* Wanting a pen name evocative of the West Indies, she assumed the pseudonym of Jamaica Kincaid. In 1975 she began contributing to the "Talk of the Town" columns in the *New Yorker.* These early essays were collected in *Talk Stories* (with Ian Frazier, 2000). From then until 1995, she worked as a staff writer for the magazine. Kincaid wrote her first short story, "Girl," a remarkable tale told in one two-page sentence, in 1978. It appeared in the *New Yorker* and later became the opening story for her collection *At the Bottom of the River* (1983), which won the Morton Dauwen Zabel Award of the American Academy and was nominated for the PEN/Faulkner Award.

In 1979 Kincaid married classical music composer Allen Shawn, son of *New Yorker* editor William Shawn. In 1985, the year her daughter Annie was born, she published her first novel, *Annie John,* and moved to Vermont. The novel was a finalist for the prestigious Ritz Paris Hemingway Award. In her home in Vermont, Kincaid has indulged a growing passion for gardening, which she describes as "an absolute luxury" (Kreilkamp 55) and which has led to two book-length essays, *My Garden Book* (2001) and *Among Flowers: A Walk in the Himalayas* (2003).

In 1986 Kincaid visited Antigua for the first time in 20 years. The visit led to a book, *A Small Place* (1998), which offers a devastating picture of political corruption and environmental mismanagement and which so incensed Antiguans that she found herself informally banned from her homeland. In 1990 Kincaid published her second novel, *Lucy,* after which she suffered from a second episode resembling a nervous breakdown (the first had followed the birth of her eldest brother). It led to a gap of three years between *Lucy* and the first installment of her third novel, *The Autobiography of My Mother* (1996). In 1995 Kincaid left the *New Yorker* in a breach with then editor Tina Brown. Her departure coincided with the death from AIDS of her brother Devon. In *My Brother* (1997), Kincaid offers a poignant narrative of her brother's struggles against the disease. In 1994 Kincaid joined the faculty of the African and African American Studies department at Harvard University.

Annie John

The key to Kincaid's success as a writer has been her ability to build a body of work out of her own autobiography, particularly her relationship with her mother. Kincaid sees her mother as the "fertile soil" that roots her writing (Kenney). The representation of the mother in Kincaid's fiction is always ambiguous—at times nurturing, but more often than not antagonistic and disapproving. There is a clear correlation established throughout Kincaid's work between motherhood and the colonial metropolis as motherland.

Annie John is one of the best examples of the Caribbean bildungsroman, or novel of development. It follows young Annie from the age of 10 until she leaves Antigua at the age of 17 and recounts her maturation as a bittersweet process of alienation and loss. *Annie John* has been celebrated for the richness of its rhythms and imagery, but above all for its gift in conveying character and its skilled evocation of the social landscape of Antigua. Although the novel has been called "charming" by many critics, the charm of the book is an unsettling one. It rests on Annie's unrepentant descriptions of how, through lies and betrayals, she foiled her mother's attempts at making a proper Afro-Saxon girl out of her. The quality through which Annie retains our interest and sympathy is her insistence on the singularity of her experience and her refusal to compromise.

Kincaid has described childhood as a state of powerlessness, a condition she has used repeatedly in her fiction to explore the process of maturation and its potential for defiance and resistance. Childhood mirrors the colonial condition and opens possibilities for symbolic representation. We follow Annie through her coming-of-age narrative as she weaves her way through a maze of colonial myths and family expectations, seeking to define a personal identity that, given her birth in a colonial milieu, must also by definition be a political identity. Kincaid invites us to read in Annie's physical and emotional maturation a mirror to her island's movement from colonialism to independence.

The initial publication of *Annie John* as stories in the *New Yorker* led to some early confusion on the part of reviewers as to what literary genre—the novel or the short story—the text belonged to. The writing of the chapters as self-contained texts for publication as independent pieces meant that when brought together as a book, they produced an episodic story with a somewhat disjointed plot. These episodes were linked as a novel by the strong presence and unmistakable voice of the young narrator, through whom Kincaid fictionalizes her experiences growing up in a small Anglo-Caribbean colony.

Annie John fits perfectly into the subgenre of the novel known as bildungsroman, or novel of development, which chronicles the moral, psychological, and intellectual development of a young man or woman. The bildungsroman has been a favorite genre of Caribbean writers, who have used its focus on the central character's development to establish parallels between their experiences and those of the small West Indian colonies in which their lives unfold. Like these novels, *Annie John* is an anticolonial narrative that chronicles the protagonist's growth toward maturity and independence as a mirror to her society's progress from colonialism to independence. Kincaid's impressionistic, richly nuanced story of young Annie John's uneasy relationship to Antiguan society is presented chiefly through her problematic relationship with her mother, allowing Kincaid to build thematic parallels between Annie's ambivalence toward her often domineering mother and the ambiguities of Antigua's history of subordination to British colonialism.

As the novel's narrator, Annie dominates the text. Her voice is the filter through which we as readers encounter her reality. As Annie moves through her adolescence, a trying period of discovery and loss, she must harden herself against her mother's efforts to recreate herself in her daughter and against the colonial myths that have informed her mother's notion of what her daughter should become.

A crucial element in Annie's characterization is the marked autobiographical nature of the text. Kincaid, in her nonfiction and interviews, has invited readers and critics to identify her with her main characters. Given her constant weaving and reweaving of her own personal story through her various books, Kincaid's readers have come to equate her protagonists' voices with her own, making it difficult to separate author from narrator. Her characterization of Annie, as a result, is a complex balance between the fictional and the autobiographical, filtered through Kincaid's extratextual commentary on the truth value of her fictionalized narrative.

Annie's perception of the world has at its core the identification between her mother and everything she feels she must reject in her world. Pitted against a mother who moves from idealized to hated figure, Annie must develop a bittersweet core of hardness as a protective shield. Annie's mother appears as a beautiful figure in her daughter's eyes when the relationship is a harmonious one at the beginning of the text, and as an almost repulsive figure, reptilian and treacherous, when the relationship turns sour. We see the mother only as Annie sees her, through her conventionality, her efforts to make a proper young lady of her daughter, her fastidiousness, her consciousness of class hierarchies, and her unquestioning acceptance of colonial notions.

The tale of Annie John's growth into maturity is set in the island of Antigua, Kincaid's birthplace. This is established in the opening pages of the text through the use of specific place names (streets, neighborhoods, buildings) and other geographical markers (hills, bay, seashore) that paint a panoramic picture of the capital city of St. John's, Annie's hometown. Details of weather, flora, and fauna contribute to establishing a distinct sense of place early in the narrative. St. John's is characteristic of Anglo-colonial West Indian capitals of the mid-twentieth century. Divided along class and race lines, the Afro-Caribbean population of Annie's Antigua has been accustomed to the presence of British expatriates in positions of authority for centuries. As a child of urban working-class parents, Annie has little occasion for direct contact with the British officials in Antigua; the English who come into her sphere are minor officials, doctors, Anglican ministers, or teachers, from whom she experiences directly the patronizing solicitude that is the most common face of colonial racism in the Caribbean.

The first chapter, "Figures in the Distance," finds Annie and her family in temporary exile from their home while the house is under repair. Living within sight of the cemetery, young Annie develops a growing fascination with death. The "sticklike figures" of mourners she sees in the distance awaken her to an awareness of both the reality of death and the body of spiritual and religious beliefs connected to Obeah that make of death such a threatening presence in her society.

In the first section, Annie's mother emerges as the repository of intricate knowledge about death and spirits as well as about the most mundane, everyday details surrounding death (undertakers, bathing the corpse, the timing of funerals and its meaning). The section introduces the notion of Obeah, the West Indian magicoreligious healing practice, as a powerful element of the native culture that will be pitted against colonial domination, signaling early in the text Annie's commitment to Antiguan cultural beliefs as the foundation of her image of herself and her society.

The second segment tells of the death of a girl younger than Annie. Although Annie did not know this bony, red-haired girl, the death strikes close to home because the girl not only dies in Annie's mother's arms, but is prepared for burial by Annie's mother. This connection to death marks the first instance of distancing between Annie and her mother: after having bathed, stroked, and dressed the dead child, Annie is temporarily repulsed by her mother's hands and cannot bear to have her caress her, touch her food, or help her bathe.

The third segment offers three examples of the social and spiritual understanding of death in Annie's world. The first concerns a girl at school whose mother had died in childbirth, thus turning her into a pariah, a "shameful thing" left alone in the world. The second—the death of a neighbor with whom Annie is intimately familiar—provides an example of a natural death that produces no anxiety or fear. The third invokes the world of superstition and folklore—a young girl is induced to stop sucking her thumb by her mother's dipping it into water in which a dead person had been bathed.

The final section describes Annie's obsession with visiting funeral parlors and private homes where the dead are laid out for viewing. When she attends the funeral of a humpbacked girl her own age, the experience is narrated in painstaking detail. The segment ends with an episode that marks the first fissures in Annie's relationship with her mother. Having returned home from the funeral to lie to her mother about not having picked up the fish for dinner, she is confronted with the truth and punished. The seeds and anxiety of separation, thematically connected to the death of a child, are planted here to be developed in subsequent chapters.

Chapter 2, "The Circling Hand," focuses on events unfolding during the summer when Annie was 12. Its central theme is the growing strain in the relationship between Annie and her mother, compounded by Annie's growing awareness of her mother's sexuality. The father's presence is a constant reminder to Annie that the blissful image of the inseparable couple she and her mother represent can at any time be shattered by his exercising his claims on his wife.

The first section opens with Annie awake in her child's bed, listening to her parents as they go through their morning routine. Annie and her mother follow their own school holiday routine, which involves Annie's apprenticeship in the domestic arts and her learning about the perils of her social world. The women her father had loved and had children with before marrying Annie's mother loom as menacing figures in this social landscape, threatening figures from which her mother must protect her since they are capable of causing Annie physical harm, either directly or through the agency of an Obeah curse.

Obeah is a set of African-derived religious and curative practices and one of the salient elements used by Kincaid to establish her cultural and geographical setting. It informs the notions of death and mourning practices in "Figures in the Distance," provides the baths that protect Annie from the evil unleashed on her by the women her father had loved, and restores Annie's physical and emotional health in "The Long Rain." As a distinctive element of Antiguan culture, Obeah provides a key element in defining the culture that informs Annie's resistance in the text.

The second segment of the chapter offers a brief history of Annie's parents' childhood. Her mother, who was born in Dominica, had left the island for Antigua after a quarrel with her father. After a difficult crossing, she had arrived safely with an enormous wooden trunk that now contains many mementos of Annie's own childhood. The occasional airing out of these things gives mother and daughter the opportunity to tell and retell the family stories that would serve as the foundation for Annie's personal history. Her father's story, in contrast, is one of lovelessness. Abandoned by his parents, he evokes Annie's pity. From her own state of bliss in her mother's unqualified love, her father's lovelessness looms like a void.

The third part of the chapter focuses on the physical maturation Annie undergoes during the summer of her 12th year and her emotional stress as she feels her oneness with her mother evaporate. As her legs become more "spindlelike," her hair more unruly, the smell of her perspiration more unfamiliar, her mother announces that she is too old to continue to look "like a little me," plunging Annie into a morass of "bitterness and hatred" that threatens to consume her (26).

In the chapter's pivotal section, Annie returns home from Sunday school to find her parents making love. Brimming with pride for a Bible school prize with which she hoped to recapture her mother's love, she finds her parents in bed, consumed with each other and completely oblivious to her presence. Her reaction is one of unmitigated hostility to both her parents, but particularly to her mother, whom she suspects of having been aware of her presence in the house before she noisily began to set the table for lunch. She considers all marks of affection as finished between her and her mother and is sure that she could "never let those hands touch me again" (27).

Chapter 3, "Gwen," focuses on Annie's physical maturation, which culminates with her first menstruation. In the first section, Annie takes us through her first day at her new school, where her teachers bear the names of English generals (Nelson) and infamous prisons (Newgate) as reminders of their exalted hierarchical positions as English teachers in a colonial school. Annie narrates the success of her first assignment—a heartrending exploration of the growing gap between her and her mother, rendered through Annie's description of how she, unable to swim, is separated from her mother while they are bathing in the sea.

In the second segment of the story, Annie's infatuation with her friend Gwen is described in the vivid but conventional terms of an adolescent love affair, from which Gwen emerges as the idealized love object that seems to fulfill every image of goodness and neatness Annie has been taught by her mother to aspire to. She represents the destiny that Annie must learn to avoid—leaving school early, descending into silliness and gossip, marrying someone she has known all her life. If she is to grow into her own individuality, Annie must outgrow Gwen and everything she represents. The eventual deterioration of their relationship can be thus seen as the outcome of Annie's movement away from the gender limitations and intellectual vacuity of her home society and into a world of possibilities as yet unknown.

In the third segment, Annie's leadership position in school brings up a thematic link between Annie's rebellion against her mother's power and her wishing to develop a powerful position of her own. She practices at being alternately kind and cruel to her classmates, exercising the kind of arbitrary power she has seen displayed by both her mother and the colonial elite the mother emulates. As rebellious as Annie wishes to be, she is still bound by a colonial education, as is made evident by Kincaid's reference to her admiration of Enid Blyton, author of "the first books I had discovered on my own and liked" (Valens 125). (Blyton is a controversial English writer of children's books widely read in the first part of the twentieth century in England and its colonies, despite their reactionary and racist characterization of blacks.)

In the last segment, Annie describes the day of her first menstruation, contrasting her fear and physical distress with her mother's nonchalance and half-mocking reminiscences of her own first day. Feeling inexorably pulled toward an adulthood she neither wants nor is prepared for, she sits among her friends, wishing she could transcend their world and live in a place where there was no future "full of ridiculous demands" (36).

The overall theme in "The Red Girl" is Annie's triumph over maternal surveillance. The Red Girl introduces Annie to the notion of transgression.

Unbathed, uncombed, unrestrained, nameless, she stands against every con-
straint Annie finds stifling. She schools Annie in betrayal of her mother and
Gwen by offering opportunities for infractions of the rules of respectability
that are so intricately bound in Annie's mind with her mother's acceptance
of colonial mores. Annie's life begins to revolve around her triumphs over
her mother's surveillance, learning lying and deceit as weapons of resistance.
The Red Girl's symbolic potential is most poignantly expressed through the
ritual of pain and pleasure that they perform during their meetings—the Red
Girl pinches Annie until she draws tears and then kisses the painful spots—
which embody the pain and pleasure that are the result of her transgressive
behavior. Annie's betrayal of her mother and the consequent crisis it causes
after she discovers Annie's marble-playing prowess leads to emotional pain,
while the exhilaration of her incursions into theft, unconventionality, and
disobedience is a source of irreverent pleasure. Ultimately, however, the Red
Girl's style of freedom is too steeped in abandon and randomness to provide
an ideal model for Annie's more ambitious and goal-oriented personality.
Annie's apprenticeship in rebelliousness under the Red Girl, however, plants
the seed of a political defiance she will display in "Columbus in Chains."

In the fourth section, Annie moves from deceit to theft, stealing mostly
from her parents, rejoicing in betraying their trust. In a pivotal scene, Annie
is discovered by her mother emerging from the special place under the house
where she hides her marbles. Discovering in Annie's hand an unusually
beautiful marble, the mother becomes obsessed with finding Annie's hiding
place. Her failure only contributes to Annie's growing contempt for her.
The section ends with Annie in suspense, barely able to swallow her supper
while she wonders if her mother's vigilance means she will have to abandon
her secret life of pain-and-pleasure encounters with the Red Girl and games
of marbles. Annie's mother, obsessed with finding the offending marbles,
uses the narrative of her past as bait to seduce Annie into revealing their
hiding place. The stories are offered as a spell that could lure Annie into a
state of rapture or sympathy that would lead her to reveal the location of
the hiding place. The episode ends with a dream that imagines an alternative
home outside the power and influence of her parents: an island where she
and the Red Girl would live, feeding on wild pigs and sea grapes, and from
which they would send confusing signals to boats cruising by, causing them
to crash onto the rocks.

Chapter 5, "Columbus in Chains," is one of the most reprinted and dis-
cussed sections from the novel. It addresses directly for the first time in the book
the colonial condition of Annie's home island and her latent resistance to
it. The chapter opens as Annie sits reflecting on her book, *A History of the
West Indies,* and her sympathy for yellow-haired Ruth, the English minister's
daughter, whose lack of familiarity with the history of the West Indies leads
to her often wearing the glittering dunce cap. It allows Annie to ruminate on
the legacy of slavery and colonialism, offering several ideas that will resonate

throughout Kincaid's fiction. Annie sees Ruth's predicament—that of being forced to live in a colony where everything reminded her of the harm her ancestors had done—as worse than the situation of the former slaves, who could take comfort in the notion that if they had been in the same situation, they would have behaved better. Annie claims that if her ancestors had traveled from Africa to Europe, they would have taken "a proper interest" in the Europeans, said, "How nice," and returned home "to tell their friends about it" (76).

Annie's ruminations on West Indian history take her to an illustration of Christopher Columbus being sent to Spain fettered in chains attached to the bottom of a ship. She savors the irony of seeing the man credited with having brought enslavement to her people and colonial control to her island humiliated in his turn as a result of his own quarrelsome nature. "Just deserts," she calls it, and takes it one step further by linking the illustration to an episode in her own family history (76). The words Annie writes under the picture—"The Great Man Can No Longer Just Get Up and Go" (77)—are the very same words that Annie's mother had used in triumph on hearing that her own father, with whom she had quarreled before leaving Dominica, now required help to walk.

The second part of the chapter describes the teacher's ire at the discovery of Annie's impertinence. Miss Edward's wrath stems from her own reverential notion of Columbus as an imperial icon juxtaposed against Annie's instinctive resistance to a distorted colonial narrative. As a result, she is removed from her position as prefect and ordered to copy John Milton's *Paradise Lost*. Annie describes Miss Edward with mocking irony, but she retains the power to punish Annie's blasphemous defamation of "one of the great men in history" and lack of remorse (77), by forcing her to endorse the power of Milton's narrative (as representative of English cultural domination).

A direct consequence of Annie's humiliation is that despite her estrangement from her mother, she yearns for her embrace and comfort, hopes that are dashed in the chapter's final episode. Her parents seem oblivious to her misery. Her mother, furthermore, tricks her into eating breadfruit by pretending it is a new type of rice imported from Belgium. Confronted with her deceit, her mother laughs, her mouth open to "show off big, shiny, sharp white teeth" like those of a crocodile (84). This imagined transformation underscores the deterioration of their relationship and Annie's need to develop different avenues for affection and comfort.

In "Somewhere, Belgium," Annie describes in poignant detail how she faces the devastation of the final and decisive rift between herself and her mother. Their climactic confrontation unfolds when Annie is 15 and imagines her deep unhappiness as a small black ball wrapped in cobwebs blighting her life. In her description of such an acute state of adolescent anger and depression, Kincaid walks a fine line between the imaginative language needed to describe something as intangible as despair and the need to keep the narrative firmly within her character's voice and personality. She achieves this by having Annie give form to her despondency through images of balls wrapped in cobwebs, thimbles, and black "things" standing between her and her mother, and by having Annie relate her dispiritedness through comparisons with books she had read and the contrast between her inner feelings and the radiant sunshine and blooming flowers surrounding her.

The chapter includes the detailed narrative of an episode that reveals the complexities of Annie's changing image of herself. Having taken a route home from school through Market Street, Annie examines her reflection before a store window. What she sees reminds her, not of her familiar image of herself, but of a painting she had seen recently of *The Young Lucifer* wearing the kind of smile that tells everyone the person "is just putting up a good front" (79). The comparison Annie establishes between herself and Satan as a lonely and vulnerable figure cast away from paradise underscores her belief that she herself has been cast out, and that, given her alienation from her mother, the loss of her friendship with Gwen, and her disaffection with everything around her, she, like Satan, should sit down on the sidewalk and weep tears of bitterness.

Her miserable reverie is interrupted by the mocking attention of several boys, who greet her with exaggerated and malicious courtesy. Her recognition of one of the boys as a childhood playmate leads to bittersweet memories of how he had taken advantage of her gratification at having an older boy as a playmate to abuse her. The mockery, and the memory of the indignities she had suffered at his hand as a child (not only had he insisted on having the upper hand in all the games they played, but once had made her take off all her clothes and sit on a nest of red ants), are connected thematically to Annie's present quandary—the fact that she is becoming a young woman and that the indignities of sexist gender relationships loom ahead of her. Her defiance of the restricted roles open to her as a girl is seen both in her dismay at realizing that Gwen has taken for granted that she wishes more than anything else to marry and in her recollection of a game she used to play with the mocking boy—a re-creation of the trial and execution of a man found guilty of killing his girlfriend and the man with whom he had found her drinking in a bar. During one of their re-creations of that drama, the boy had found himself hanging by the neck from the front gate, unable to extricate himself, and Annie had been too petrified to summon help. Although Annie displays remarkable maturity and poise in greeting the boy politely, despite her obvious embarrassment, the encounter reminds her of a time when her relationship with her mother was still harmonious; her mother had come fiercely to her defense when the boy had made her sit on the ants' nest.

The chapter's final section narrates Annie's crushing encounter with her mother when she returns home after the incident with the mocking boys. Kincaid returns Annie to the image of the thimble of unhappiness within her, described here as spinning inside her, bumping against her heart, chest, and stomach, scorching from within. She is confronted by her mother's claim that she had seen her "making a spectacle" of herself by acting like a "slut." Annie feels the word *slut* overwhelming her and replies, "Like mother like daughter," a response that resounds like an earth-shattering blow between them, pitting against each other the "two black things" that stand for their mutual hostility. But her mother's reply—"Until this moment, in my whole life I knew without a doubt that, without any exception, I loved you best"— deals Annie a more devastating blow as it seems to withdraw her mother's love from her with splintering finality, opening "a deep and wide split" between them and turning Annie's world upside down (86).

Sitting in her bedroom, surrounded by the furniture her father had lovingly made for her, Annie finds the trunk in which her mother had put all her belongings after quarreling with her father and leaving his house forever. The memory of her mother's quarrel with her father is here connected to Annie's own quarrel with her mother, linking them as natural progressions in their family history. Her mother's trunk now contains Annie's things— the mementos of her own past that she once enjoyed perusing with her mother—and the memory rends Annie's heart. Part of her wants to retreat into a safe and beautiful space with her mother; the other part wants to see her dead and coffined at her feet. Her decision is rendered when her father, sensing the tension at home, offers to make his wife a new set of furniture and in turn asks Annie what she would want him to make for her. Her immediate response, "a trunk," signals her desire to make the quarrel stand and ultimately to leave home, like her mother before her.

Chapter 7, "The Long Rain," tells of the prolonged illness that follows Annie's quarrel with her mother, during which Annie retreats into a semblance of her childhood, when she was completely dependent on her parents and could count on their unqualified love and support. It is as if, having felt deprived of maternal care, she wills herself into a state of infantilism, where she must be coaxed into eating and, like a baby, wets her bed. Ultimately, she must reenter the turmoil of adolescence, but not before she finds the resolve to carve a persona and a future separate from her mother.

Kincaid weaves the tale of Annie's illness around a series of thematic threads, chief among them the images of rain and drought. Her illness is preceded by a prodigious drought lasting for over a year and develops during a "long rain," pouring continuously for three and a half months. The torrent makes the sea rise, permanently covering what used to be dry land; in much the same way, Annie will grow taller, coming out of her illness towering over her mother and father and having gained a remarkable degree of inner personal strength. In this first section, however, Kincaid limits Annie's narrative to her parents' bewildered reaction to this mystifying illness, while Annie seeks to describe a condition akin to a nervous breakdown. She seems to be floating in a state of semiconsciousness—weightless, detached, hearing conversations as if through a thick fog. Kincaid has Annie return to the image of the black thing lying inside her head, the thimble blotting out the memory of her past. To this image she adds the sound of the rain on the galvanized roof as something pressing her down, bolting her to the bed. Kincaid relies heavily on water imagery to convey Annie's sense of disconnectedness: the rain anchors her to the bed; the sea mirrors her growth in the cocoon of illness Annie builds around her like a protective shell; sounds rock in her ears like a large wave dashing against a seawall; in a dream, she drinks in the sea in huge great gulps, leaving only the dry seabed; when she starts to leak out the seawater through little cracks in her body, she wets her bed and must be changed by her parents, as if she were still an infant. Her awareness of her father's near-nakedness as he holds her comes as a reminder of the sexuality that she seems to be trying to avoid by her refuge in sickness.

In the second part of the chapter, Annie is propelled by her mother's offer of chocolate milk into a hallucination. As she feels part of the black thing inside her head break away, replaced by a yellow light, she sees herself as a small toy Brownie, dressed in the regalia of the troop to which she belonged. The vision centers on the hierarchical character of the Brownies, emphasized through the many insignias, emblems, badges, citations, and rituals that are most clearly connected in Annie's waking dream to colonial control.

In the third segment of "The Long Rain," Annie's mother resorts to Obeah to heal her daughter. The father, disapproving of Obeah practices, arranges to leave the house before Ma Jolie comes to cleanse Annie's body and bedroom of any potential evil lurking menacingly over her. The rituals of anointing Annie with special oil and special candles leave an impression of beauty on Annie but otherwise fail to draw her out of her condition. The segment closes with a reminder of cultural hierarchies as the father's disapproval of Obeah practices forces the mother to rearrange the medicine shelf in Annie's room, hiding the equally ineffective medicines prescribed by the doctor before the remedies brought by Ma Jolie.

In the fourth section of the chapter, Annie's parents try to resume their normal routine when her illness goes into its third week, only to have to rearrange their lives again when Annie, left unsupervised for a short while, destroys the family photographs. The incident sheds light on Annie's inner turmoil; its bizarreness reads like her effort to obliterate the stresses and tensions that have led her to illness and derangement. In her delirium-ridden mind, the photos blew themselves up until they touched the ceiling, keeping beat to a music Annie could not hear, perspiring until their smell was unbearable to her. They seem to move as in a parody of sexual intercourse, falling back on the table limp with exhaustion when their strange dance is finished. Annie, faced with this row of photographs of people dressed in white in a travesty of purity—Annie in her white dress uniform and her Communion dress, her Aunt Mary in her wedding dress, her father in his white cricket uniform—rises from her bed to give them all a good wash in a sort of purification ritual. She washes them thoroughly, cleaning crevices, trying to straighten creases, removing the dirt from her father's trousers before dusting them with talcum powder and covering them with a blanket so they can sleep. In the process, she eliminates the faces from the people in the wedding picture, except for herself, in a gesture of self-affirmation and alienation; in a photo of her mother and father, she had erased them from the waist down, obliterating the sexuality Annie found so problematic; in a picture of herself in her Confirmation dress, she had erased everything except a pair of shoes with decorative cutouts on the sides that her mother had found inappropriate and over which they had quarreled bitterly. The shoes, a memento of a time when she had told her mother she wished her dead, remain as an affirmation of her right to her own sexual identity.

Annie's grandmother, Ma Chess, a more knowledgeable Obeahwoman than Ma Jolie and a Carib woman, coaxes Annie back into health, not through remedies, but through her willingness to nurture Annie from her symbolic infancy by accepting the stages through which her granddaughter must progress back to health. She curls up with her in a fetal position, providing a womblike space for Annie's healing. She feeds her and bathes her, replacing the mother who now turns increasingly to the father for companionship. Ma Chess is Annie's link to both the pre-Columbian ancestry that lies at the foundation of Caribbean identity and to the cultural and religious syncretism characteristic of West Indian societies. This syncretism—this reconciliation or fusion of systems of belief deriving from Amerindian, African, and European cultures and practices—is a vital element in Annie's search for an identity that allows her to come to terms with a disjointed past. Ma Chess offers a primordial maternality. Her success is an affirmation of Annie's connection to a past other than the one her teachers have tried to impose on her and of the validity of native cultural roots and traditions connected to precolonial history.

In the seventh and final part of "The Long Rain," a recovered Annie seeks to reinvent herself through her eccentric clothes and her new strange accent and newfound power. Her self-dramatization is evident in her efforts to present herself outwardly as different from anybody her fellow students have ever met, as the new persona she will need when she leaves everything behind and goes to the new dreamed-of space for which she longs. The period of her illness has given birth to a freer and more independent self.

The final chapter, "A Walk to the Jetty," opens with an affirmation of identity: "My name is Annie John." The five parts into which the chapter is divided follow the progression of Annie's last day at home, as she prepares to board the boat that will take her to England to train as a nurse. The chapter is marked by the duality of Annie's position: at 17, she is at once still firmly planted in her old world, while already distanced from her past, looking into a future she is already refashioning into something different from what her mother planned for her.

The first segment finds Annie still in bed taking stock of her room, disconnecting herself from everything she is determined never to look at again.

Her summing up of her life underscores the emotional distance from her parents that has only widened since she began to regard them as sexual beings in their own right—"Now they are together and here I am apart," she says (132). Lying in the bed her father had made for her, she relishes the thought of every act of the day being one she will perform for the last time. The room, where everything was made by her mother or father, leaves no space for the expression of Annie's own subjectivity. Her strong desire to leave this space forever is a reflection of her desire to define a space of her own, where she can no longer feel that "the two of them made me with their own hands" (133).

The second segment of the story opens with Annie's announcement that the Anglican church bell had struck seven. The tolling bell—a reminder of Antigua's colonial history—signals the start of Annie's preparations for departure. With ceremonial studiousness, Annie dons clothes and jewelry doctored by the Obeahwoman, has her hair pressed, shares a Sunday-style breakfast with her parents, and receives the many friends of her mother who come to show the appropriate amount of joy and sorrow at her departure. Throughout these ceremonial farewells, Annie's public and private selves play out conflicting roles: she looks at her parents at breakfast "with a smile on my face and disgust in my heart" (137); she says good-bye to Gwen affectionately, while wondering why she continues to behave like a monkey. In her description of the morning's events, Annie returns to the image of her parents as a unit that excludes her; their festive mood strikes her as proof of their relief at her leaving. The brief section contains two instances of Annie's rejection of the notion of marriage: she replies to her parents' suggestion that in due time, she will write to announce that she is getting married with a contemptuous "How absurd!" (137), and Gwen's parting announcement that she was more or less engaged to a boy from Nevis is met with a "Good luck" that manages to conceal her disdain for the way in which Gwen had degenerated into "complete silliness" (137).

The third segment follows Annie's actual walk to the jetty. The description of their half-hour walk reads like that of a ceremonial procession through the salient moments of Annie's past. "I was passing through most of the years of my life," Annie asserts, and the bittersweet procession marks the last time in which Annie and her parents will walk "in the old way" (143), with Annie between her mother and father. The details Annie offers of this dreamlike walk read like her effort to encapsulate the idealized memories she intends to treasure.

As she reaches the bay, Kincaid returns Annie's narrative to the water symbolism she had used so effectively before, evoked here through Annie's old fear of "slipping between the boards of the jetty and falling into the dark-green water where the dark-green eels lived" (143). Annie will invoke images of self-obliteration as the means of conveying her feelings of loss as she leaves the island—she feels held down against her will, as if she were burning from head to toe, and she imagines that someone is tearing her up into little pieces that will float down to nothing in the deep sea. In this section, Annie's narrative voice uses the phrase "I shall never see this again" like a mantra that makes her heart alternately swell with gladness and shrivel inside her (146). Once in the launch, as they move away from the jetty, the haunting quality of her surroundings vanishes, the familiar sights resume their ordinary nonevocative aspect, the sea regains its habitual blue. Gripping her parents' hands tightly, Annie has a fleeting feeling that "it had all been a mistake," that she can still remain in the comforting security of the world she knows, but in a moment of epiphany remembers that she is no longer a child and that "now when I made up my mind about something I had to see it through" (146).

The final section of "A Walk to the Jetty" completes the process of Annie's severance from her parents and her past. The awkward farewells from her parents in her small cabin are punctuated by Annie's now familiar duality and the contrast between Annie's desire to flee and the performance of sorrow expected from her. She has to remember that it was expected of her to stand on deck and wave the red handkerchief given to her by her mother for that purpose and to continue to do so until the launch bearing her mother disappears in the distance. The book closes with an evocation of water and rebirth. After the figure of the mother vanishes, Annie returns to her cabin, from which she hears the waves lapping around the ship, sounding as if a vessel full of liquid was "slowly emptying out" (148). The image, juxtaposed as it is in the text to that of the water vessel emptying out, invokes the flow of the amniotic fluid that precedes birth, signaling Annie's emergence from the womb into an independent self.

Chapter 11

Mayra Montero's The Messenger

Mayra Montero—one of the most prolific and acclaimed contemporary Caribbean novelists—was born in Havana, Cuba, in 1952. The salient historical event of her childhood, the triumph of the Cuban Revolution in 1959, brought abrupt and unwelcome changes to her life. Her father, a well-known television writer and actor, was sanctioned for ideas expressed in his radio scripts and lost his position. As a result, the family experienced great hardships, having to live on the generosity of their relatives. Her family's situation precluded Montero's integration into the new Cuban society under Fidel Castro's regime. Barred from the Young Communists or the Pioneers, the youth organizations of the socialist regime, she experienced the privations characteristic of those who were seen to oppose the new government: hunger, shortages of clothes and medicine, and limited freedom of movement. After her father had declared his decision to emigrate, she was no longer allowed to attend her college preparatory school. These experiences made for an unhappy adolescence, exacerbated when the family moved to Puerto Rico in the late 1960s and she had to adapt to a new environment and new circumstances.

In Puerto Rico, and later in Mexico, Montero pursued studies in journalism. Her first journalistic assignment, at the age of 20, had her covering baseball games for the Puerto Rican newspaper *El Nuevo Día*. Her work for various magazines and newspapers led eventually to her becoming a columnist and later the Central America and Caribbean correspondent for Puerto Rico's leading newspaper, *El Mundo*. In this capacity, she had a firsthand view of momentous events in the region's history—elections, coup d'états, and the victory of the Nicaraguan revolution among them. She has often spoken about the excellent training journalism provided for her as a budding writer: "It has given me flexibility, ease in front of the blank page, and something more important...an economy of language which is the result of journalistic practice" (Prieto). Although writing fiction is now her main occupation, she continues to write a Sunday column for *El Nuevo Día* and often collaborates with the Spanish newspapers *El País* and *ABC* and *Revista Rumbos* in the Dominican Republic.

Montero was brought up a Catholic but from a very early age was exposed to Santería, an African-derived magicoreligious system of belief practiced widely throughout Cuba. In the 1980s, her contact with university professors and researchers in Puerto Rico made her aware of the similarities between Haitian Vodou and Cuban Santería practices. Through many visits to the border between Haiti and the Dominican Republic, she came to know the role of Vodou in the lives of the Haitian laborers who harvest sugarcane in often slaverylike conditions. She found in the correspondences in liturgy and hagiography between Catholicism and these Caribbean Creole religions a compelling approach to understanding history and culture. These practices, she has explained, are "at the origin of an important aspect, perhaps the most beautiful and sublime aspect, of our *mestization*" (Prieto). Although not a practitioner of Santería or Vodou, Montero nonetheless feels "a great aesthetic, even philosophical affinity" for these belief systems (Montero, "The Great Bonanza of the Antilles" 196). Her home altar is a syncretic space where Vodou *lwa* (spirits) mingle with Cuban *santos* and with Catholic Madonnas and saints, all testament to the role these practices play in Caribbean spirituality.

Mayra Montero began her literary career with the publication of a collection of short stories, *Ventitrés y una tortuga* (Twenty-Three and a Turtle) (1991). The best known of her short stories, "Corinne, muchacha amable" (Corinne, Amiable Girl) (1991), is the tale of a young woman turned into a zombie by the lover she has spurned. It is set against the backdrop of the Haitian people's struggle against the Duvalier government, here represented by the dreaded Tonton Macoutes, the regime's feared militia. Her first novel, *La trenza de la Hermosa luna* (The Braid of the Beautiful Moon) (1987), is a brilliantly rendered tale of an exile's return to Haiti after 20 years as a wandering sailor and of the transformation that leads him from disillusionment to passionate action against the Duvalier regime.

In her second novel, *Del rojo de tu sombra (The Red of His Shadow)* (1992), Montero tells the disturbing tale of the contest of wills between the leaders of two Vodou societies—Mistress Zulé, an inexperienced but gifted priestess, and Similá Bolesseto, a notoriously violent and devious priest—and the disastrous impact on their religious communities, composed mostly of Haitians who have crossed the border into the Dominican Republic to cut sugarcane. *Tú, la oscuridad (In the Palm of Darkness)* (1995), Montero's third novel, tells the tale of American herpetologist Victor Grigg, who, with the aid of his Haitian guide Thierry Adrien, is on a quest for an elusive and threatened blood frog, extinct everywhere but on a dangerous, eerie mountain near Port-au-Prince. *El capitán de los dormidos* (The Captain of the Sleeping Ones) (2002) is a tale narrated by two voices: that of Andrés Yasin, a 12-year-old boy from the island of Vieques, off the coast of Puerto Rico, and J. T. Bunker, an American pilot known as the Captain of the Sleeping Ones because he ships the corpses of the dead across the Caribbean. In *Vana illusion: Las memorias noveladas de Narciso Figueroa* (Vain Illusion: The Fictionalized Memoirs of Narciso Figueroa) (2003), Montero offers a fictionalized rendering of the experiences of the pianist and founder/director of the famous Figueroa Quintet, the paterfamilias of a Puerto Rican family that has devoted their lives to classical music. In her most recent novel, *Son de Almendra* (2006), she recreates the world of the pre-Castro Cuban Mafia of the 1950s.

During the 1990s, Montero also established herself as the Caribbean's foremost writer of erotic fiction. Her two erotic novels, *La última noche que pasé contigo (The Last Night I Spent with You)* (1991) and *Púrpura profundo (Deep Purple)* (2000), fuse two deep interests: the nature of erotic desire and its connection to Caribbean popular and classical music. Montero, who had been a finalist in 1991 for the Sonrisa Vertical Prize—given in Barcelona by the prestigious Tusquets Press for the best erotic novel written in Spanish in a given year—for *La última noche que pasé contigo,* won the prize in 2000 for *Púrpura profundo.*

In addition to her prize-winning fiction, in 1996 Montero published an anthology of the essays she had written since 1992 for her weekly column in the Puerto Rican newspaper *El Nuevo Día.* The sometimes irreverent pieces of *Aguaceros dispersos* (Scattered Showers)—whose topics include an elderly woman reminiscing on her youth in Port-au-Prince (Haiti), a rooster roaming through San Juan, the story of a general who dies on the same day of his arrival in the island he came to govern, and the assorted items forgotten at the cleaners'—offer a fascinating glimpse into the everydayness of life in Puerto Rico and surrounding islands.

The Messenger

Montero's concerns with Caribbean spirituality, particularly as represented by the Afro-Caribbean religious practices that have been at the heart of so much of her fiction, maintain their centrality in her 1998 novel *The Messenger.* The title in Spanish, "like a messenger from you," is drawn from the "Canto Quarto" of *Sentimento del tempo* (1932) by Italian modernist poet Giuseppe Ungaretti (1888–1970), born in Alexandria, Egypt, and thus connected to the tale that serves as a background to Montero's novel—the plot of Verdi's *Aïda.*

Set in Havana, Cuba, in 1920, *The Messenger* tells the story of a pair of doomed lovers, Enrico Caruso (1873–1921), the most admired operatic tenor of the early twentieth century, and Aida Petrinera Cheng, a young Cuban woman of mixed Chinese and African ancestry who becomes his lover. The novel imagines the secret events that transpired when, during a series of performances in Cuba in 1920, Caruso fled for his life into the streets of Havana after a bomb exploded in the Teatro Nacional, where he was performing the role of Radames in Verdi's opera.

In an interview with *Bomb* in 2000, Montero explains the genesis of the novel in the anecdote of the explosion:

I took this anecdote and built a story around it—which has since turned out to be not so fictional after all—in which Caruso is helped by a Cuban woman, a *mestiza* who is half mulatto and half Chinese. . . . After the novel was published I started to hear rumors that, in fact, Caruso had fallen in love with a Cuban woman in those months he spent in Cuba. (Prieto)

The historical circumstances that serve as a background to the novel are as follows. Caruso's visit to Cuba was arranged during a period known as the "Dance of the Millions," a time of unprecedented and very short-lived prosperity ushered in by extremely high prices for cane sugar (of which Cuba was one of the world's leading producers) after the destruction of the European beet-sugar industry during World War I. Caruso was invited to give 10 performances for the then astounding sum of $100,000. He arrived on May 5, 1920, with voluminous luggage and a retinue that included his manager, personal secretary, and several singers and musicians from the Metropolitan Opera House hired to support his performance in various operas. He was also accompanied by a number of servants, among them a valet, hairdresser, and cook. The group settled in an expansive set of suites at the Hotel Sevilla. Caruso's visit to Cuba was unquestionably the social and cultural high point of the "Dance of the Millions." His sold-out performances and the dinners and receptions offered in his honor attracted everyone from the Cuban president to the richest of the planters, whose profits had bankrolled the tenor's visit. As captured by Montero in the novel, he would offer the signed caricatures he penned of his hosts and other guests as tokens of his gratitude.

Caruso's commitments while in Cuba included performances at the Teatro Nacional in Havana, which boasted the best acoustics of any opera house in Latin America, and at the Caridad Theater in Santa Clara and the Terry Theater in Cienfuegos, all three still carefully preserved architectural treasures. The operas he performed in Cuba included Verdi's *Aïda,* Georges Bizet's *Carmen,* Giacomo Donizetti's *L'Elisir d'Amore,* Giacomo Puccini's *Tosca,* Friedrich von Flotow's *Martha,* and Ruggero Leoncavallo's *I Pagliacci.*

The explosion that serves as a springboard for the plot of *The Messenger* took place during the second act of Caruso's last appearance in Havana, the last of two afternoon performances of *Aïda* to which he had agreed to accommodate patrons who could not afford the exorbitant prices demanded for his other appearances. Casualties and damage were very limited, but its repercussions were serious. The attack was blamed by many on labor and political unrest caused by the elite's excesses during this period of unprecedented prosperity. Others speculated that the attack was the result of reprisals against Caruso by the Black Hand, an Italian criminal organization active in Italy and the United States, whose specialty was extortion, blackmail, and kidnapping. The investigation never yielded enough evidence to prove anyone's guilt with certainty.

In August 1920, shortly before leaving for Cuba, Caruso began experiencing the symptoms of the illness from which he would die a year later. His last performance at the Metropolitan Opera House in New York—number 607 at the theater with which his career is so closely linked—was on December 24, 1920, as Eléazar in Jacques Fromental Halévy's *La Juive*. He died on August 2, 1921, in his hometown of Naples.

The fictional events stemming from the historical explosion at the Teatro Nacional, as imagined by Montero in *The Messenger,* find the seriously ill Caruso rescued from the Hotel Inglaterra, to which he had fled, by Aida Petrinera Cheng, with whom he will embark on an intense affair that will result in the birth of Enriqueta, one of the novel's two principal narrators. The couple goes in search of a Santería priest who can heal him—or at least protect his lover from sharing his fate. That fate, as determined by their roles as avatars of the Radames and Aïda of the opera, would entail their dying together in an airless tomb. Aida takes Caruso to her godfather, José de Calazán, a powerful *santero*, or priest, who tries to protect the singer from the murderous agents of the Italian society of the Black Hand. Knowing Caruso to be deathly ill, and having been warned by the orishas (the spirits of the ancestors in Santería) about the singer's arrival in Cuba, his dangerous involvement with his goddaughter, and his tragic fate, Calazán will try to save Aida, who vows not to give up her lover, and prevent Caruso from dying in Cuba.

The Messenger is narrated primarily by Aida and her daughter Enriqueta Cheng, the daughter born of the affair between Aida and Caruso. Enriqueta draws on her interviews with witnesses to the affair, the tale told by Aida herself from her deathbed, and newspaper accounts to unveil a mystery played against the rituals of Santería and Chinese mysticism. The novel is steeped in two parallel traditions, that of Aida's godfather's African-derived Santería and the complementary healing practices of Afro-Chinese magic, a blend that results in what enthusiastic critics have called a "many-layered," "mesmerizing" tale.

Giuseppe Verdi's *Aïda* was first performed to great acclaim in Cairo in late 1871, with a libretto based on a fictional tale based on narratives of Egyptian antiquity. Montero assumes her readers' familiarity with the plot of the opera, as she builds parallels between the fate awaiting Caruso and Aida and the events that lead to the entombment alive of the operatic Radames and Aïda.

In Verdi's tale of the ill-fated lovers, Radames, a young warrior, is in love with Aïda, slave to the Princess Amneris, who loves Radames. Radames leaves to lead the Egyptian defense against an attack led by Amonasro, King of the Ethiopians, who, unbeknownst to him, is Aïda's father. Radames returns in triumph, bringing Amonasro among his prisoners. Aïda reveals her parentage and Radames offers a successful plea to free the prisoners. He is rewarded with Amneris's hand in marriage. On the eve of their wedding, Amonasro calls on Aïda to discover the route the Egyptian army will follow to plan an ambush. Torn between love and duty, she and Radames decide to flee. Amonasro overhears the conversation, which discloses to him the movements of the Egyptian army. Surprised by Amneris, Amonasro, Aïda, and Radames are taken prisoners. Radames is declared a traitor and sentenced to be entombed alive, and Aïda finds her way to the tomb so they can die together.

The structure of *The Messenger* is a relatively simple one. The book is divided into 12 chapters that take their titles from the libretto of Verdi's *Aïda,* stressing the links between the plot of the novel and the opera's plot. Each chapter, except for chapter 2, is divided into two parts. The first part of chapter 1, "A Messager s'avanzi" (A Messenger Approaches), is narrated by an omniscient and unidentified third-person narrator; the second part is narrated by Enriqueta Cheng, Aida's daughter, and introduces her mother's narrative about her relationship with Caruso. All remaining chapters are identical in structure, except for chapter 2. They are divided into two parts: the first one, taken from Aida's narrative, tells of the events of 1921 and her romance with Caruso; the second, narrated by Enriqueta, tells of her research and interviews to verify her mother's account. Enriqueta's narrative is found in italics throughout the text. Chapter 2, the sole exception, only includes Aida's narrative.

Chapter 1, which serves as an introduction and frames the narrative, is set in the present and opens with an unidentified man coming to visit the elderly and jaded Enriqueta Cheng. He is coming to collect a memento purportedly given to Aida by Caruso to commemorate the day they met—a gold nugget into which a small piece of wood from the explosion at the Teatro Nacional had been embedded. The tiny plaque says, in Italian, "In Memory of the Bomb That Made Us Burn." The inscription serves as a leitmotif in the novel, as one salient element of the story of Aida, Enriqueta, and everyone who witnessed or was in any way connected with the bomb and the unhappy repercussions they endured for the rest of their lives. It is a leitmotif that ties thematically with the street on which Enriqueta lives, Calle de la Amargura, or the Street of Bitterness. The memento had been promised to her visitor by Enriqueta in exchange for photographs of Milan, including the Scala and the Galleria, photos of Caruso's birthplace, and photos of the grave in Naples on which he had placed flowers in Enriqueta's name. He also receives in exchange, unexpectedly, a manuscript with two narratives: Aida's story as told to Enriqueta, and Enriqueta's own narrative of her quest to verify her mother's narrative and learn the truth of her parentage. Once the two narratives that will form the text of the novel are introduced, we hear no more about the mysterious stranger.

Chapter 2, "La sacra Iside consultasti?" (Did You Consult Sacred Isis?) takes place on January 6, 1920, on the feast of the Epiphany, with all its symbolic connotations of new beginnings. Its focus is on a divination ceremony conducted by Aida's godfather José de Calazán, a *babalawo,* or priest of the Santería religion. Santería, or the Regla de Ocha, as it is commonly known in Cuba, is literally the worship of the pantheon of spirits known as orishas. The birth of most of the orishas preceded the creation of humans by the principal but remote and inaccessible deity Olofi; some orishas were once humans who evolved into deities because of some remarkable quality. The orishas intervene in their devotees' daily lives and, if properly appeased with sacrifices *(ebbó),* can intercede on their behalf before Olofi. Santería interprets human life, both sacred and profane, as motivated by *aché,* "the force toward completeness and divinity" (Murphy 130). Human life, for Santería devotees, is surrounded by sources of *aché* that can be awakened in objects and people: "Ashe is a current or flow, a 'groove' that initiates can channel so that it carries them along their road in life. The prayers, rhythms, offerings, tabus of santería tune initiates into this flow. They are lifted out of the self-absorption and frustration of ordinary life into the world of power where everything is easy because all is ashe, all is destiny" (Murphy 131). There are four major avenues for humans to approach the orishas' world: divination, sacrifice, possession trance, and initiation (Murphy 134).

In chapter 2 of the novel (10–12), we are offered an accurate description of an *Ifá* divination ceremony as the means of preparing Aida for the crisis in her life that will begin when she meets Caruso. The *Ifá* divination practice, which only trained *babalawos* can perform, involves the *ékuele* chain (usually made of coconut halves or turtle shells). On the basis of the number of shells facing up or down with every throw, the *babalawo* is referred to one of the many parables and proverbs that codify the ancient wisdom of African religious culture. The *babalawo*'s role is that of interpreting those narratives (called *patakís*) to access knowledge about the problems the devotee must face and prescribe sacrifices, ceremonies, baths, or other means of avoiding a bad fate. "The Ifá itself," Eugenio Matibag has argued, "is a vast information-retrieval system that preserves, accesses, and processes the texts of mythological, naturalist, medicinal, and spiritual knowledge. At the heart of the Ifá system lie the thousands of narratives that the babalawo has memorized as part of his training and that he recites to clients in consultations" (153). What the divination ceremony tells Calazán is that Caruso brings death with him and that Aida can be tainted by that death. She must, therefore, bring Caruso to Calazán for a cleansing ceremony to protect her from sharing his fate. Nothing can be done for Caruso except for sending him to die elsewhere because "he is not coming to die; he is already dead when he comes" (11). The beginning of the process of saving Aida involves *ebbó*—for example, the throwing of coins into the ocean to appeased Yemayá, the orisha that rules the sea—and healing baths in the ocean, accompanied by rinsing her head with indigo. These elements, the sea-bathing and the color blue of the indigo, indicate to the reader that Yemayá, spirit of the sea, is Aida's protective orisha.

In *The Messenger,* the power of Santería is more than matched by the practices that have evolved out of the syncretism of its African-derived practices with those of the Chinese immigrants that came to Cuba as indentured servants in the latter part of the nineteenth and beginning of the twentieth centuries. Aida is deeply connected to Chinese Santería through her biological father, not her mother's husband Noro Cheng, but Yuan Pei Fu, a powerful Chinese priest, who was the repository of the relics of the Chinese spirit Sanfancón. In "The Great Bonanza of the Antilles," Montero writes about her own knowledge of the strength of Afro-Chinese practices in Cuba:

I was exposed to phenomena of syncretism as singular as that of Chinese Santería, and I visited the legendary Calle de Zanja, crucial heart of the Chinese barrio of Havana, altars in which the African Orishas blended with the improvised Orishas of Asian origin, such as the very miraculous San Fan Con, who derived from the mystical warrior Cuang Con. It was said in Cuba that Chinese Santería—that is, the cult of Ocha with its typical Yoruba deities but duly transculturated and adapted to Asian idiosyncracies by Chinese-Creole *paisanos*—was infallible in the accomplishment of certain types of magic. (199)

The chapter narrates an episode that encapsulates the worldview of Cuban practitioners of Santería. Montero is careful to provide for Aida an ancestry that links her to both the powerful keeper of the relics of Sanfancón and to Lucumí and Mandingo slaves that brought the practices that would evolve into Santería to the Caribbean. The interaction of the spirits of the dead and the living is exemplified here in the tale of how the restless spirit of the late wife of Aida's husband, Baldomero, works from the grave to cause the death of Aida's child. The expiation needed for her guilt in having contributed to Ester's suicide is revealed in Aida's acceptance of her first daughter's death and on her apprehension when remembering that the day she received the news about Caruso's pending arrival during divination was the anniversary of Ester's suicide. This elemental guilt, therefore, is linked to the bitterness that surrounds everyone that comes near the events of the Teatro Nacional.

Chapter 3, "Il mistero fatal" (The Fatal Mystery), which ends with the explosion and the first encounter between Caruso and Aida, elaborates on the notion of guilt. It opens with Calazán's advice against opening Baldomero's tomb to take out the photo of Ester they had buried with him (the photo had had a nefarious role in the death of Aida's daughter and may still be capable of harming Aida by setting in motion the calamitous events surrounding the romance between Aida and Caruso).

The chapter advances the plot in two significant ways. It clarifies for the reader the relationship between African-derived Cuban Santería and the elements of Chinese spirituality it incorporates, underscoring the notions that the saints or spirits are "blood brothers," regardless of their origin. And it elucidates the continuity of practices that makes it possible for Aida and her mother to realize that Calazán's magic will not be sufficient to protect her, to seek in turn the protection of the more powerful "Chinese *nganga*," and to go to a Catholic church with offerings for the altar that holds relics of Santa Flora in hope of yet another level of protection.

The second part of chapter 2, narrated by Enriqueta, summarizes for the reader the historical events surrounding Caruso's arrival in Cuba and his activities prior to the explosion at the theater and his meeting Aida. There are two episodes of note here. In one of them, Caruso draws a fictional caricature of a young woman, Lydia Cabrera (1988–1991), who some years later would become the most important of the early researchers on Cuban Santería and the author of two seminal texts, *Cuentos negros de Cuba* (Black Tales from Cuba) (1936) and *El monte* (The Bush) (1954). In the second, a black woman stops Caruso while on his way to meeting the then Cuban president and counsels him to wear white, the color of initiation in Santería, the color of those seeking purification through service to the spirits.

Chapter 4, "Che veggo! Egli?" (What Do I See! Them?) narrates the couple's arrival at Calazán's house to begin the process of separating Aida's fate from that of Caruso's. The detail of dressing Caruso in Baldomero's clothes and shoes is a suggestive one on Montero's part since it emphasizes—particularly when linked to the old woman's advice in the previous chapter—the importance of clothing in the characterization of the tenor and the transformations he must undergo in the text. These are all signaled by changes in clothing—from his appearance dressed as Radamés, to his embodiment in the late Baldomero's suit, to the nakedness in which he must confront the orishas.

The chapter explores the concept of fate in Santería, introduced by Aida's comments that she "didn't dare tell him that everything that had happened was written" (37). Santería practitioners believe that Orula, the master of divination, a tutelary orisha in the Lucumí pantheon, was present during the creation of mankind and thus knows everyone's destiny and can give proper guidance about the future. He communicates through his *ekuelé* divining chain and the *tablero,* or divining board. The prophecies humans receive through Ifá divination, as a result, are always fulfilled. Respected and venerated, Orula is the true secretary of Olofi, mediator between humans and the gods, the orisha who must be consulted before all major events in life to seek guidance and instruction for proper procedure, including those related to such religious ceremonies as initiation, sacrifice, and possession. Before Aida's portion of the chapter ends, she tells Caruso that they must remain and offer a sacrifice to the orishas since that is what Calazán has determined must be done.

The concept of *ebbó*—the sacrifice or offering that must accompany every request—is central to divination and to healing practices in Santería. The primary purpose of divination is that of ascertaining precisely what must be done to appease the spirits. "Doing *ebbó* is placating the saints," Calazán explains (39). In this case, Calazán's intercession with the orishas has resulted in a sort of truce, where the spirits "had arranged for him to die somewhere else, in a place by the sea that once had fire" (39), a reference to the eruption of the Vesuvius volcano near Naples. What the spirits request in turn is a ceremony involving drumming from noon to sunset to summon the spirits.

Drumming, executed in an exact, prescribed manner, is integral to all ritual activity in Santería. The music of the drums will bring the orishas down from the heavens to possess their children and commune with their devotees. The most sacred of drums in Regla de Ocha worship are the consecrated *Batá*, a set of three instruments, the *Iyá* (the mother), the middle-sized *Itótele,* and the smallest, the *Okónolo.* They can be sacred *(tambores de fundamento, de Añá)* or profane, unbaptized *(tambores judíos).* Consecrated *Batá* drums are more than musical instruments: they are the powerful materializations of the spirit Añá, referred to in Aida's narrative as "the messenger of children who wanted to talk to their parents" (42), or of devotees who need communicating with their orishas.

Chapter 5, "Oh! Chi lo salva?" (Oh, Who Can Save Him?), narrates how Calazán foils the Italians' efforts to reach Caruso in Regla, which indicates that Montero follows the theory that the explosion at the Teatro Nacional was arranged by vengeful members of the Black Hand. It is in this chapter that Caruso sings Verdi's aria "Celeste Aïda" for the Cuban Aida for the first time, the melody that the orishas had blown through the *ékuele* and which had stayed with her all her life, a "melody that hurt me and made me despair, and that despair allowed me to live" (58). This quality of despair is precisely what Enriqueta explores in her portion of the chapter, which follows how the explosion that had such a profound impact on her mother's life, and on her own, was like a bolt of lightning in the lives of others. The story of Manuel Martínez, who encounters the singer Gabriella Besanzoni in circumstances similar to those of the meeting between Aida and Caruso, underscores the notion that "the bomb did us more damage on the inside than it ever could have caused in the theater" (65).

In chapter 6, "Si levano gli estinti" (The Dead One Rise), Caruso and Aida move to Matanzas, 60 miles from Havana and best known for the richness of its African-derived culture, to prepare for the ceremony of healing. Here, Caruso tells Calazán, Aida, and the Lucumí women who have come to assist in the ceremony the tale of Verdi's *Aïda*. His audience reacts to the plot of the opera by seeking to synchronize Caruso's narrative with the master narrative of the orishas of Cuban Santería. The ancient tales of the orishas, with their loves, jealousies, betrayal, and heartbreaks, is presented here as predating that of Aïda and Radamés, who, like Aida and Caruso, become avatars for the orishas, endlessly reenacting their stories.

It is here that Caruso sings "Celeste Aïda" for the second time, now in the context of the parallels established between the plot of Verdi's opera and the world of Santería. Montero establishes a second level of parallels, those between the Añá, the messenger that calls the orishas, and Caruso's voice, described here as waking "the *orishas* in the woods" (75). Yemayá, Aida's tutelary spirit, "must have come up to the surface, trembling with hunger in the trembling water" (75). Caruso's singing prompts his listeners to identify him with the orisha Changó—the throat of Changó, he is called later. Changó is perhaps the most venerated and popular of the Cuban spirits, one of the tutelary or protector/guardian gods. Both feared and venerated, his domain is music and he rules over the sacred *Batá* drums, fire, thunder, and lightning. Caruso's voice, like Changó's, incorporates the sacred power of the *Batá* drums. Congo woman's reminder that "Changó didn't know his real mother was Yemayá" (Aida's tutelary spirit) underscores the connection between Caruso and Aida, who did not know that their love was prohibited by the orishas. "He didn't know she was his mother," Congo woman reminds us. "He wanted her to be his wife" (74).

In chapter 7, "Amor fatal" (Fatal Love), as Aida struggles with the notion that her love for Caruso is doomed, she, as narrator, brings us back to two notions presented earlier in the text. One of that of the sacrifice Calazán was making by daring the orishas in his attempt to change the path they had established for Aida; the second is that of making a child with Caruso that can avoid the burden of the guilt tied to Ester's suicide and to the birth and death of her late daughter. Aida wanted a baby "different from us so it wouldn't gather any harm" (83).

Most of the chapter, however, is dedicated to a description of the Santería ceremony offered to appease the orishas and make it possible to keep Aida in Cuba, away from Caruso's dreaded fate. The centerpiece of that ceremony is Aida's possession by the orisha Yemayá, the great universal mother, deity of maternity, the sea, and salt water, whose colors are blue and white, and who, when she takes possession of her children, swirls around quickly, swaying like the waves of the sea.

Possession is the foremost manifestation of the reciprocity that marks the relationship between Santería practitioners and the orishas who protect them. The mystic trance of possession, when the orishas communicate with their children by embodying themselves in one of them, is the most fundamental element in the practice of Santería. This surrender of the devotee to the orisha is usually induced by the rhythms of the sacred *Batá* drums. In the novel, Yemayá possesses/embodies Aida, "mounting" her and commanding her to carry her to the water.

The ceremony described in the text (85–91) begins with the shaking of the *acheré*, a small rattle used for summoning the spirits. It incorporates Aida's possession, ritual dancing to the beat of the *Batá* drums, and ceremonial animal sacrifices destined to appease the spirits and help the living reach their objectives—that of delaying Caruso's fate so he can die away from Cuba, and that of separating the lovers so Aida does not share his fate. Through the ceremony, Aida and Caruso are identified with their tutelary spirits, Yemayá and Changó, respectively.

Of special note during the ceremony is the moment when Caruso is immersed in the water and appears to be about to drown. Aida, fearing that Calazán is going to let him die, rushes into the water to save him. For Aida and Caruso, the immersion in the water becomes a revelatory moment, when each of them can see the future and what it has in store for them, to which they respond with terror and resignation. Later, when Aida confronts Calazán about his intentions, she realizes that Calazán indeed intended to let Caruso drown, as a sign of mercy once he had understood what his future entailed:

Do you know how he's going to die? I'll tell you: he'll die howling like an animal, his screams will be heard night and day, he's going to suffer a great deal before he leaves the world.... Just think, Aida, you lost the chance to let him die in peace. (93)

The ceremony ends with the sacrifice of a guinea hen, from which a drop of blood is offered to every orisha. After the ceremony, Caruso gives Aida the gold nugget that her daughter will later exchange for the photographs and memories of her father's last days in Milan.

In chapter 8, "Presago I core" (My Heart Forewarned Me), Aida ponders her decision to remain with Caruso, despite her godfather's warnings that if she stays, "then nothing can be done for you now" (106). During their stay in Santa Clara, where Caruso performed and where they received another threatening letter, she explains her commitment to the singer through the parallels established between them and the orishas Yemayá and Changó. "When the bomb exploded," she argues, "a piece of my life had blown away" (112). Her love for Caruso, she explains, was more like the way you love "another life that shows up in this one" (113). This other life refers once again to their roles as avatars for the Radames and Aïda of Verdi's tale, and for the ancestral spirits Changó and Yemayá. It is a sentiment echoed in Enriqueta's portion of the chapter, in which the man she interviews, Abadelio Trujillo, refers to the events unleashed by the bomb as caused by the power of fate: "Destiny was to blame" (115). "There wasn't one bomb," he adds, "there were many. All the ones that changed us that summer, all the ones that blew us to bits" (124).

Chapter 9, "Fuggire!" (To Flee!), draws close parallels to Verdi's *Aïda* through the despair felt by the lovers when they realize that, surrounded as they are by enemies whose conditions they cannot meet, their only option is flight. Caruso's worsening condition and his feelings of being trapped are echoed in Enriqueta's narrative of her meeting with the cook at the Inglaterra Hotel who witnessed her parents first meeting. Like Aida, she has kept a memento of the explosion, of "the half a tree that seemed like my other half" (143, 142).

In chapter 9, "Ed ella?" (What about Her?), Aida plans her escape to the city of Trinidad (now a UNESCO World Heritage city), with the aid of the local Congo brotherhood (as Santería societies are often called). Aida explains her determination to flee as stemming from her being "a horse of a power that controlled me" (148), an allusion to the phenomenon of possession, where the person mounted, or possessed, is referred to as the "horse." Her rider was Yemayá, who, with Aida, was struggling against Orula (the orisha who knows the future) and against Oddúa (master of the secrets of death). In her explanation, Aida identifies Osún as the messenger of Olofi and underscores the goal she shares with Yemayá to "change the future Ifá had shown us" (149). The sheer difficulties of their struggle are summarized in her statement that it was "the two of us against the will of the other *orishas*" (149).

Enriqueta's narrative in chapter 10 addresses the question of the *paisanos'*, or Chinese *santeros,* involvement in the events that transpired in Trinidad after the couple's flight. The topic had already been introduced in Aida's narrative when, while meeting with Tata Sandoval, the local *babalawo,* he alludes to the presence of many Chinamen in the neighborhood and explains that "they kill with paper, they do their work with crickets and dragonflies" (151). Enriqueta's narrative speaks of her visit to the Chinese district and her grandfather's former house to inquire about Yuan Pei Fu's possible involvement in the events of Trinidad in 1920. (Aida had believed that her father Yuan Pei Fu had intervened in propelling the catastrophe that ensued after their flight.) Enriqueta's account clears her grandfather of blame but leaves a certain ambiguity surrounding the actions of Pancho Wong, the cripple who made the paper animals (many of them decorating the altar in Yuan Pei Fu's old room), and who had been in Trinidad at the time. Speaking to Enriqueta, Felipe Alam explains the nature of Yuan Pei Fu's work: "[He] worked with herbs, with birds and other animals.... He was the only one who understood the 'refined' Chinese that the spirits of the ancestors spoke" (161). He understood, as Aida did not, that "you cannot struggle against...the messenger that is yours" (162), and that therefore Aida and Yemayá's efforts to struggle against Orula's ruling and the will of the orishas was doomed to defeat from the very beginning.

Chapter 11, "Tu...in questa tomba!" (You...in This Tomb!) tells of Aida and Caruso's flight from Cienfuegos to Trinidad. As in Verdi's opera, this flight—and Caruso's dreams of taking Aida to New York and on to Naples—is doomed to failure. Aida's narrative prepares the reader for that failure through references to her *aché*, described here as "my ability to see the other side of life, the broth of uncertainty and mystery where the will of man is always floating" (168). The gathering clouds that will frustrate the lovers' desire to thwart their destiny are embodied here in a syncretic wave of spirits whose demands for water Aida cannot fulfill: "On the ocean, in that quiet night, all the Chinese phantoms awoke, all the ghosts from the steamship *Oquendo;* and the black phantoms, all the ones who came with my grandmother Petrona of the Lucumí nation. There was a power, a great gathering, many *egungún* hovering around" (176). The feeling of doom is underscored in Enriqueta's portion of the chapter, when, after the fateful events of Trinidad (described by Aida in the following chapter), Calazán is quoted as saying that "he couldn't take care of [Caruso] because he was dead and only Oyá can take care of the dead" (185).

Chapter 12, "Ciel!...Aïda" (Heavens!...Aïda), reenacts the entombment of Aïda and Caruso in Verdi's opera through Caruso and Aida's kidnapping, after which she is left to die alone in a cave, only to be rescued through the agency of the Congo brotherhood. The separation of the lovers, which constitutes a break from the original opera plot, could be interpreted as having taken place through Calazán's intervention with the orishas, who are credited here with saving Aida from what should have been a slow and despairing death. One of the avatars of the "mistress of her head," Yemayá, is believed to have remained with her: "I don't know which one stayed with me, fighting off everything that was around me" (194).

The centrality of the world of Santería in Montero's *The Messenger* is maintained through the last moments of Aida's narrative, when, at the moment of death, Caruso's spirit sends "a messenger from his soul" on a journey to Cuba to say farewell to Aida and Enriqueta "in sorrow and in love" (204, 205). This last installment of Enriqueta's narrative underscores the notion that "things happened as they had to happen" and thus Caruso "couldn't escape the libretto, he couldn't skip a line. Fatality is the only opera we never have to study" (212). The notion of fate, so important in the classical narratives from which Montero partly draws her plot (through its connection with Verdi's *Aïda*), provides a deep connection to the Santería belief that our future is determined at the time of birth by Olofi and that Orula, keeper of the secrets of the future, will advise us as to how best to follow our path. To this notion, Montero has added the idea—taken from a belief prevalent among natives from a Pacific island—of a misfortune "that sometimes falls like an open blanket over certain people, and each of them gets a piece of the blanket" (213). The conceit allows Montero to build a narrative that projects—through the explosion that brings Aida and Caruso together—the effects of the calamitous events at the Teatro Nacional into the lives of its many victims and witnesses.

Chapter 12

V. S. Naipaul's The Mystic Masseur

Vidiadhar Surajprasad Naipaul, one of two Nobel Prize in Literature winners from the Caribbean (the other one is Derek Walcott), was born in the village of Chaguanas, Trinidad, on August 17, 1932. He was born into a Hindu family of Brahmin descent, one of the many who had arrived in Trinidad in the late nineteenth and early twentieth centuries to work as indentured workers in the sugar plantations. At the age of six, his family moved to the capital of Trinidad, Port of Spain.

Naipaul was aware from a very early age of the social and political tensions that existed between his fellow Indo-Trinidadians (about 40% of the population of Trinidad and Tobago) and Afro-Trinidadians (about 39% of the population), which enter his fiction from his earliest works. Race, nationality, religion, and traditions were issues that created deep fissures between the two groups and that prevented Naipaul from feeling completely comfortable in the culture of his home island. His disconnection as an Indo-Trinidadian from the mainstream culture of his island would follow Naipaul throughout his life, and he is often described as a wanderer never entirely comfortable anywhere.

From an early age, Naipaul's path to a career as a writer seemed clear. His father, Seepersad Naipaul, worked as correspondent for the *Trinidad Guardian* and was himself a writer of modest fame. He heartily encouraged his son's writing ambitions and was immortalized as the model for the central character in Naipaul's autobiographical masterpiece, *A House for Mr. Biswas* (1961).

Naipaul attended Queen's Royal College in Port of Spain and then won a scholarship to study at Oxford, from which he graduated in 1953, the same year his father died in Trinidad of a heart attack. Naipaul has continued to live in England, although he has traveled extensively, becoming in the process one of the most celebrated travel writers of the twentieth century. He began work as a freelance writer immediately on graduating from college, supplementing his income with a job as broadcaster for the BBC's *Caribbean Voices* (1954–1956). From 1957 to 1961, he worked as a fiction reviewer for the *New Statesman.* In 1955 he married his college sweetheart, Patricia Hale, who died in 1996. His present wife is Pakistani journalist Nadira Alvi.

Naipaul began his illustrious career as a novelist with the publication in 1957 of *The Mystic Masseur,* a lighthearted satire of a country healer or masseur, whose ambition leads him to a career in politics (adapted into a 2001 film by Ismail Merchant). It was followed in quick succession by other bittersweet renditions of life in Trinidad and Tobago, such as the satire of Trinidadian democracy titled *The Suffrage of Elvira* (1958), his collection of vignettes of urban life in Port of Spain, *Miguel Street* (1959), and what is unquestionably the masterpiece of this early stage of his career—some would say the best of his fiction—*A House for Mr. Biswas.*

The success of *A House for Mr. Biswas* has allowed Naipaul to dedicate himself entirely to his writing since the early 1960s, and he has produced dozens of novels, essays, reviews, and other works. In the 1960s, his fiction became darker, reflecting a more pessimistic view of the world, particularly in its assessment of postcolonial societies in works like *A Flag on the Island* (1967), *The Mimic Men* (1967), *Guerrillas* (1975), and *A Bend in the River* (1979). In the late 1980s and early 1990s, Naipaul's fiction turned introspective, blending fiction with autobiography and memoir, as in *The Enigma of Arrival* (1987), where he explores his early journeys between Trinidad and England as a metaphor for his life, and *A Way in the World* (1994), where he investigates his rootlessness and feelings of displacement, linking them to the realities of colonialism. In his most recent novels, *Half a Life* (2001) and *Magic Seeds* (2004), he follows the experiences of Willie Chandran, a man born in India but who wanders around the world looking for a meaning to his life.

Naipaul has also gained a reputation as a gifted—if sometimes oddly misanthropic—travel writer. His at times controversial meditations on the societies he has visited include *The Middle Passage* (1962), *An Area of Darkness* (1964), *The Loss of El Dorado* (1969), *The Overcrowded Barracoon* (1972), *India: A Wounded Civilization* (1977), *A Congo Diary* (1980), *Among the Believers: An Islamic Journey* (1981), *A Turn in the South* (1989), and *Finding the Center* (1984), among many others. His gaze is not always a sympathetic one; his descriptions can be brutally honest and his judgments, more often than not, quite harsh. As a result, these writings have met their share of criticism, with some readers deeming their conclusions to be overly judgmental, perhaps racist, uninformed, or otherwise inaccurate, despite their literary merit.

Throughout his career, Naipaul has received numerous literary prizes. In addition to his 2001 Nobel Prize, he has received the John Llewellyn Rhys Memorial Prize for *The Mystic Masseur* (1958), the Somerset Maugham Award for *Miguel Street* (1961), the Hawthornden Prize for *Mr. Stone and the Knights Companion* (1964), the W. H. Smith Prize for *The Mimic Men* (1968), the Bennet Award (1980), the Jerusalem Prize (1983), the Ingersoll Prize (1986), the Trinity Cross (1990)—Trinidad and Tobago's highest honor—and the first David Cohen Prize for lifetime achievement (1993). In 1989 Naipaul received the distinction of being knighted in England. Naipaul's archives are kept at the University of Tulsa, where they have been maintained since 1993.

The Mystic Masseur

The Mystic Masseur, Naipaul's amiable tale, has been described quite accurately by Bruce Bawer as a "brief, hilarious *tour de force* about Ganesh Ramsumair, a bumptious, good-natured young Trinidadian of modest education and limited spiritual proclivities who stumbles into a successful career as a holy man and healer (and, eventually, a national political leader)" (372). Set in the 1940s and 1950s—the epilogue is dated the summer of 1954—Ganesh's story chronicles Trinidad's rocky path to modernization with a sweetness and humor that hides a marked satiric critique. The novel also represents the comic version of Naipaul's own path out of Trinidad through his education and writing career.

Structurally, the novel is divided into 12 chapters and an epilogue. Except for the first chapter (which tells of the narrator's first encounter with Ganesh, the mystic masseur), all the chapters are arranged chronologically. They follow Ganesh Ramsumair's transformation from a failed rural healer to G. Ramsay Muir, Trinidadian politician. The last chapter (which narrates another significant encounter between the narrator and the pundit some 14 years later), depicts Ganesh as the island's representative to an important conference in England.

The novel is told in the mock-heroic mode, written in a grandiose style that is incongruous with Ganesh's modest accomplishments and humble status. Mock-heroic works like *The Mystic Masseur* are commonly satires or parodies that poke fun at heroic genres such as the epic. They often (as in our case here) invert the heroic model by focusing on a fool as the hero. In *The Mystic Masseur,* Naipaul follows the heroic narrative—to the point of naming one of the chapters "Trials," as in the archetypical heroic saga—until the hero's grandest triumph (that of representing Trinidad as one of its leading politicians). His "hero," however, is seen satirically as a flawed character, who reaches his position, not by talent and commitment, but by sheer luck and a degree of manipulation and chicanery. He is presented, moreover, as being typical of his social landscape, so that Naipaul can be seen as satirizing not only Ganesh, but the premodern society that makes his career possible. In *The Mystic Masseur,* "the narrative takes the form of a rogue's progress, as the picaroon hero gradually rises to the top of the society" (Thieme 1355). This society, however, is a colonial backwater, whose people, uneducated and naïve, fail to recognize the fool under the trappings of false erudition and mystic powers.

The Mystic Masseur is set in rural Trinidad amid the numerous East Indian communities that sprang up throughout the countryside following the transportation of indentured servants from India (1845–1917) to replace the newly emancipated African slaves. East Indians constituted the largest of the various groups that arrived from China, Portugal, Syria, and Lebanon to supply labor for the sugar and tobacco plantations of the late nineteenth and early twentieth centuries. Their arrival to arduous work and deplorable living conditions nonetheless transformed Trinidadian culture and society. During the first century of their lives in Trinidad, despite the end of their original period of indenture, East Indians remained tied to the rural communities of central and southern Trinidad, the areas most closely associated with sugarcane cultivation. Most of them remained cane workers until well into the twentieth century, supplementing their incomes with subsistence crops they planted as squatters in Crown lands.

The Mystic Masseur captures a pivotal moment in the history of Indo-Trinidadians, as they move from a rural base to a strong social and political presence in cities and towns throughout the island. This transition coincided with the profound changes brought about by World War II, credited with deeply changing the fabric of Trinidadian society. Oil production, which had been increasing in economic importance since wells began operating in 1909, expanded significantly during the war. This, coupled with the presence of significant contingents of American soldiers stationed at the American military bases in Chaguaramas and Cumuto, led to significant investment in developing the island's infrastructure. The building of improved roads, bridges, port facilities, and housing offered employment opportunities away from the agricultural sector, leading to the movement of workers away from rural areas into urban centers. Indo-Trinidadians were among those who benefited most from these socioeconomic changes.

The changes undergone by the Indo-Trinidadian community during the war and postwar periods are best exemplified in the figure of Bhadase Sagan Maraj, a union leader who founded and led the Sanatan Dharma Maha Sabha, the most influential of the Indian community's religious and political organizations. Like the fictional Ganesh, he would finagle his social and religious influence—gained through the association's sponsoring of the building of Hindu temples and schools for the teaching of Hindi and Sanskrit—into the foundations of a successful political career that opened the way for a powerful Indian presence in Trinidadian politics. Louis Simpson points out that there was a pundit in Trinidad that could have served as a model for Ganesh: "a Camār from Janglī Tolā—that is, an East Indian of lower caste, who set himself up as a Brahmin pundit" (574).

This Indo-Trinidadian political presence manifested itself for the first time quite clearly in the elections of 1946, the first to take place under universal adult suffrage and thus to allow for broad popular participation. For East Indians in Trinidad, the run-up to the elections offered a precious opportunity for political unity along the antidiscrimination and civil rights tenets of Mahatma Gandhi's movement. In *The Mystic Masseur,* Ganesh's first act as president of the Hindu Association is to send a telegram of support to the All India Congress, exhorting them to "keep Mahatmaji ideals alive" and encouraging the struggle for independence (185).

The growth of Indo-Trinidadian organizations such as the Maha Sabha was closely tied with events in India and Pakistan, both of which had achieved their independence in 1948. These political developments, closely linked to Gandhi's religious and political philosophy, were attentively followed in Trinidad, fostering increased interest in Indian culture, religion, and traditions. This interest led to extended tours of Trinidad by swamis, as visiting Hindu missionaries came to be known, who came to spread the true teachings of Hinduism to a community whose religious practices had become creolized after extended contact with Afro-Caribbean religious practices.

These historical elements provide the raw material for Naipaul's satire of Indo-Trinidadian upward mobility during the war years in *The Mystic Masseur.* We meet its narrator—an Afro-Trinidadian young boy who is brought to Ganesh for a consultation about an injured foot—in chapter 1, "The Struggling Masseur." This "mock-biographer," as Kenneth Ramchand describes him (38), has only two encounters with Ganesh: the one that opens the novel "just at the beginning of the war," where he speaks of his subject as "a struggling masseur, at time when masseurs were ten a penny in Trinidad" (1), and a subsequent meeting in 1954 in England, where the young man is a university student and Ganesh has adopted a new anglicized identity as a successful politician, that of G. Ramsay Muir.

The narrator's status as a mock-biographer stems from both the satiric tone of the tale and from the nature of his so-called research, which is limited to Ganesh's autobiography and other self-published pamphlets. Indeed, the novel's satiric intent is evident in the two scenes that frame the narrative, both of which underscore the narrator's view of his character as a fraud, fixing his trajectory as one that moves from posing as a skilled masseur with pretensions to being a pundit at the beginning to denying his roots as an Indo-Trinidadian mystic masseur at the end.

The result of this mock-biographer's work is a satiric version of Trinidadian history. As Fawzia Mustafa writes, "when the narrator of *The Mystic Masseur* suggests in his introductory remarks that, 'I myself believe that the history of Ganesh is, in a way, the history of our times' he announces the mock-heroic dimension of the novel's political fable" (46). "Later he was to be famous and honoured throughout the South Caribbean" (1), the narrator announces in his opening statement, thus prefacing the tale of a so-called hero whose trajectory will owe more to the naïve exploitation of people's ignorance than to true intelligence and ability.

The book's opening chapter establishes the satiric tone of the text through the narrator's detailed description of his own consultation with Ganesh the masseur. Naipaul sets a humorous tone through the exaggerated articulation of the various local versions of English that help define the parameters of the Indo-Trinidadian and Afro-Trinidadian populations, especially through their comic attempts at speaking standard English in formal situations. He underscores the comic foundation of the text through the misconception about the nature of books and reading—of literacy and literature, in short—which will be a leitmotif throughout the text. The narrator's awe is awakened by the proliferation of books in Ganesh's house, which would, in a nonsatirized world, point to the masseur's laudable intellectual achievements, but which are here measured by the inch, deemphasizing content and quality in favor of ostentatious display of pseudo-learning.

The chapter also emphasizes the emptiness of Ganesh's claims to curative powers. The healing ceremony, conducted in a room covered with pictures of Hindu deities and religious quotations in Hindi and English, resembles an Afro-Caribbean Obeah ceremony, with its laying of hands and mysterious incantations. "If I had been sharper," the narrator comments, "I would have paid more attention to that, for it showed, I am convinced, the incipient mystical leanings of the man" (6). The ceremony, with all its magical trappings, however, is ultimately ineffective, as the narrator must at the end, in the chapter's debunking of Ganesh's claims, see a properly trained doctor to heal his foot.

The attention to books in chapter 1 points to the novel's interest in addressing—as satire—the topic of the emergent writer, of the impulse to write in a premodern colony that may be as unprepared for swiftly coming democracy as for spawning good writers. The irony of the chapter resides in part on the circularity of this impulse to write: the novel satirizes Ganesh's mercenary relationship to books and to writing itself (he writes self-serving autobiographies or appropriates the writings of others in nonsensical compilations), while the narrator purportedly becomes a writer through cannibalizing Ganesh's writing for his own satirizing account of the career of Ganesh the mystic masseur.

In chapter 2, "Pupil and Teacher," Naipaul addresses Ganesh's flawed education as stemming from a series of failures, of instances of having to settle for less than true success. His father had for years held on to "five acres of waste land near Fourways," hoping to have an oil well dug into it, "but he could not afford to bribe the drillers and in the end he had to be content with a boundary well" (9). Ganesh, in turn, had to contend first with his failed attempt to leave behind his Indian identity—spreading a story that his real name was Gareth—and later seeing his friend Indarsingh receive a scholarship to England, while he had to settle for a second grade in the Cambridge School Certificate and a brief career as a teacher in a school where he was admonished to "form, not inform" his pupils (9). The book will return to the figure of Indarsingh in the concluding chapters, where he becomes Ganesh's unsuccessful and somewhat embittered political opponent. Having returned from England with a degree and a veneer of intellectual accomplishment, he has nonetheless lost the ability to communicate with his peasant protoconstituency, as Leela clearly indicates: "All this fancy talk in all this fancy accent he are giving the people here, it are beat me why they don't fling something big at his head" (189).

Ganesh's ambivalence about his Indian ancestry—which he will later exploit to develop a career as a pundit and healer—is evident not only in his attempts to pass for a non-Indian, but in the resistance to the marriage his father has arranged for him, a resistance that leads to a permanent estrangement from his father. His initiation ceremony as a "real Brahmin" offers another example of Ganesh's misgivings about embracing his Hindu identity, which he is bound to take too literally. Told to go to Benares to study, as is typical of the ceremony, he continues to walk despite the admonishments to return, prompting one of the neighbors to remind him that true fulfillment of the instructions is impossible as Benares "is in India, and this is Trinidad" (11). The episode points to the difficulties inherent in how to be an Indian in Trinidad, while at the same time fulfilling a dream of upward mobility through education (however deficient) and modern entrepreneurship. Underscoring this struggle is Ganesh's evident mediocrity, which the text depicts as evident both in his trajectory as a pupil and his brief career as a teacher.

The death of Ganesh's father, which coincides with the loss of his teaching job, brings the character's crisis of identity to a decision point. It draws him back to his village, now that he is in control of his father's oil-derived income of $60 a month, and looking for a path back into his Indian identity now that he had "the double glamour of a college education and a father recently dead" (21). The novel offers us two versions of this crucial moment in Ganesh's career: one offered by the narrator, which shows the protagonist being rescued from his Port of Spain failure by his father's timely death, the other presented in Ganesh's own words as a quotation from his autobiography, displaying his spin on the events and making virtue out of necessity. His father had died just about the same moment he was resigning his job in Port of Spain: "it was indeed a singular conspiracy of event that pulled me away from the emptiness of urban life back into the stimulating peace and quiet of the country" (21). Necessity becomes virtue in this account.

Chapter 3, "Leela," narrates Ganesh's quest for an occupation in the village of Fourways, where the respect for education of the community leads to high expectations. Here he finds a father substitute, Ramlogan, who seeks to direct his future, just as his own father had attempted to do unsuccessfully. Ramlogan's presence as a father figure signals Ganesh's return to the Indian fold, a return narrated through irony. He first suggests that Ganesh take up massaging or healing since "your father was the best massager we had" (25). In the Trinidadian countryside, massagers, or masseurs, provided a specific type of physical healing known as cracking, rubbing, and vein pulling, brought as a practice from India by indentured workers: "The masseur's ability to massage away pain affecting the muscular and skeletal system is learnt by experience, and from their fathers. The skilled ones are visited before the medical practitioner" (Lans 51). Ramlogan's suggestion is laden with irony as we learn immediately that Ganesh's father had stopped massaging after he had misdiagnosed a case of appendicitis and a young girl had died. "He was still the best massager we ever had," Ramlogan insists (25).

The tensions in this chapter build around Ganesh's urban-generated impulse toward modernity and the comfort zone of life in Fourways as a respected sahib. He "remembered the queer feeling he had of being separated from the village people, and he felt that there was something in what Ramlogan said" (25). His encounter with the eccentric Mr. Stewart, an Englishman who had appeared in Trinidad dressed as a Hindu mendicant, offers Ganesh a role model that can embrace both tradition and modernity; he can assume a traditional role as a masseur and pundit, while pursuing a career as a writer. It is the same advice offered by Leela, Ramlogan's semiliterate but modernity-bound daughter, who suggests a literary career as a way out of his impasse. Ganesh will begin to look on book writing as a preordained thing, despite the skepticism with which his announcement is usually met: "You ever hear of Trinidad people writing books?" (38).

Chapter 4, "The Quarrel with Ramlogan," illustrates these tensions most eloquently. Here the stresses between tradition and modern cupidity, as illustrated by the events surrounding Ganesh's wedding with Ramlogan's daughter, come to the fore thematically through the struggle between the two men over money matters. Ramlogan's unwillingness to send a messenger with the traditional saffron-dyed rice to friends and relatives to announce the wedding—together with the more significant struggle over the kedgeree—shows how both men are willing to manipulate the gap between tradition and modernity to their own advantage. Ramlogan's crying plea to Ganesh not to shame him publicly over the dowry money (the amount of money he must give as the father of the bride before the groom deigns to eat the kedgeree) is built on a modernity argument: "I know that for you, educated and reading books night and day, it wouldn't mean much, but for me, sahib, what about my cha'acter and sensa values?" (40). Ganesh's reply that "it is the custom" is ironically mercenary, anticipating his exploitation of the tradition to extract the largest possible dowry from his father-in-law. The incident would lead to a recurrent quarrel between the two men over

Ramlogan's desire to profit from Ganesh's growing fame and prosperity. It also sets Ganesh's character as that of a person willing to manipulate tradition for personal profit.

A secondary aspect of the performance of tradition amid developing modernity is found in the courtship between Ganesh and Leela, which takes place outside the traditional conventions of Indian culture (the groom must not meet the bride before the wedding, for example) but is performed in a traditional way to satisfy a notion of propriety. While Ramlogan, as the older of the two, is consistently ready to eschew tradition since it favors him financially, Ganesh profits from the accepted customs. This includes his quasi-ritualized first beating of his wife, which is here presented, ironically, as a ceremony almost as important as the wedding for the solemnization of their marriage: "It was their first beating, a formal affair done without anger on Ganesh's part or resentment on Leela's…it meant they had grown up and become independent" (49).

It is a testament to Naipaul's conscious decision to work in the mock-heroic mode that chapter 5, "Trials," begins with a clear acknowledgment of Ganesh's nonheroic stature: "For more than two years Ganesh and Leela lived in Fuente Grove and nothing big or encouraging happened" (57). In an inversion of the heroic trials that the hero must overcome in the epic, in this chapter, Ganesh confronts a series of failures against which he seems powerless. The chapter ends, ironically, with Leela's return to her father's house.

These disappointments, which included his acceptance of his incompetence as a masseur and Leela's inability to bear children, will force Ganesh to return to the notion of reading and book writing as a way out of Fuente Grove. In pursuing this topic, as Louis Simpson has argued, Naipaul was "reenacting his own escape by way of an education" (574). Naipaul has spoken frequently of feeling trapped and asphyxiated in Trinidad, a world from which he escaped into the rarefied literary world of London while still in his twenties. In *The Mystic Masseur,* he bestows this dream of escape to his main character, but it is projected in the text as an absurdist fantasy that plays against Ganesh's lack of real education and his community's inability to grasp the significance of true creative or scholarly writing.

This comic reenactment is built in *The Mystic Masseur* through the absurdity of Ganesh's obsession with accumulating books, which he begins to buy by the yard. He is, as David Ormerod has argued, less interested in the contents of the books "than in the escape symbolism inherent in their possession" (78–79). In this chapter, which precedes the writing of Ganesh's first pseudo-book, Naipaul is especially concerned with how the phenomenon of book possession is in itself a marker of difference and uniqueness in a backward little village like Fuente Grove. Their possession is "an assertion of one's stature" that allows Ganesh to "transcend the squalid hamlet" and "assume an identity in the minds of others" (Ormerod 78). Ganesh's reputation, "lowered by his incompetence as a masseur, rose in the village" (Naipaul 69).

Naipaul underscores the satire of Ganesh's shallow relationship to books and uninspired approach to writing by painstakingly describing his method of copying passages from the books he had read as something that started "in a fine, sloping hand," only to deteriorate into "a hasty, tired squiggle" (72). His "writing," imitative and plagiaristic, is founded on what Ormerod calls "a warped aestheticism" (79), manifested by his seeming obsession with varieties of papers and types unavailable in an island colony such as Trinidad. On expressing his wish to have his future books printed in Fournier, a type he associates with Aldous Huxley, he is scolded by Beharry: "You think they have that sort of type in Trinidad. All they have here is one sort of mash-up type, ugly as hell" (7). These difficulties are interpreted by Ganesh as evidence of the tribulations that all writers must endure before they achieve fame and recognition: "Leela, is the thing everybody who want to write have to face. Poverty and sickness is what every writer has to suffer" (77).

Chapter 6, "The First Book," narrates the events leading to the publication of Ganesh's first book, the self-published "antheology" of information culled from a multiplicity of sources, *101 Questions and Answers on the Hindu Religion*—"a set of things about religion, from different authors" (82). The publication of the book, despite its lack of initial success, will propel Ganesh toward widespread recognition and political power, and this chapter illustrates how this process begins.

Naipaul's treatment of the creative process is laden with the same sense of irony that permeates the novel. The "thrilling, tedious, discouraging, exhilarating process of making a book" (86), as described in the text, is concerned primarily with appearance and surface, rather than with content and creativity. In fact, creativity is entirely absent from the process, as Ganesh offers what is merely a compendium of other authors' work. Beharry marvels at the power of Ganesh's writing once he sees it in print, while the budding author's joy is tempered by his disappointment over the book's size ("no more than thirty pages, thirty small pages" [86]) and the smallness of the type ("that ugly type he call Times" [86]). Ramlogan's enthusiasm for the book ("the book is smooth smooth" [89]) is likewise lessened by the book's having been dedicated to Beharry.

In this chapter, Naipaul is primarily interested in showing how reactions to the publication of the book prefigure the book's impact on Ganesh's future career. Leela, despite her father's rage at the book not being dedicated to him, returns home to Ganesh after a separation lasting several months. She joins Beharry and his wife, the Great Belcher, and others in orchestrating what will ultimately be a successful marketing campaign to sell, not the unsaleable book, but the figure of the mystic masseur himself.

Chapter 7, "The Mystic Masseur," marks the very center of the book, both structurally and thematically. It features the story "Black Boy under a

Black Cloud," through which Ganesh succeeds in marketing his skills to the larger world—to "use his learning to help out other people," as the Great Belcher puts it (104)—through showmanship and chicanery. The episode is emblematic of Ganesh's understanding of the use of deception, as he carefully sets the stage with mystical symbols and images of the Hindu gods, chants in Hindu, and talks of the devil to effect a cure that will resonate throughout the island thanks to the "local grapevine, the Niggergram, an efficient, almost clairvoyant, news service" (125).

Behind Ganesh's success is a mimetic impulse that finds him copying the methods and promotional savvy of the Hollywood Hindus, "cultivated men who issue frequent bulletins about the state of their soul, the complexities and variations of which are endless and always worth description" (106). Ganesh has no complexities of scholarly learning or soul searching to reveal, a fact of which he is completely cognizant. The outside trappings of the Hollywood Hindus, however, are more than sufficient to Ganesh's purpose, which is to find a way to profit from the money that begins to circulate in the Trinidadian economy with the beginning of the war and the increased American military presence.

The narrator enters this chapter as a character to reminds us once again of the gap between Ganesh's representation of himself and the truth behind his flawed autobiographical account. Quoting from Ganesh's autobiography, *The Years of Guilt,* the narrator alludes to Ganesh's philosophical acceptance of his first book's failure—"if . . . my first volume had been a success, it is likely that I would have become a mere theologian, writing endless glosses of the Hindu scriptures" (101). The irony is implicit, both in the narrator's comment that "in fact, when the war began, his path was none too clear" (101) and in the reminder that rather than being a "mere theologian," Ganesh's career, for a mystic, will only have the thinnest veneer of religiosity. The chapter, therefore, will underscore Ganesh's embracing of sham, pretense, and subterfuge as substitutes for knowledge, faith, and honesty. Therefore his path to financial and social success begins with his deceitful treatment of the boy who saw the cloud and will be signaled in the next chapter by the belated success of his first book, which becomes "the first best-seller in the history of Trinidad publishing" (132) after its marketing is linked to Ganesh's success as a healer and mystic.

The extent of his success is succinctly presented in the early pages of chapter 8, "More Trouble with Ramlogan," which show Ganesh's surprise at the extent of his own powers. He establishes his reputation through the deployment of four qualities: his apparent sincerity, as he quickly begins to believe that he is indeed a mystic; the reputation for learning he has acquired through his possession of yards and yards of books; his avoidance of any set fees, which allows him to treat everyone who comes to him; and his excellent qualities as a listener, which appears to be his one and true skill. Through this mixture of cunning and innate good qualities—and with a credulous population as a backdrop—his reputation rises, and he gets "as many clients as he could handle" (127). This reputation, however, is closely linked to an authenticity as a mystic he only half possesses and that needs to be carefully protected, hence the second quarrel with Ramlogan that gives the title to this chapter.

Central to the quarrel is the question of who gets to benefit from Ganesh's success. Once again, here notions of success are intricately tied to modernity, which the villagers understand as entering into capitalistic modes of economic development. As Ganesh begins to gain control of his enterprise—for example, by monopolizing the sales of his book and retaining all profits—his entrepreneurial spirit sets him at odds against those who had helped him. He does not need Bissoon the peddler to sell his books anymore—this mode of selling books belongs to a premodern world—and the old man ends up in the Poor House of Port of Spain. Suruj Mooma dreams of "building up a brand-new modern shop...with lots of tins and cans on good good shelf" now that their shop enjoys the custom of Ganesh's clients (143). The economic success he brings to the village is acknowledged by the Public Works Department in improved infrastructure and services for the village. Moreover, Ganesh builds a mansion with his prosperity, while Leela adopts a hilarious pseudo-refinement that mimics that of a world she has never seen.

It is in this context that one must read Ganesh's response to the news that Ramlogan has, behind his back, established a fleet of "official" Fuente Grove taxis that charge the mystic's clients a higher fare than the norm. Ganesh's "genuine" response is one of outrage at the exploitation of his naïve clients by his father-in-law, and he indignantly demands that Ramlogan sell the taxis to him. Keeping his father-in-law from sharing in the profits of his enterprise, however, does not lead to fairness for his clients, as he sets up the taxi fleet as his own, with fares that, although not as high as Ramlogan's, are still "a little more than it ought to have been" (139). Greediness wins the day, with the only difference being that Ganesh secures most of the profits for himself.

The same profit impulse guides the publication of Ganesh's second book, *The Guide to Trinidad,* through which he seeks to capture the untapped American GI market. In this episode, as throughout the chapter, Naipaul uses Beharry's reactions as a mirror to the readers'. The textual strategy is particularly clear here, as his response moves from his being "dismayed at the subject" of the book, through his finding it difficult "to hide his bewilderment" when Ganesh sends free copies to all the American camps (148). Beharry will embody the narrator's consternation when Ganesh, who has been profiting from increasingly frequent visits from the Americans, will refer to them as perhaps "the most religious people in the world": "'Hollywood Hindus,' muttered Beharry, but he nibbled so badly Ganesh didn't catch what he was saying" (148).

Chapter 9, "Press Pundit," narrates how Ganesh's prestige and growing economic power translates into political power as Trinidad moves to its first election under universal adult suffrage. These developments are preceded by an account of how his reputation allows him to move out of the confines of Fuente Grove into a career as a mediator and speaker at prayer meetings. These appearances are orchestrated by his growing entourage and involve rich displays of his by then numerous published books: "Seated on the platform under a tasseled red canopy, and surrounded by his books, Ganesh looked the picture of authority and piety.... People were awed by this display of learning" (149, 150).

This learning, as displayed by his growing list of titles—which includes his "ponderous analysis of the evils of constipation" (Ormerod 78), *Profitable Evacuation,* "a vital subject...that has adversely dogged human relationships since the beginning of time" (Naipaul 153)—centers on a shallow approach to Hinduism and the other religions, such as Buddhism, whose teachings he amalgamates into a sui generis contradictory philosophy. Naipaul's satire here focuses on a trivialization of faith that is presented as stemming from the cultural losses incurred by a community separated from the true roots of its Indian identity. Above all, however, this trivialization is depicted as rooted in Ganesh's faulty education and deep sense of opportunism. Selwyn Cudjoe argues that there is "a complex Hindu consciousness evident in *The Mystic Masseur* in the spiritual guidance of Mahatma Gandhi, in the teaching of the *Gita,* and in the role of mysticism" (42). The importance of the *Gita* is particularly relevant, as, being one of the foundational texts of Hinduism, it has the power of sacred scriptures. In his shallow spirituality, however, Ganesh trivializes its complexity, reducing it to a short list of simplified principles, the most important of which is Gandhi's *Gita*-derived concept of desirelessness, "which culminates in the attainment of self-realization or freedom" (Cudjoe 42). "His main point," the narrator tells us, "was that desire was a source of misery and therefore desire ought to be suppressed" (150). This does not stop Ganesh from focusing on his own desire for success, recognition, and financial power. On listening to his nonsensical philosophies, his audience is depicted as feeling "a little nobler" (151)—thereby asserting the naïveté that characterizes them as a class and that leaves them open to manipulation and exploitation by more venal politicians—especially those hiding behind a pretense of faith.

Selwym Cudjoe has argued that "Ganesh's life parallels that of Ghandi in many essential details...[particularly in] his participation as a mystic in social and political life" (45). But in Ganesh's tale, Gandhi's remarkable faith-driven career is reworked as farce. The ludicrous aspects of politics Trinidadian style are underscored in the text through the absence of a coherent political philosophy or a movement supporting either independence or the improvement of the condition of the island's people. Political thought, as represented in the novel, is limited to a variety of slogans, behind which stand the actual issues of Trinidad's first election under universal adult franchise: "Workers United!," "A Fair Day's Pay for a Fair Day's Work," "Homes for the

Destitute," freedom of speech, access to education, and the elusive goal of so-called progress.

Ganesh's political campaign, on the other hand, is built on his pretended religious uniqueness. Politically, he "had no platform," and his campaign is built around the nonpromise that he can "do what he can" (187). Moreover, following the message of the books he had published reporting on his conversations with the deity, his supporters were encouraged to vote for him because he was holy: "A vote for Ganesh," therefore, was "a vote for God" since Ganesh is a man of good and God (187). Naipaul's satire on this political process is enhanced by his giving Ganesh's rival the most important political issues facing Trinidad at the time as his platform. Indarsingh's campaign is the one truly rooted in Gandhi's anticolonial stance, as the book based on his campaign speeches will show. He based his speeches to the masses on analyses of the economics of colonialism, the anatomy of oppression, and a people's approaches to freedom (189). His "carefully thought-out" speeches (188), however, are inaccessible to his uneducated audience since his instructive model is academic, rather than populist.

Ganesh's election to the island's Legislative Council is the culmination of a career that proves him to be indeed endowed with the attributes of his namesake, the Hindu god Ganesh, the "remover of obstacles." Naipaul offers a summary of his career that contextualizes his rise to power and prominence (192–93) and underscores the notion of destiny—the idea that "my maker meant me to become a mystic"—as the only credible explanation for Ganesh's fate. This notion of destiny, however, is not tied to divine forces, but to the premodern environment in which Ganesh's career develops. The joke, ultimately, is on the Trinidadian people, depicted in the novel as unprepared for modern democracy.

Leela embodies in the text Naipaul's belief in the Trinidadian villagers' lack of preparation for modernity. Long accustomed to watching the behaviors and antics of colonial masters, they have become mimic men, whose entry into modernity is imitative, rather than truly internalized. Naipaul humorously uses Coca-Cola as symbolic of this indigestible modernity in various scenes in which it produces gas and burping. The Great Belcher, for example, claims she is "done with Coca Cola," as she "ain't modern enough for it" (159). Leela, who displays her new Coca-Cola-stuffed refrigerator in the most public room of their new grand house, serves it to Ganesh's political supporters in her "prutty prutty" glasses. The drink, unfamiliar and full of gas, stands for the discomfort of the transition into modernity as Ganesh moves into a political career in chapter 10, "The Defeat of Narayan."

The chapter takes aim both at the venality of the many associations to aid the Hindu villagers that sprouted in Trinidad in the postwar years and, in particular, at the Hindu press in Trinidad. Depicted as mere vehicles for the promotion of social schemes and, most importantly, for the selling of ads, they emerge in the text as yet another example of the incompatibility of a representative democracy with the ignorance and gullibility that prevail among the uneducated masses of the colony of Trinidad.

The heavy-handed satire of Naipaul's description of the dinner at Government House in chapter 11, "M.L.C."—where the newly elected native legislators are depicted as contemptuously ridiculous—has prompted West Indian critic Gordon Rohlehr to observe that despite the amiability of the characterizations of Ganesh and his associates, the "suspicion persists that Naipaul himself regards these people with more contempt than compassion" (124). The description of the dinner is indeed loaded with heavy doses of sarcasm, aimed at showing the newly elected officials as unmodern, uneducated oafs, as if universal adult suffrage has given entry into political power to buffoons and demagogues unsuited for the enlightened practices of democracy.

This unsuitability is underscored by the brief description of Ganesh's political career in chapter 12, "M.L.C. to M.B.E.," and the brief epilogue, "A Statesman on the 12.57," which outlines the trajectory of Naipaul's failed Indo-Trinidadian politician Ralph Singh in his 1967 novel *The Mimic Men.* Ganesh's own path is that of a mimic man, who moves from a career as a mystic, which, although marked by cupidity, was still openly rooted in a superficial recognition of his Hindu culture and religion, to a renunciation of his ethnic identity in favor of a colonial one. Ganesh transforms himself into an anticommunist demagogue who finds success in imitating the colonizer's lifestyle, values, and political opinions (see, for example, his transformation into an anticommunist pamphleteer). In the process, and through the eyes of one of his earliest patients as a masseur, he becomes a pathetic, Anglicized version of himself, the honorable G. Ramsay Muir.

Chapter 13

Patricia Powell's A Small Gathering of Bones

Patricia Powell was born in Spanish Town, Jamaica, in 1966. From the age of three, she was raised by a great aunt, who owned a rum shop in the Jamaican village of Manchester, a masculine space full of characters and tales that the young girl would later use as inspiration for her fiction. Her aunt drank as much as the men, but was never seen drunk or incoherent, and argued "just as vehemently, and as passionately" as the men (Smith 326). Powell remembers her as "a great swooping bird, breaking up fights and throwing out the drunkards" (Smith 326), a larger-than-life figure who is behind the way Powell imagines all her female characters. Her aunt, a "shrewd businesswoman" (Smith 326), also had a marked sentimental streak.

Powell migrated with her family to the United States in 1982, at the age of 16, just two years before entering Wellesley College to pursue a degree in English. She began her studies at Wellesley College as an economics major but soon realized that her true interest lay in literature. Missing her family and her native Jamaica, and finding it difficult to make friends in Massachusetts, Powell found solace in writing. For her graduation in 1988, she wrote an honors thesis in creative fiction that became her first novel, *Me Dying Trial* (1993). The novel, drawn from her family experiences, tells of a young Jamaican schoolteacher trapped in an abusive marriage who challenges cultural expectations by breaking away from her constraining circumstances and leaving with her six young children for the United States. Powell has described her first novel as "completely raw and vulnerable, with all its insides spilling out and exposed" (Smith 329).

Following her graduation from Wellesley, and not thinking of herself as a writer (her first novel would not find a publisher for five years), Powell applied to Brown University's master of fine arts program on the advice of friends. Her writing project at Brown would become the manuscript for her second novel, *A Small Gathering of Bones* (1994), written in memory of I. Facey, a Jamaican friend who had died of AIDS in 1989 and to whom the book is dedicated:

When I began the work, I didn't know I would end up writing a novel about gay male life in Jamaica during the 1970s, about sexual identity and coming out, about night clubs and pick up spots, about the hardships and pressures of homophobia and how it affects the private life, about AIDS and destroyed bodies, about failed relationships, about mothers and their gay sons, about rejection and hypocrisy and strong and lasting friendships, about homosexuality and religion, about forgiveness and love. All I knew then was that since I couldn't have attended his funeral, to share the grief of his passing, I would figure out a way to transform that grief. To speak out about what had really killed him. (Smith 327)

The publication of her first two novels to critical and popular success before her thirtieth birthday transformed the young writer's life. She received numerous awards, including the Lila Wallace Readers' Digest Writers Award in 1992, the Ferro-Grumley Award for Fiction, the Bruce Rossley Literary Award, and the PEN New England Discovery Award. In 1995 she was a finalist for the prestigious Granta/Best of Young American Novelists Award. She also received a number of important fellowships: Yaddo Fellowships in 1993 and 1996 and McDowell Fellowships in 1992 and 1997. These were accompanied by countless invitations to lecture and teach at some of the most prestigious American universities, and Powell has taught creative writing at Harvard University (as a Briggs Copeland Lecturer in Creative Writing in the English department), at her alma mater, Wellesley College, at the University of Massachusetts in Boston, and as a Martin Luther King Visiting Professor at the Massachusetts Institute of Technology (MIT).

In 1999 Powell published her third novel, *The Pagoda,* the tale of a Chinese shopkeeper in the village of Manchester, Jamaica, in the nineteenth century. Drawn in part from the figure of her great aunt and the world of the rum shop she knew so well from childhood, the protagonist of her novel is a Chinese immigrant posing as a man to secure a living for herself and her daughter. She is working on her fourth novel, *The Good Life*. In an interview with Lynn Heinemann of the Office of the Arts at MIT in 2003, Powell described her writing thus:

I write because I have so many questions and there are no reasonable answers in sight. Writing becomes a way of investigating. I'm concerned about the way we live in the world, the injustices we heap onto other people because of difference—race, class, gender, sexual identity, cultural identity, etc. I should not have to be Chinese to write about the plight of the Chinese back in the 1800s or even today. I should not have to be gay or a gay man with AIDS to be concerned about the ways in which homophobia kills all of us, gay and straight alike. I care about people and their suffering and the ways they try to move out of their suffering, or build defenses around it, perhaps even bury themselves even more deeply inside it, because they can't imagine any other possibility.

A Small Gathering of Bones

The historical setting of *A Small Gathering of Bones* is the year 1978 in Kingston, Jamaica, in the early months of the AIDS epidemic and during a time of strident homophobia in Jamaica. The events of the novel are set against the local elections of 1978, a moment of political tensions marked by violence and bombings. "Fifteen dead, fifty injured. Only three buildings bombed," is how the narrator summarizes the political events that provide a background to the tale (120). In the novel, AIDS is still a disease with no name; indeed, during the 1970s, without salient symptoms identified and with no information available about its spread through sexual contact or bodily fluids, as many as 300,000 people were infected with the disease.

Ian Kaysen is portrayed as only the second person with symptoms of what would become known as HIV to have been seen by the physician at the local Kingston hospital: night sweats, swollen glands, and other symptoms caused by the opportunistic infections that attacked the body as the immune system became compromised; the liver-colored marks of Kaposi's sarcoma, a rare and usually benign form of cancer that usually occurs in elderly people; the cough produced by a rare form of lung infection, *Pneumocystis carinii* pneumonia; the blood-tinged phlegm; and the beginning of dementia as the disease attacked the brain. The disease would not be named until 1982, four years after the events narrated in the novel; the virus that causes it (HIV) was not discovered until 1983, when it was confirmed that it could spread through sexual activity and contact with bodily fluids. By then, as we now know, it would be too late for most of the gay characters we meet in the novel, whose relationships and sexual behavior put them at such risk, to have all escaped infection. Indeed, the novel prefigures the multiplication of cases in Jamaica in the intervening years between 1978 (when the action takes place) and 1982 (when the virus is discovered) through the almost casual way in which it locates early symptoms in many of the members of the gay community with whom Ian and the novel's main character, Dale, have had love affairs—Loxley, Gavin, and even Dale himself—and through its graphic narration of anonymous sexual encounters in Nanny Sharpe's park.

Crucial to the background of the novel is an understanding of the profound homophobia that characterizes Jamaican society and that has placed the island under the scrutiny of the Human Rights Watch Organization and Amnesty International. Homosexuality is illegal in Jamaica, and there is amply documented evidence of discrimination against homosexuals. Article 76 of Jamaica's Offences against the Person Act makes anyone committing the "abominable crime of buggery" subject to up to 10 years in prison. Article 79 makes physical intimacy between men in public or private punishable by up to two years in prison, with the possibility of hard labor. Amnesty International USA has documented reports of violence ranging from "vigilante action by members of the community to ill-treatment or torture by the police" (Amnesty International USA). Gay men and women, they report, "have been beaten, cut, burned, raped and shot on account of their sexuality" (Amnesty International USA).

In *A Small Gathering of Bones,* Powell describes in subtle yet powerful ways the burden that widespread homophobia has placed on gay men in Jamaican society. During a visit to his friend Ian at the hospital, after an AIDS-related seizure that has left him partially paralyzed, Dale walks away from the receptionist with an intense awareness of the possibility of betraying himself as a closeted gay man because he is visiting a gay man who had been found at Nanny Sharpe's (a park known as a place for anonymous homosexual encounters). The passage encapsulates the everyday indignities of being gay in Jamaica:

Him was manly enough to pass. Didn't sport the same limp wrist cock off to the side as if about to express some great wonderment, or gentle sway of the pelvis thrust forward like Ian.... Him was barrel-chested, stocky around the middle, and walked with a confidence common to most married men. Furthermore he was wearing man clothes today, dungarees, the heavy post office boots and a cap for it was drizzling outside. But him could still feel the words embellished on her brain, poised, ready to pounce from off her tongue. (80)

Human Rights Watch reports that "political and cultural factors, including religious intolerance of homosexuality, Jamaican popular music, and the use of antigay slogans and rhetoric by political leaders, also promote violence and discrimination based on sexual orientation and gender identity." Internationally known Jamaican singers like Capleton, Sizzla, Elephant Man, Bounty Killer, Beenie Man, TOK, and others frequently use derogatory terms for gay men *(chi-chi men* and *battybwoys)* and urge their audience in their music to shoot, burn, rape, stone, drown, and shoot homosexuals. In January 2004, at the Rebel Salute concert in St. Elizabeth, Jamaica, Capleton and Sizzla sang almost exclusively about gay men: "kill dem, battybwoys haffi dead, gun shots pon dem...who want to see dem dead put up his hand" (kill them, the queers have to die, gun shots in their head...put up your hand if you want to see them dead) (Younge). Politicians have embraced these homophobic songs, incorporating them into their campaigns for office. During the 2001 elections, Human Rights Watch reported, the Jamaican Labour Party (the main opposition party) used as its campaign song "Chi Chi Man," a song that celebrates the burning and killing of gay men. The ruling People's National Party, for its 2002 campaign, used as its campaign slogan the phrase "Log On to Progress," which alluded to a popular song and dance ("Log On") advocating the kicking or stomping of gay men (Human Rights Watch).

The church has been instrumental in the intensification of homophobia in Jamaica. Evangelical Christianity is particularly strong on the island, and it advocates the reading of the Bible for its strong antihomosexuality message. As a result, pastors preach vehemently against homosexuality as a sin, often invoking cultural arguments, such as Jamaican society's intolerance, as reasons to support the continued criminalization of homosexuality.

This climate of repression, especially as it concerns the church, is the subtext in the narrative of how the homosexual community of *A Small Gathering of Bones* relates to its cultural and political environment. In an interview about her work, Powell explained the difficulties of addressing the fear homosexuals in Jamaica face daily:

I've been struggling for a while trying to figure out how to write gay/lesbian sexuality so as to best illustrate the charged interactions that my characters face. And by charged I mean the constant fear, or internalized hate, the terror that's gnawing in the back of the subconscious. I didn't want to write it in the conventional way, as a shared, wondrous, idyllic experience, because it was more complicated than that for them. (Smith 325)

A Small Gathering of Bones is divided into seven chapters that narrate events unfolding in the nine months that elapse between February and November 1978. Presented chronologically, each chapter addresses one or two days but is interspersed with flashbacks to earlier events and conversations that give the chapters their complex texture. In his review of the book, John McCluskey says of these flashbacks that it is "the shrewd weave of memory that adds texture and poignancy to the novel" (317). Dreams are interwoven into the narrative to address the various characters' hopes, fears, and expectations.

The opening of the novel—which speaks of Ian Kaysen's "offensive dry cough" (1)—leaves no doubt that Powell's primary concern in the novel is that of addressing the very early stages of the AIDS epidemic in Jamaica in 1978. The novel ends with Ian's death, albeit in a surprising way that points to a parallel concern of Powell's—that of the stigma attached to homosexuality in Jamaica and how this stigma leads to a mother's withdrawal of her love and commitment to her son. The narrative, framed between these two thematic threads, explores the complexities of being homosexual in Jamaica's homophobic society in the age of AIDS. In Anglophone Caribbean literature, this is the sole fictional exploration of homosexuality, AIDS, and homophobia. The only other salient text addressing these issues as a primary focus is Jamaica Kincaid's nonfictional memoir of the death of her brother from AIDS, *My Brother,* published in 1997. In the Spanish-speaking Caribbean, the subjects have been repeatedly addressed by writers of the stature of Reinaldo Arenas (*Before Night Falls,* Cuba, 1993), Senel Paz (*Strawberry and Chocolate,* Cuba, 1990), and Manuel Ramos Otero (*Invitación al polvo,* Puerto Rico, 1994), among others.

The novel is a third-person account narrated through a sensitive rendering of the cadences of Jamaican English from the perspective of Dale Singleton. Dale, a perceptive and religious young man, is still recovering from the end of a romance with his former lover, Nevin Morgan, with whom he still shares a house at the beginning of the novel. The plot draws its pathos from what would be fairly banal romantic complications if this were a novel about heterosexual affairs: Dale, who moves on to a relationship with Loxley toward the end of the novel, is still pained by the breakup of his relationship with Nevin, due to his jealousy of Johnnie, Nevin's shop assistant; Ian, also a former lover of Nevin's, has become a good friend of Dale's, who seeks to help him resolve his estrangement from his homophobic family; a subplot finds Nevin's sister Rose, intent on marrying her Rastaman boyfriend and having a child, unaware that her mother has been secretly inducing her miscarriages. These somewhat melodramatic plotlines escape a descent into pathos through the poignant humanity of Dale's voice and the pathos of relationships that must be lived in fear of violence and through self-protective lies. The reader, moreover, has a fuller understanding of the significance of the symptoms exhibited by the various characters and knows, as the characters do not, that difficult as are the circumstances they face in the text as homosexuals in Jamaica, they have ahead of them a yet more disturbing and tragic trial.

The opening chapter of the novel, "February 1978," describes, through Dale's at times jesting admonitions, his deep concern over his friend Ian Kaysen's "hardeared, persistent" cough (3). The chapter's first section—before the narrator introduces the cast of characters and describes their relationships to each other—establishes the insightful and heartrending quality of Dale's viewpoint. This is accomplished through the combination of his efforts to hide his concern over Ian's worsening condition and the reader's awareness of the hopelessness of the disease that is producing this "offensive dry cough" (1). "Dale feel a wave of tenderness wash over him so strong," the narrator explains, "him wanted to stroke the thin stately neck in front him" (3).

The second section of the first chapter speaks to the tensions within the gay community: incidents of homophobic violence, lack of solidarity between friends and lovers, and the disapproval of family members. The latter is exemplified here—as it will be throughout the text—by Miss Kaysen, Ian's mother, who, after her son is attacked, comes to see him only to tell him that "nothing good can amount from all the bad company Ian keep" (3). Dale emerges from this introduction as an exception—a sensitive and generous young man who cleans, washes clothes, and brings food to Ian for the sole reason that "him take after his mother that way; he can't stand to see bad things happen to people" (4). Above all, the section explores the characters' capacity for friendship and establishes the routines of the subset of the gay community in Kingston that surrounds Dale: Clovy's Bar, where they dance and flirt on Saturday nights; the concerns about clothes and demeanor; and the struggle with relationships, studies, life, and careers. Of particular importance are the two relationships that are introduced here, as the plot of the novel revolves to a great extent around them: Dale's romantic liaison with Nevin Morgan (which has already finished when the novel opens but remains central to Dale's emotional life) and his friendship with the AIDS-stricken Ian.

The chapter introduces a theme of great significance to the development of the novel: that of the nature and possibilities of gay spirituality within traditional churches, which look on homosexual relationships as sinful and, in some cases, as aberrant behavior. The opening chapter establishes both the faith that underpins Dale's generosity of spirit to friends like Ian and the importance of the work he does for the community from within his church, the Gospel According to St. Luke's Episcopal Church. His deep involvement in the church includes his teaching three sessions of Sunday school; his stepping in to lead prayers and conduct baptisms, communions, and weddings; his leading a group in Bible study; and his sensitive handling of the Young People's Meeting.

Of primary importance to Dale is his protective role in helping other young men like himself come to accept their homosexuality, as he himself had been helped to do from within the church. Pastor Bowles, of the Pentecostal church he used to attend with his mother, had counseled acceptance of the "the doings of the Almighty": "It is for us to accept, son, to accept and bear persecution," he had advocated (10). It is a message of self-acceptance heavily imbued with notions of Christian martyrdom, but one that resonates with Dale because it contextualizes his life as gay man in a homophobic society. He had resolved, then, "to bear it majestically, to turn the other cheek when the sharp edge of the stone clapped against his head, when the steel-toed tips of police shoes elbow him in the sides, when his friends pile ridicule upon ridicule on his curved shoulders" (10). And aware of the homophobia that characterizes his own church's official posture toward homosexuality, he fears for those who would have to endure the church's purgation should Dale not be there to counsel silent acceptance: "there'd be endless prayer meetings, endless consultations, endless accumulations of shame and guilt...and in the end, maybe that youngster would gird his waist, fasten his eyes tight and choose a Sister" (11).

In this opening chapter, Powell builds her characterization on a skillful blending of present and past narratives, using memory to contextualize the personalities and intertwining relationships whose understanding by the reader is crucial to the elaboration of the plot. The character traits that define Dale, for example, are seen as much through his present actions (caring for Ian through his injury and alarming cough) as through the flashbacks to events in the past (such as the conversation between him and Nevin, and later between him and Ian, about his career possibilities). By addressing Dale's multiple ways of being, Powell avoids the subsuming of his character and personality under his homosexuality and underscores the traits he shares with all Jamaicans, regardless of sexual orientation. Powell accomplishes this partly through descriptions of the spaces Dale inhabits, inscribing his humanity into the objects that surround him in his room and in his office: his collection of fountain pens; his newspaper clippings of strange stories; and particularly the old schoolteacher desk, with faded etchings (among them "Batty-man"). The garden, for example, offers Dale a space of reflection and a connection to memory (especially that of his mother) and to traditional Jamaican culture. The memories of his mother, in particular, the descriptions of the time they spent together—"sitting quiet in the garden, she in the rocker by the oil stove in the corner, him on a hard bench against the wall, hunched over yards and yards of wool" embroidering and weaving (11)—provide a powerful contrast to the descriptions of Nevin's homophobic and violent family. Mrs. Morgan, among other violent acts, had sent her husband tumbling down the stairs, leaving him confined to a wheelchair.

Mrs. Morgan's violence—which includes inducing her daughter's miscarriages to prevent her having a Rastaman's child—is linked thematically to Miss Kaysen's emotional violence toward her son Ian. The pain his mother's rejection inflicts on Ian—who loves her "to distraction" (19)—is graphically depicted through his emotional collapse when she rejects the gifts that accompanied his letter "explaining the state of his heart where men were concerned" (20). Dale finds him wearing the silk dress, earrings, and necklace he had sent his mother, "whimpering softly, thumb and forefinger tenderly caressing ashes from a small white envelope that had his name scrawled on it with a piece of charcoal" (20).

Chapter 2, "Late February 1978," briefly conjures the violence, jealousy, and promiscuity that is the result of sexual and emotional lives lived under cover of secrecy and menace. Dale himself bears the scars of Nevin's assault after he discovers him with his lover Alexander. Through the brief narrative of the development of Dale's relationship with Alexander, a religious education teacher who hides his homosexuality from his wife and children, Powell explores the complexities of homosexual love in a society where same-sex relationships are repressed through violence and social and legal censure.

Chapter 3, "April 1978," opens with Dale's meditation on proper motherhood, which underscores his maternal side, presented here as drawn from his warm rapport with his mother. This, and a brief conversation with Ian about their failed relationships before the latter is hospitalized for collapsed lungs, ushers in an extended narrative on motherhood (and parenthood) and homosexuality presented through three conversations Dale has with mothers (and a father). Two of these take place in the present (with Miss Kaysen and Mrs. Morgan); two take place in the past between Dale and his now deceased mother and between him and his married lover Alexander.

Dale's conversation with Miss Kaysen, to whom he goes to inform her of Ian's hospitalization, underscores her rejection of Ian because of his homosexuality. "When your child choose a course God didn't cut out for him, you dish him dirt," she explains. "You wash your hands clean. You banish him from your life" (37). Maternal rejection, which here becomes symbolic of the ultimate possible erasure of homosexuality in Jamaican society, is even a possibility in Dale's relationship with his own mother, despite their loving relationship. Intent on telling her openly that he is gay, Dale announces to her that he is "funny that way," as his Uncle Ralph had been, only to have her collapse into a deep faint. She recovers, but chooses denial and silence, rather than acknowledging her son's homosexuality: "Her face look fresh and vibrant again," Dale recalls. "But not a word about it mentioned" (40). This erasure extends to parents, even when they are homosexuals themselves, as Dale understands after a conversation with his lover Alexander, who clearly declares that he would rather have his son marry and have children, even if it means remaining in the closet, like he is.

The fourth conversation, with Nevin's mother, Mrs. Morgan, assumes her knowledge of her son's homosexuality, while regaling Dale with stories of parents who resorted to Obeah to punish children who had embraced homosexuality. Obeah, a set of hybrid or Creolized beliefs dependent on ritual invocation, fetishes, and charms, incorporates two very distinct categories of practice. It involves "the casting of spells for various purposes, both good and evil: protecting oneself, property, family, or loved ones; harming real or perceived enemies; and bringing fortune in love, employment, personal or business pursuits" (Frye 198). Here Mrs. Morgan acknowledges that she has practiced Obeah to tie Mr. Morgan to his home and family through a potion concocted by her father. She also assumes that others have used it against their children, like in the case of the father who persecutes his daughter with spells to punish her for living with a woman. She wonders, then, if Ian's affliction is the result of some Obeah work prepared against him by a former lover or creditor since the symptoms of the disease are incompatible with those for recognizable diseases.

Chapter 4, "End of April 1978," analyzes the collapse of Dale's relationship with Nevin, and through it the possibility of a deeply committed relationship between two men in Jamaican society, a society in which loyalty and monogamy in heterosexual relationships are far from the norm. Through Dale's poignant struggle between his love for Nevin and his heartbreak at the sexual and emotional betrayal brought about by Nevin's philandering, Powell scrutinizes the details that lead to the end of their five-year relationship. Aware of the pathos involved in the petty quarrels and misunderstandings that are typical of relationships under stress, Powell gives them the accompaniment of country songs heard on the radio, particularly songs by Charley Pride. Pride (1939–), a Negro League baseball player who moved on to a successful career in country music (one of the few African American performers to do so), was famous for lovesick ballads like "I'm So Afraid of Losing You Again," "Someone Loves You Honey," and "When I Stop Leaving I'll Be Gone." She stresses the normalcy of the difficulties between them by having Dale take counsel from Mrs. Morgan and contextualize advice drawn from heterosexual relations as perfectly applicable to his collapsing homosexual affair. In this, Dale assumes the more dependent female role, as it is the one imposed on him by his younger age and financially dependent situation. Faced with what he sees as Nevin's interest in Johnny, Dale asks Mrs. Morgan "politely how she's manage if Mr Morgan openly keep woman with her" (56).

Powell uses the devise of Dale's visit to a psychiatrist to introduce into the text the memories of his childhood assessment of his parents' troubled marriage and the narrative of the early and promising days of his relationship with Nevin. She underscores Dale's subordinate position by identifying his predicament with that of his mother: "Must be him searching for a younger version of me," Dale explains bitterly. "Like my father and mother all over again" (64). The psychiatrist, a woman herself, has little to offer in their shared cultural setting: "It's tough, isn't it? Finding yourself trapped in the same position as your mother. Cycle repeating itself" (65).

Underpinning the analysis of the end of Dale and Nevin's relationship in this chapter is the issue of financial independence, which keeps Dale subordinated to Nevin. Powell underscores the connection between the emotional state of the relationship and Dale's quest for independence through the couple's bickering about Nevin's desire to have Dale join him in his business (his refusal leads to the fateful hiring of Johnny as Nevin's assistant) and Dale's acceptance of a position with the postal service that Nevin thinks is beneath his qualifications.

Chapter 5, "June 1978," parallels the previous chapter in important ways, as it opens with Dale meeting Ian—increasingly feeble from the complications of AIDS but defiantly flirtatious—and ends with Dale angrily tossing the check Nevin wanted to give him to pay his university fees into a waterfall. The central theme of the chapter, however—despite the attention given to the final collapse of Dale and Nevin's relationship and Dale's new relationship with Loxley—is the puzzling nature of Ian's disease and his worsening condition. Ian's admission into the hospital with a crippling stroke that leaves him partly paralyzed—together with his having been found while in search for anonymous sex in Nanny Sharpe's Park—awakens in Dale both a fear of approaching death and transgressive desires that, unbeknownst to him (but not to the reader), put him at greater risk of sharing Ian's fate.

This chapter establishes firmly the connection between death and sex that is AIDS's contribution to the sexual politics of the late twentieth and early twenty-first centuries. In it, Powell explores the complexities of sexual desire against the background of early death. The sex-death duality invades Dale's dreams about his mother's funeral, as Ian's body replaces that of his beloved mother's: "Every time him look in the casket, it was Ian's face that stare back at him, one half smooth and stiff like a piece of china, the other half tender with the laugh lines spreading like branches around his mouth" (96). Coming out of the hospital after seeing Ian shortly after his stroke, Dale responds to his emotional upheaval and need to forestall communicating the news to Ian's family and friends by letting a stranger pick him up at the bar: "This was the very same thing him been cautioning Ian against. But it was starting to feel so exciting. . . . And without even waiting for the bartender to return with the drink, Dale grab the paper bag with Ian's trousers and follow briskly behind the fellow to the car outside" (88).

Among the secondary themes developed in this chapter is that of Dale's puzzlement over Ian's stories about his mother's visits and gifts, especially presents of home remedies to help him battle the ever more visible signs of AIDS. It is a theme continued from the previous chapters, but it is here presented as joining the symptoms of Ian's nameless disease. The symptoms are those of the AIDS dementia complex, one of the most important complications associated with late HIV infection, which causes symptoms similar to those of Alzheimer's disease, memory loss, and some forms of psychosis. Ian's stroke is also a sign that his HIV infection is entering into its late stages, as neurological complications are a sign that the infection has crossed the blood-brain barrier and entered all levels of the nervous system. Ian's doctor informs Dale that he has seen only one patient with symptoms similar to those exhibited by Ian, and he had slipped into a coma two weeks before. It is not surprising, given the centrality of the disease and its spread in this chapter, that Powell extends here the reach of AIDS to incorporate Dale and his close friends. She reminds of Nevin's affair with Ian while he was still sexually involved with Dale and has Loxley, Dale's present lover, show the early symptoms of the disease: "And in the early morning hours, when Dale would awaken to the sounds of Loxley's chest rattling out the same 'ke-hem ke-hem' accompanied by a mouthful of purple phlegm like Ian's, him didn't even stop for a second to contemplate that this might be the same disease plaguing Ian" (96). Here Dale is also described as exhibiting the night sweats that are an early indication of HIV infection.

In chapter 6, "Mid-July 1978," Powell returns to the subject of homosexuality and the church that was so important to the novel's introductory chapter. Here it becomes central to Dale's spiritual crisis, as his unhappiness about his unresolved feelings for Nevin and his pain at seeing Ian slip away toward death push him into the addictive thrill of anonymous sex at Nanny Sharpe's and the concomitant feeling of guilt and sin. The chapter opens with indications of Ian's recovering strength and his resolve to renounce his homosexuality after he becomes convinced that his illness is God's punishment for the sins of homosexuals all over the world: "God punishing him, making him poorly. It's happening all over, abroad, everywhere" (106). Ian becomes determined to return to the church and be baptized, in an open declaration of his renunciation of sin.

For Dale, Ian's illness—and his intimations that this is an illness that is indeed affecting gay men around him—leads to a different conclusion. He feels he is being driven away from the church by the devil, who demanded he "choose between Salvation and the love between men" (107).

The chapter includes a detailed narrative of the sexual encounter in the park that symbolizes Dale's acceptance of the overwhelming power of the temptation represented by the anonymity and pleasure of these encounters he once warned Ian against because of their sordidness and the risk of physical attack and possible death. In an interview with Faith Smith, Powell spoke of the importance of the scene to Dale's development as a character, calling it a "crucial moment" in the character's development:

A devout Christian and minister, he was leaving the church for he could no longer bear the hypocrisy and lies; his best friend was dying in the hospital; he had just left a long term relationship and was trying to begin another; it was his first anonymous encounter and his friend Ian had already been beaten up here; etc.... The arousal is interrupted by the character's constant reminder of the hostile world around him, and his own fragile, vulnerable position. So there are the street sounds of people passing and of laughter, but there is also the fear of beating or incarceration if found, the fear of death—through the anonymity and the illicitness of the situation bring their own charge. (324)

Ian's baptism is the culminating moment in this collective crisis of faith, as Ian, glowing with hope, offers the sublimation of his sexuality in return for a chance to live a full life. For Dale, the ceremony is emblematic of a renunciation of the self that should not be required of God's creatures. As a result, he turns away from the church, avoiding the midday service and Bible study and only focusing on Young People's Meeting, where he could lose himself in other people's problems. "This wasn't what religion should be used for, to hide behind like a veil, to plunge into like a dream," he concludes after watching Ian surrender his self through baptism. "Him should be able to accept himself and his religion, embrace the two like twin. Not suppress one, while the other reign triumphant" (119).

Chapter 7, "November 1978" (the novel's final chapter), features the "small gathering" of the title—a small party to celebrate Ian's birthday on the evening before his death from a fall. It is a gathering of the soon-to-be-dead, as Powell underscores through the description of the ever expanding signs of Kaposi's sarcoma on Loxley's back as he undresses the evening after the party. This small gathering presages the one in Ian's imagination, where he would marry Bill's light-skinned sister as his fiancée and there would be a "close little gathering with her family, most of whom would be coming from England, a few friends, and of course his own family" (128). It is emboldened by his renunciation of homosexuality, his willingness to marry and have children, and the baptism that would prove to his mother the substance of his change, on which Ian insists during his ill-fated visit to Miss Kaysen, unleashing the tragic set of events that end with his death at the bottom of her stairs.

The haunting quality of the novel's ending stems from the absolute hatred for homosexuality that can transcend a mother's love, turning it into deadly rage. Miss Kaysen's development from cruel mother to the hellish fiend that she has become at the end of the novel—from rejecting mother to her son's murderer—is Powell's metaphor for the power of the hatred that sustains homophobia in Jamaican society. *A Small Gathering of Bones* becomes a searing indictment of homophobia through its mesmerizing narrative of maternal violence.

Chapter 14

Jean Rhys's Wide Sargasso Sea

Jean Rhys was born Ella Gwendoline Rees Williams on August 24, 1890, in Roseau, the capital of the island of Dominica, then a British colony. Her father, William Rees Williams, was a Welsh doctor and a recent arrival to the island. Her mother, Minna Lockhart, was a third-generation Dominican Creole of Scottish descent. A white Creole in a predominantly black, small island society, Rhys never quite fit into her community. Her whiteness was intensified by her family's connection to the Geneva estate, an old slaveholding sugar plantation. Thus, from an early age, Rhys felt the burden of race, class, and history as an obstacle to her identification with her home island. Yet her life in Dominica—which she left at the age of 16 and to which she did not return, except for a brief visit in 1936—became the centerpiece of her literary work.

In 1907, Rhys moved to England to attend the Perse School in Cambridge and later the Royal Academy of Dramatic Art in London. Her education was cut short by the death of her father, and she subsequently earned her living as a chorus girl under the name of Ella Gray. During the First World War, Rhys volunteered in a soldier's canteen, and afterward worked in a pension office. In 1919 she married Johan Marie (Jean) Lenglet, a French-Dutch journalist and songwriter. They had two children together, one of them a son who died three weeks after birth. Their daughter Maryvonne, Rhys's only surviving child, was born in 1922. From 1923 to 1924, when Lenglet was jailed for financial fraud, Rhys had an affair with British author and publisher Ford Madox Ford, who was instrumental in mentoring her as a writer. He published her first short story, "Vienne" (1924), in his magazine,

The Transatlantic Review. The affair inspired her first novel, *Postures* (later retitled *Quartet*), published in 1928. Rhys and Lenglet divorced in 1933, and Rhys spent the rest of her life in England, where she had returned with Lenglet and their daughter in the late 1920s. *Quartet* was made into a film, directed by the famed producer/director team of Ismail Merchant and James Ivory, in 1981.

The years following her return to England marked the beginning of Rhys's life as a full-time writer. The first of many collections of short stories, *The Left Bank and Other Stories,* appeared in 1927, followed shortly by her first novel, *Quartet.* Three other novels appeared in quick succession during the 1930s: *After Leaving Mr Mackenzie* (1931), *Voyage in the Dark* (1934), and *Good Morning, Midnight* (1939). These are dark novels about young West Indian women stranded and isolated in Europe, dependent on men for survival, often penniless and vulnerable to sexual abuse and emotional pain. They enjoyed critical success, and Rhys seemed to be on her way to a successful career as a modernist writer.

Rhys's path to success, however, took a strange detour after the publication of *Good Morning, Midnight,* and she inexplicably stopped writing and disappeared from literary circles for the next two decades. In 1934 she had married Leslie Tilden Smith, a copy editor, and the two of them were plagued by the alcoholism against which she would battle intermittently for the rest of her life. In 1936, with the aid of a small inheritance received by her husband, Rhys returned to Dominica, her first and only visit since her departure in 1907. The visit was not as successful as she would have hoped, as there were growing social and political tensions on the island, and the society Rhys had known as a child had been utterly transformed. The trip served as a catalyst for her writing, and after her return to England, she produced the first draft of a manuscript she called *The Revenant* and which in time would become her most successful book, *Wide Sargasso Sea.*

The novel, however, would not be completed for almost three decades, as the couple sunk together into a life of relative poverty and deeper alcoholism, and the war years were difficult ones for them. Tilden Smith died in 1945, and in 1947 Rhys married her third husband, Tilden Smith's cousin Max Hamer. Life with Hamer, however, was even more difficult than it had been with her late husband, as he spent a considerable portion of the time they were married in prison, chiefly for misappropriation of funds. Rhys herself spent a very brief period in jail for assaulting a neighbor, an experience she turned masterfully into one of her best short stories, "Let Them Call It Jazz" (1962).

Rhys's rediscovery in 1959 has become the stuff of literary legend. She had settled in obscurity and poverty in Devonshire, where she was found by actress Selma Vaz Dias, who was preparing a dramatized version of *Good Morning, Midnight* for a radio broadcast on the BBC. Found to be working on a new novel, she was helped into a second literary flourishing by editors

Francis Wyndham and Diana Athill. Her short stories began appearing in venues such as *London Magazine, Art and Letters,* and *The New Yorker,* and she resumed work on *Wide Sargasso Sea,* whose publication in 1966—the year of her husband, Max Hamer's, death—was greeted with great critical acclaim. Of her providing a voice and a story for the silenced madwoman in the attic of *Jane Eyre,* Rhys would later say that she was "convinced that Charlotte Brontë must have had something against the West Indies, and I was angry about it" ("Jean Rhys"). The novel was recognized with a number of awards, including the W. H. Smith Award, the Royal Society of Literature Award, and an Arts Council Bursary. A film version of the novel, directed by John Duigan, appeared in 1993 to indifferent reviews.

Rhys relished her return to the limelight and the financial stability that the success of the novel brought her but continued living and working in Devonshire until her death in 1979. She published two new collections of short stories, *Tigers Are Better-Looking* (1968) and *Sleep It Off, Lady* (1976), and saw the reissue of her earlier novels and short stories. Her unfinished autobiography, *Smile Please,* was published in 1980. Rhys's letters were edited by Francis Wyndham and Diana Melly and published in 1984 in England as *Jean Rhys's Letters: 1931–1966.* Her papers, which include a number of unpublished manuscripts, letters, and drafts of her early novels *Triple Sec* and *Black Exercise Book* have been deposited in the Special Collections department of the McFarlin Library at the University of Tulsa in Oklahoma.

Wide Sargasso Sea

On its publication in 1966, *Wide Sargasso Sea* immediately became one of the most critically acclaimed of Caribbean texts. Critics and readers alike were fascinated by this story of the first Mrs. Rochester, the infamous madwoman in the attic of Charlotte Brontë's *Jane Eyre* (1847), one of the most widely read novels in the English language. Rhys's effort to rescue Bertha Mason from the oblivion into which she is sent in Brontë's text produced, in the opinion of many critics, the most significant critique to date of *Jane Eyre* and of the early Victorian assumptions that sustained its plot. Indeed, most of the literary criticism on *Wide Sargasso Sea* centers on the clarification of the novel's connection to Brontë's text.

Rhys repeatedly described the impulse to write about Bertha Mason, the woman who must die if Brontë's heroine is to find happiness with Mr. Rochester, as stemming from a sense of injustice at the erasure of the shadowy and incoherent Creole woman in Brontë's text. It was tantamount in her eyes to the erasure of the West Indies and its importance to the British imperial economy throughout the Victorian age. Reduced to being merely the bearer of a fortune that secures Mr. Rochester's finances before the death of his elder brother makes him the heir of Thornfield Hall, Bertha has no role to play in Jane Eyre's story, other than as a mad—and thus irrelevant—figure whose presence is necessary to the gothic atmosphere of Brontë's novel and whose death is mandated by the romance plot.

In *Jane Eyre,* the history of Mr. Rochester's first wife is offered in a brief explanatory narrative after he is confronted in church by his brother-in-law, Richard Mason, as he is to be wed to Jane. Bertha is presented as the Creole heiress he weds in return for her fortune of £30,000 (a significant amount with its burden of betrayal) after his father and brother have unfairly left him financially adrift. His discovery of Bertha's inherited madness, which her family has concealed from him until it is too late, destroys any affection he has felt for her. Her increasingly erratic and violent behavior leads him to lock her up in the attic of Thornfield Hall under the care of the mysterious Grace Poole.

Rhys built the plot of her novel on the skeleton of that brief narrative, bringing to life the details of Mr. Rochester's sojourn in the West Indies and allowing the silenced and shadowy West Indian character of Jane Eyre to tell her story in her own words. The primary setting of *Wide Sargasso Sea,* then, will be the West Indies (parts 1 and 2), where we read about events that take place during the years Jane Eyre spends at school, before her arrival at Thornfield Hall; the secondary setting will be that of Thornfield Hall, as Bertha, renamed Antoinette by Jean Rhys, tells of her confinement in the cold attic and her longing to return home (part 3). This section contains some scenes familiar to readers of *Jane Eyre,* but here they are described through the eyes of Bertha/Antoinette.

Part 1 recounts Bertha/Antoinette's childhood to the moment she learns of her prospective marriage to the character we assume to be the Mr. Rochester of *Jane Eyre*—but who remains nameless in *Wide Sargasso Sea.* It is set in Jamaica, in her late father's Coulibri estate, and in nearby Spanish Town, the capital of the island from 1534 to 1872, where Antoinette goes to school and where she eventually meets her future husband. Coulibri, the name for the West Indian crested hummingbird, was also the name of a sugar estate in Rhys's native Dominica, near her family's old estate, Geneva. Part 1 is narrated by Antoinette herself, which allows Rhys to convey the idiosyncrasies of her character's personality as well as the cadences of creolized English.

Part 2—which follows the married couple's inauspicious honeymoon—is set in an unnamed Windward island easily recognizable as Dominica, especially after the mention of the village of Massacre, located on the leeward coast of Dominica and known as the site of the murder in 1674 of Thomas "Indian" Warner, the half-Carib son of Sir Thomas Warner (one of the most prominent figures in the early settlement of the Windward and Leeward islands) and the party of approximately 70 Caribs in his company. The description of the honeymoon cottage at Granbois (Grand Forest), a house inherited from Antoinette's mother, follows that of the small Amalia estate owned by Rhys's father and located north of the Dominican capital, Roseau.

Part 2—narrated by Antoinette's unnamed husband (to which I will refer here as Mr. Rochester, as has become customary in discussions of the novel)—captures his bewilderment at the profusion of nature, the Creole language he does not understand, the island's pervasive sensuality, the baffling stranger he has just married, and above all a culture that seems mysterious and frightening and that includes Obeah potions and spells.

The historical setting of *Wide Sargasso Sea* differs from that of *Jane Eyre*. Whereas the events of the latter take place between 1798 and 1808 (the novel is narrated by Jane around 1819), Rhys sets her story some 20 years later, so as to coincide with the aftermath of the emancipation of slavery in the Caribbean. The Slavery Abolition Act of 1833 declared that all slaves in the British Empire would be emancipated as of August 1834, but would remain indentured to their former masters until 1838. Within this chronology, Mr. Rochester marries Antoinette sometime in the early 1840s. The historical shift allows Rhys to incorporate into her narrative the uncertainty of the socioeconomic upheaval caused by emancipation in Jamaican plantation society. It also allows her to build the details of Antoinette's family background on her own family history. The avowed model for the character of Antoinette's father, Mr. Cosway, Rhys's maternal great grandfather, had died in 1837, and Rhys models the pivotal scene in part 1, where Coulibri is attacked by its former slaves, on a similar attack on her family's Geneva estate in 1844, after a census was taken that led to fears that slavery was about to be reinstituted.

The novel's opening sets up the racial and class parameters that constrain Antoinette's troubled childhood. The trouble that has come is that of emancipation, which left many of the former sugar estates in ruins and halted production in all but the most prosperous plantations. The Coulibri estate had fallen into decay without able management after her father's death, and the compensation promised to the planters for the loss of their slave property was left unpaid in countless cases. Mr. Lutrell's suicide, and the abandonment of his estate, is presented here as representative of the extreme dejection faced by planters, who saw estates held in the family for generations destroyed by emancipation.

Financially ruined, since the former slaves had withdrawn into sullen hostility, Antoinette and her mother are marooned and fearful for their safety. They are also shunned by white society because the Jamaican ladies do not approve of her mother, "a Martinique girl." Martinique, as a French territory, belonged to the rival camp in the ever lasting hostilities between the French and the British in the Caribbean. Martinican society, moreover, was considered more lenient in matters of interracial marriage than the British colonies, and the possibility of racial mixture was always present when prejudices against the French were aired. The possibility of an interracial relationship with her cousin Sandi, which opens for Antoinette after her marriage collapses, so horrifies Rochester that it leads directly to her imprisonment in the attic of Thornfield Hall.

The characters that surround Antoinette in her isolation at Coulibri help foster the colonial gothic atmosphere of the narrative of her life at the estate. Her mother, driven into paranoia by the loss of her former comforts and the hostility that surrounds her—here exemplified by the jeering of the blacks as she goes out riding in her now threadbare clothing and by the poisoning of her horse—seems incapable of offering her daughter a sense of order and stability. She is described as growing "thin and silent" (9) and finally refusing to leave the house. Rhys will develop the theme of maternal rejection as one of the central leitmotifs of her novel, from her mother's acting in the early pages of the novel as if Antoinette were "useless to her" (9), to her violent rejection during their last encounter, when the mother has already succumbed to madness. The rejection of Antoinette is exacerbated by the mother's preference for her younger child Pierre, who suffers from some developmental condition that makes him stagger when he walks and does not allow him to speak distinctly.

The mother's nervous condition—which will later be attributed to inherited madness—is exacerbated here by racial tensions. "The Lord make no distinction between black and white, black and white the same for Him," her servant Godfrey lectures her (10). This claim of equality, one of the most immediate changes brought about by emancipation, represents for former plantation mistresses like her a complete social upheaval. Not so for her daughter Antoinette, whose has found in Christophine, a former Martinican slave given to her mother as a wedding present, the emotional anchor and mothering she needs. Christophine's presence in the household, nonetheless, contributes to the family's isolation. Her intense blackness—she is described as "blue-black"—is meant to identify her firmly with an equally intense Africanness that terrifies those around them because she is associated with the magicoreligious practices of Obeah.

Race is the pivotal element in Antoinette's world, more powerful than class in determining relationships and establishing community. Antoinette internalizes, like her mother does, the hatred implicit in their being called "white cockroaches" now that they are no longer rich and powerful. For the character, the change brought about by emancipation is articulated most eloquently by nature running rampant after being held under tight control by the structures of the plantation. The family's garden is now an overgrown space gone wild; and although she compares it to the Garden of Eden, it is a space full of orchids with long tentacles and a sweet and strong smell that terrifies her. The estate, like the garden, has gone to bush, erasing the marks of the plantation.

The taunting of Antoinette as a white cockroach belongs to this new social and economic landscape, and Antoinette accepts the justice of it, being able to place herself in the shoes of those who feel themselves finally able to taunt. This is perhaps what makes her deep friendship with Tia possible since Antoinette must accept Tia's impulse to strike back at whites, including, on occasion, her friend. The friendship with Tia is seminal to Antoinette's ability to recover some of the joys of childhood—swimming in the bathing pool, boiling green bananas in an old iron pot, drying herself in the sun. It is also the source of rejection as it cannot transcend the constraints of their race and class barriers to true understanding. Tia, in fact, is Antoinette's chief taunter, mocking her for her family's loss of wealth and class status after emancipation: "Old time white people nothing but white nigger now, and black nigger better than white people" (14).

Antoinette's life at Coulibri is changed by the arrival of new occupants at the neighboring estate, Nelson's Rest, whose previous owner, Mr. Lutrell, has committed suicide in the first page of the novel. Lutrell's heirs bring into her mother's life a Mr. Mason, who is to become Antoinette's stepfather. He and the Lutrells are representative of a new kind of planter, entrepreneurs who came to the West Indies to take advantage of the general economic collapse that followed emancipation and who bought bankrupt estates at very low prices. Rhys establishes a distinction in the novel between the former slave masters and the new ones in terms of class origin and familiarity with the West Indies. The old plantation masters belonged to a higher social class and had been in the West Indies for generations. Although the plantation system they had instituted ended with the Emancipation Act, the new ones presided over a new system that was not necessarily an improvement: "The new ones have Letter of the Law. Same thing. They got magistrate. They got fine. They got jail house and chain gang. . . . New ones worse than old ones—more cunning, that's all" (15).

The Mr. Mason that will become Antoinette's stepfather belongs to the "new ones," as the commercial exchange that is Antoinette's marriage to Rochester will attest. The Mr. Mason of *Wide Sargasso Sea,* however, represents a departure from Brontë's text, where the character was Bertha's biological father. Rhys gives Antoinette a different biological father—the Mr. Cosway who belonged to the former plantation masters—which allows her to incorporate the differences between pre- and post-emancipation plantation society into her text. The addition of Mr. Cosway also allows Rhys to develop two family lines—the English family represented by Mr. Mason and his son Richard and the mulatto family that is the result of Mr. Cosway's liaisons with several black mistresses. Members of this colored family—Sandi and Daniel Cosway—feature prominently in the plot of the novel.

The marriage of Antoinette's mother with Mr. Mason has ambiguous repercussions for the narrator. It brings her family financial stability and renewed contact with her aunt Cora, who tries to become Antoinette's protector. It also, however, brings her into closer contact with the white ladies of Jamaica who had shunned her mother while they were marooned at Coulibri. And it brings recurrent nightmares that foreshadow her sad fate in the hands of her future husband. The contact with the taunting ladies will have dire ramifications since it is through them that Antoinette hears for the first time that Christophine is thought to be an Obeahwoman. The implication is that Antoinette's mother used her services to secure the magic or potions to ensnare Mr. Mason—thus providing an explanation as to why the unbalanced and bankrupt woman could catch "a very wealthy man who could take his pick of all the girls in the West Indies" (17). The realization that Christophine practices Obeah—not a religion as such, but a system of beliefs rooted in Creole notions of spirituality that acknowledges the existence and power of the supernatural world and incorporates into its practices witchcraft, sorcery, magic, spells, and healing (Frye 198)—forever changes the way Antoinette perceives her beloved Coulibri.

The arrival of the Lutrells into Coulibri—and by extension Mr. Mason—is greeted by Christophine with dread: "Trouble walk into the house this day," she says. "Trouble walk in" (15). It also prompts the first of Antoinette's recurring dreams, in which she is walking in the forest being pursued by "someone who hated [her]" and whose footsteps kept coming closer (15). Antoinette's relationship to Coulibri, as Rhys develops it throughout the book, is the fundamental relationship in her life, hence the importance of the change brought about by discovering Christophine's links to Obeah, which introduces an element of fear into Antoinette's connection to the estate to which she believes she emotionally belongs. Rhys will develop this element of fear through the central sequence of part 1—the attack and burning of Coulibri—which is the longest sustained narrative in this part of the novel.

The destruction of Coulibri is the pivotal moment in the development of Antoinette as a character, as it leads to the destruction of her home—literally an expulsion from paradise—and to the death of her brother and, eventually, her mother, who loses her reason as a result of the shock. Rhys constructs the attack episode carefully, developing Antoinette's and her mother's growing fear through the gap between their perception of the former slaves' mood and Mr. Mason's lack of understanding, as "one of the new ones" who now own plantations in the West Indies but have no insight into its peoples or cultures. "You don't like, or even recognize, the good in them," his wife tells him, "And you won't believe in the other side" (19). The episode offers a number of examples of this gap in understanding, from Mr. Mason not seeing the danger of speaking before the servants about importing indentured servants from the East Indies to work the fields now that slavery is over, to his wife not realizing the danger of leaving Pierre in the servant's care until he is almost burned alive. Antoinette understands the situation as stemming from their renewed wealth—and the renewed fear of oppression it brings with it:

The black people did not hate us quite so much when we were poor. We were white but we had not escaped and soon we would be dead for we had no money left. What was there to hate? (20)

The narrative of the attack itself plays on a number of intertwined themes: Mr. Mason's bewilderment and belated surprise at his own misjudgment of the situation; his wife Annette's increasing hysteria as she grows aware of Pierre's danger and of the betrayal implicit in the attack; the courage of the two servants who remain loyal; and Aunt Cora's summoning of the authority of the old planters—whose class and mores she represents—to extricate them from the riot, although even she cannot save the house. Antoinette's lucid description of events—which contrasts sharply with her assertion that she "was so shocked that everything was confused" (22)—includes the poignant burning of the parrot, symbolic of bad luck and in that sense a distraction for the mob, but also a scene that will reverberate for Antoinette, as the parrot's cries are what she will recall her mother crying in her madness.

The poignant ending of the narrative of the attack is built on a crucial encounter between Tia and Antoinette that encapsulates the latter's feelings of desolation and will be echoed at the novel's end. The passage demonstrates the ambiguity in the feelings of the erstwhile friends, divided by class and race—and thus forced to side with their own at moments like this—yet connected by a friendship that transcends race and class. The impossibility of such relations across race and class will reverberate through Antoinette's remaining time in the West Indies, becoming in turn the tragic force behind her ultimate self-destruction. On being attacked by Tia as they are leaving Coulibri, Antoinette will see her friend's face as in a mirror: "We stared at each other, blood on my face, tears on her. It was as if I saw myself. Like in a looking-glass" (27).

The aftermath of the burning of Coulibri finds Antoinette settled at Aunt Cora's house after a long illness and would at first seem to indicate that her emotional recovery will match her physical healing. There is a meeting with her mother—now living in isolation in the country—in which Annette physically rejects her daughter by flinging her against a partition. But most of the remaining portion of part 1 is devoted to Antoinette's education in the convent school, where she remains for a time as a boarder. The convent school, modeled after the Convent School in Roseau, Dominica, that Rhys attended and where she spent some of the happiest times of her childhood, becomes for Antoinette a "refuge." Antoinette writes of her classmates that "they are safe" and have no notion of "what it can be like *outside*" (35). The school attended by Antoinette, Mount Calvary Convent, is named after the Mother Superior of the Roseau school, to whom Rhys became very attached.

The Convent School sequence begins and ends with two scenes of thematic significance. The first, where two children are waiting for Antoinette as she leaves Aunt Cora's house for school, threatens to turn her again into a victim of taunting and bullying by black children. She is rescued from this predicament by her "cousin" Sandi Cosway (the son of her illegitimate and colored half-brother Alexander, and as such Antoinette's half-nephew), who promises—and has the power to—stop the harassment altogether. Sandi's measure of power in the society of Spanish Town stems from his father's commercial interests and is typical of the established colored class in West Indian societies of the early twentieth century. It also establishes Sandi as the possible knight in shining armor that can become Antoinette's protector since the character's development points to the need for such a firm protective hand to ensure her well-being.

Ironically, the chapter ends with a visit from her stepfather to announce that she will be returning home to live with him and Aunt Cora, and with intimations that he has tried to arrange for her happiness through marriage. The framing of this section of the narrative between these two possibilities of romance and male protection—Sandi and a future and yet unnamed husband—is of significance in Antoinette's characterization as someone in need of male protection (as a version of early-nineteenth-century womanhood) and of the emotional crisis that ensues when that protection is unavailable or withheld. It is not surprising, then, that the announcement of a possible suitor brings about the second of Antoinette's dreams, in a more ominous version that illustrates the character's fatalistic acceptance of her fate and foretells her imprisonment in the attic of Thornfield Hall. In this dream, she is walking in the forest wearing what appears to be a wedding dress ("white and beautiful"), while following a man whose "face [is] black with hatred" (36). Their destination is "an enclosed garden surrounded by a stone wall," where the trees "are different trees" (36). And she knows it will end "when I go up these steps. At the top" (36). The dream becomes intertwined with the memory of her mother's death in her own prison of madness and, as we will learn later, sexual abuse.

The dream will resonate with a theme of importance to Rhys—that of women's lack of control over their own fortunes and how this lack of control victimizes them and deprives them of self-determination. Annette had alluded to this when defending Aunt Cora from Mr. Mason's accusations that she had not helped them while they were marooned at Coulibri, claiming that "when [her husband] died not long ago she came home, before that what could she do? *She* wasn't rich" (18). This will be the thematic focus of part 2, where Aunt Cora will take Antoinette's stepbrother to task for handing Antoinette and her extensive fortune to Mr. Rochester without making any provision for her to have access to any of her money. It will also feature prominently in Christophine's struggle against Rochester to allow Antoinette to remain in Jamaica.

Part 2, narrated by Rochester, offers an account of his marriage to Antoinette, one characterized by ardent desire on his part but by what he acknowledges is a lack of love or tenderness toward her. Their relationship is fraught with cultural misunderstandings that have at their root racial misconceptions on his part. He distrusts Antoinette's whiteness since to him she appears foreign, unknowable, and—as a West Indian—of questionable race: "Long, sad, dark alien eyes. Creole of pure English descent she may be, but they are not English or European" (39). Through his narrative, Rhys builds on the notion of Antoinette's whiteness being compromised or tainted by her close emotional connection to Christophine and other blacks, her colored family, her command of what he terms "the debased French patois" (53), and the ease with which she can insert herself into Creole culture. This distrust is exacerbated by his discomfort as they move away from the urban spaces of Spanish Town (where he has been ill with fever) to the wilderness that surrounds them at Granbois in the "wild but menacing" environment of Dominica, a "beautiful place—wild, untouched, above all untouched" (51). Dominica, still the most unspoiled of all Caribbean islands, is an environment where all the features characteristic of the West Indian landscape seem magnified: the mountains are taller, the rains more forceful, the ravines deeper. The interior is covered in thick, almost impenetrable tropical rain forests and vegetation grown in a profusion of greens. Rochester, in his narrative, seems overwhelmed by the almost Edenic nature surrounding them at Granbois: "Too much blue, too much purple, too much green. The flowers too red, the mountains too high, the hills too near" (41).

Part 2 includes a brief flashback that narrates the events of the day before the wedding, when Antoinette had sent word with her stepbrother that she could not go ahead with the ceremony. There are three thematic strands in this brief section that bring greater coherence to part 2 of the novel. One is the notion that blacks are more observant than whites and can discern hypocrisy and lies more readily than whites. Aware that he is merely playing the part of a lover, since he is about to marry a girl he does not know entirely for her fortune, Rochester does not perceive any disbelief from whites, hence his feeling, when surrounded by blacks at Granbois, that they can see through him, that he is exposed before them. The second is Rochester's fear of being made a laughingstock by Antoinette's refusal to marry him, which points to vanity and an excessive concern for what others think of him. The fear that "this would indeed make a fool of me" (46) pervades his attitude of slight paranoia toward all those whom he feels are watching him at Granbois. The third is that of the bargain that he makes with Antoinette, which will be the source of his greatest betrayal of her. She agrees to the wedding after he declares that "I'll trust you if you'll trust me" after she inquires whether he can give her peace (47).

Rochester's initial fascination with Antoinette is physical, built on an identification between her and the wild nature that surrounds them. She is to him like the night-blooming moonflowers, like someone who has slept too long in the moonlight. He is as fascinated by her as he is by the bathing pool where he stayed for hours, "unwilling to leave the river, the trees shading it, the flowers that opened at night" (47). The notion of the surrounding nature being "untouched" is part of its appeal. The crisis in the marriage arrives precisely when he begins to mistrust the untouched quality of both nature and Antoinette and his jealousy, possessiveness, and sense of having been made a fool of surface.

The first indication of trouble comes when, confronted with a large crab in the bathing pool, she throws a large pebble at it "like a boy, with a sure graceful movement" (52). To his inquiries, she replies that "Sandi taught me, a boy you never met" (52). A more serious threat to his comfort and vanity is the letter she receives from a man claiming to be Antoinette's colored half-brother, Daniel Cosway. He destroys Rochester's peace of mind by preying precisely on those fears he had unveiled throughout the earlier part of his narrative: that he has been deceived by the Mason family and therefore been made a laughingstock by being tricked into marrying the daughter of a lunatic and a philandering drunk; that he has been bewitched by the beauty of his wife, awakening fears of Obeah; that his wife had loved and may have been intimate with her "cousin" Sandi, who is "more handsome than any white man" (75). Like Rochester's Iago, Daniel Cosway destroys his victim's peace of mind.

Once his mind has been poisoned against Antoinette, Rochester ceases to find beauty in the surrounding landscape, and when he gets lost in the forest he felt "lost and afraid among the enemy trees" (62). The sense of a profound change in him sends Antoinette to ask for Christophine's help just as he sits at home reading a book about Vodou and Obeah. Rhys inserts Antoinette's narrative of her conversation with Christophine into part 2 (otherwise narrated by Rochester) since the scene is crucial to the progress of the narrative and is outside the scope of what Rochester can witness. Christophine's advice is to leave him (to go to Martinique, as Christophine suggests, or to England, as Antoinette hopes) and make a new life for herself, unaware of the English law that hands a husband complete control of his wife's fortune. An heiress before her marriage, Antoinette is now powerless to leave her husband because she no longer has any money of her own. Her narrative recalls overhearing a quarrel between her stepbrother Richard and Aunt Cora about his allowing Antoinette to marry without a settlement that would legally protect her fortune. Christophine agrees to give Antoinette what she desires—a potion that will reawaken Rochester's passion, at least for one night—in exchange for Antoinette trying to explain to her husband, calmly and rationally, the truth about her family, around which Daniel Cosway had built such lies.

Christophine's love potion leads to a night of violent passion, but also to Rochester's greatest betrayal of Antoinette's trust. Their attempt at conversation leads nowhere, as he doubts her version of events and she realizes that talk can change nothing between them. Her story of the sexual abuse of her mother that she witnessed in her last visit repels him, and he never again refers to her as Antoinette—a name she shared with her mother—but rechristens her Bertha, a rechristening that becomes his first attempt at erasing her true self. Their night of love leaves him hating Antoinette, and he seeks to punish her for what he sees as her betrayal in giving him a potion by making love to her servant Amélie within Antoinette's hearing. This violation of their agreement to trust each other brings Antoinette to the verge of madness, not because of Amélie, she claims, but because he has violated Granbois, a place she had loved.

Through the slow disintegration of the marriage that follows, we see Rochester through the eyes of Christophine and, to a lesser extent, the rest of the servants, Amélie among them. Christophine sees him as a man who loves money above all: Rochester "can't see nothing else" (68). After he has made love to her within Antoinette's hearing, Amélie tells him that she is sorry for him, "but I find it in my heart to be sorry for her too" (85). Christophine, who looks after Antoinette after she leaves the house at Granbois, seeks to bargain with him so he can return to England and leave Antoinette behind, but her mention of the possibility that Antoinette may remarry if he leaves her awakens his jealousy. In Christophine's eyes, however, Rochester is a villain that will do anything to secure Antoinette's money: "It is in your mind to pretend that she is mad. I know it. The doctors say what you tell them to say" (96). At this juncture, as at other crucial moments of betrayal in the text, a cock crows to signal the moment of treachery. To accomplish her separation from Christophine, he threatens her with an accusation to the police. Here, as right on his arrival at Granbois, Rochester writes in bitterness to his father, reproaching him for what they have gotten him involved with. His plan, which mirrors Christophine's charge, is to take Antoinette to Spanish Town, to a house with two separate suites of rooms, and live the kind of separate lives that will ultimately destroy his wife, and where he knows he will be the object of mockery. His ultimate goal, however, is to lock her into the room in the attic at Thornfield Hall.

The last section of Rochester's narrative narrates in detail their departure from Granbois, which he intends to sell, as his ownership of what used to be her property gives him a right to do. His description offers a portrait of Antoinette as having assumed a frozen smile that masks her inner turmoil, her understanding that she is now trapped, left without recourse other than, like in her dream, to follow Rochester through the path that leads to her destruction. Her recurrent dream here becomes a reality. For Rochester, the will to control her seems nurtured by hatred and sexual jealousy.

Part 3 brings us back to locales and scenes we recognize from Brontë's *Jane Eyre*. Its opening paragraphs are narrated by Brontë's character Grace Poole, Bertha's nurse at Thornfield Hall, who makes reference to two other characters from *Jane Eyre,* Mrs. Eff (Mrs. Fairfax) and Leah. Grace's role as narrator is that of summarizing very briefly the events that followed Rochester and Antoinette's departure from Granbois—his writing to engage a nurse and his travels through Europe to forget. Mrs. Eff summarizes the changes that his West Indian adventure has brought on him thus: "He was gentle, generous, brave. His stay in the West Indies has changed him out of all knowledge. He has grey in his hair and misery in his eyes" (105).

Antoinette's narrative tells of how she is trying to determine what she has been brought to this cold and damp place to do. "What is it that I must do?"

she repeatedly asks. She also asks who she is since Antoinette began to erase away when he started calling her Bertha, and "I saw Antoinette drifting with her scents, her pretty clothes and her looking glass" (107). Her recollections of coming to England, "this cardboard world," are vague memories of cold and pain, but they are at times interrupted and incoherent. She does not remember, for example, Richard Mason's visit, and has to be told by Grace Poole of how she attacked him with a knife and bit him. She recalls, however, seeing the unnamed girl (Jane Eyre) in the passage and the red dress she was wearing when she last saw Sandi and he had asked her to come away with him.

When writing about Antoinette's fate, Rhys uses dreams to foretell what will happen to the character. The ending of *Wide Sargasso Sea* builds on these dreams, while pulling together the threads of Antoinette's earlier narrative. A dream in her cold attic traces for her the path she must follow to fulfill her destiny at Thornfield Hall—a destiny already written for her in her master narrative, that of Charlotte Brontë's *Jane Eyre,* and which requires that she burn down the mansion and leap from the upper ramparts to her death. In Antoinette's dream, however, she takes flight over the ramparts to return to Coulibri and her happy days with Tia, and the dream points to the answer to her question about the purpose of her being there.

Chapter 15

Simone Schwarz-Bart's

The Bridge of Beyond

Simone Schwarz-Bart was born in 1938 in Charente-Maritime, on the west coast of France, to Guadeloupean parents (a soldier and his teacher wife). Her parents returned to Guadeloupe in 1943, when she was five. Her childhood years, spent in Guadeloupe under the Vichy regime, were marred by an Allied blockade that led to severe food shortages on the island. Her father, a soldier with the Free French soldiers, was away during most of her childhood.

Schwarz-Bart studied in Pointe-à-Pitre, the Guadeloupean capital, and at the universities of Paris and Dakar (Senegal). In 1959, while a student in Paris, she met her future husband and collaborator, André Schwarz-Bart (1928–2006), a Jewish writer and former member of the French Resistance who had lost his parents during the Holocaust. He had just published *Le Dernier des justes (The Last of the Just)*, the story of a Jewish family spanning almost 10 centuries, regarded by many critics as one of the finest literary works of the post–World War II period. They married in 1961, the same year in which André won the coveted Prix Goncourt for his novel, and spent the early years of their marriage in Senegal, where their oldest son was born. They subsequently lived in France, Switzerland, and Guadeloupe, where Simone ran a home furnishings shop at Pointe-à-Pitre, "Tim, Tim," and later, a Creole restaurant. Their son Jacques, born in 1962 in Les Abymes (Guadeloupe), is a noted and innovative New York–based jazz saxophonist and composer known popularly as "Brother Jacques."

Together, Simone and André Schwarz-Bart embarked on a remarkable collaboration that they hoped would produce a cycle of seven novels narrating the history of the French Antilles from slavery to the present. They completed only two books together. The first, *Un Plat de Porc aux Bananes Vertes* (A Dish of Pork with Green Bananas) (1967) tells the story of Mariotte, an old Martinican woman living in an asylum for the elderly in Paris, who speaks of her alienation from French society and nostalgia for her Caribbean past. It was followed in 1972 by *La Mulâtresse Solitude (A Woman Named Solitude)* (1972), the story of a Guadeloupean slave in the late eighteenth century. *A Woman Named Solitude* initially listed only André as author, while the English translation listed Simone as a coauthor. The coauthorship has been accepted as the accurate reflection of their collaboration on the novel.

In 1972 Simone published the first of her two novels as sole author, *Pluie et Vent sur Télumée Miracle (The Bridge of Beyond)*, the story of three generations of Guadeloupean women who work on the cane fields while developing the knowledge of curative herbs and supernatural phenomena that makes them powerful healers. It was followed in 1979 by *Ti Jean L'Horizon (Between Two Worlds)*, the magic-realist narrative of the adventures of a Caribbean mythological hero. In 1987 Simone published a one-act play that has enjoyed significant success, *Ton beau capitaine (Your Handsome Captain)*, about the "niggers of the niggers," the exploited Haitian workers who migrate to Guadeloupe to cut cane and constitute an oppressed and denigrated class.

In 1989 André and Simone Schwarz-Bart published a six-volume work, *Homage à la Femme Noire* (In Praise of Women of Color), an encyclopedic work that recovers the silenced history and achievements of the women of the African diaspora. Neither has published any fiction or drama since then, although rumors abound about numerous unpublished manuscripts by both writers. André died in Guadeloupe in 2006 from complications after surgery to repair a heart ailment.

The Bridge of Beyond

Simone Schwarz-Bart's first novel *Pluie et vent sur Telumée Miracle* (literally, Rain and Wind on Telumée the Miracle Woman), a tale set on the island of Guadeloupe, traces the stories of five generations of the Loungador women from the period just following the emancipation of slaves in 1848 to the mid-twentieth century. It is set in a remote settlement in the northeast corner of Basse Terre, near the village of La Ramée. Through a focus on two of the Loungador women—Toussine, known as "Queen without a Name," and her granddaughter Telumée—Schwarz-Bart weaves a narrative that is above all a homage to the hidden strength and the power to endure through adversity of poor and exploited women who are sustained by their connection to the land and to the world of the spirits.

The novel—which is told in the first person by the central character, Telumée—is divided into two parts. Part 1 ("My People") consists of two chapters and focuses on the story of the narrator's grandmother, Toussine Loungador, who is honored by her community with the name of "Queen without a Name" for the strength with which she confronted multiple misfortunes. Part 2 ("The Story of My Life"), which is divided into 15 chapters, tells Telumée's own story of hardship and pain and of how she rises above her troubles with the help of Ma Cia, a healer with powers bestowed on her by the spirit world. The narrative underscores the vital link between grandmother and granddaughter—a connection rooted in African-derived cultural practices and spiritual values—that establishes a continuity of traits and experiences that will ultimately help Telumée rise above her sufferings and degradation.

The novel is told in Schwarz-Bart's own recreation of the French Creole language spoken by the peasantry of Guadeloupe, filled with proverbs and aphorisms that capture the dynamic, living philosophy of a nearly illiterate peasantry, whose wisdom is encapsulated in a richly nuanced linguistic tradition that borrows as much from French as from the African languages that plantation masters tried so hard to eradicate. The novel opens (part 1, chapter 1) as Telumée, aged and awaiting death, stands in her garden reminiscing of her grandmother Toussine Loungador and her "unshakable faith in life" (3). The tracing of Toussine's parentage allows Telumée to establish Guadeloupe's past of slavery as a presence that continues to rule over the life of the local peasants. Her great grandmother Minerva, a former slave with roots in the town of L'Abandonnée, a settlement of runaway slaves, is linked to the struggle against slavery and to the Maroon communities that played an important role in the preservation of African culture and religious practices. Her great grandfather's abandonment of Minerva during her pregnancy allows Schwarz-Bart to incorporate into the text the strength of the ancestral spirits who accompanied the enslaved peoples from Africa, here exemplified by the strength of Xango, the man who rescues her from her perceived shame. Xango's presence in the text functions as an avatar of his namesake, the Yoruba spirit of thunder and lightning and one of the most popular of the African orishas or *lwa* in Afro-Caribbean religion.

The story of Toussine's youth—like that of her mother's life after meeting Xango—belongs to the storybook world of the fable, in which love ensnares humans like a spell, plunging them into a sweet dream blessed by the sunshine. Like in the fairy tale, this Maroon world—set apart from the evils of slavery and the plantation—where Jeremiah had lived "hearing the sound of the waves in his ears" (4) and where Toussine was charmed by her lover's "satiny, iridescent skin" (7), is threatened by jealousy and resentment, forces that prove more powerful than witchcraft in bringing bad luck into Toussine's and Jeremiah's lives.

The notion of bad luck deployed by Schwarz-Bart in the description of the downturn in Toussine and Jeremiah's fortunes is one closely linked to African-derived Caribbean practices, which include a belief that third parties can in various ways determine an individual's luck. The novel depicts ill fortune as "that madwoman bad luck" (11). Here the community's jealousy stems primarily from other women and is based on the importance marital status conveys on Toussine. It is seen as stemming from her possessing "some unique and exceptional quality" (7), which will ultimately take racial overtones. Years of moderate prosperity for Toussine and Jeremiah lead the community to question whether they think "all these things make them white" (11), positing the basis of their malice as being grounded on social hierarchies born out of the evils of plantation life. The narrator, Telumée, will seek to distance the reader from the community's ill will by explaining the true foundation of this prosperity: Jeremiah worked with "enormous patience" so that he never brought back an empty boat, and would tend his garden with Toussine in harmony with themselves and nature. "While he dug, she would mark out the rows; while he burned weeds, she would sow" (9).

This harmonious life, when it comes tragically to an end with the burning to death of one of Toussine and Jeremiah's daughters and the destruction of their house, is seen by the community as "poetic justice"—a catastrophe that matches in its magnitude the happiness and prosperity they had enjoyed beforehand. It is ushered in, as many events central to the plot are, by a proverbial statement: "Woe to him who laughs once and gets in the habit, for the wickedness of life is limitless" (11). It encapsulates a philosophy of life borne out of the oppressive conditions of slavery, which, in postslavery Guadeloupe, still limits the possibilities for fulfillment and happiness open to the peasantry of villages like L'Abandonnée. The text underscores the reality that the attainment of the sort of middle-class status achieved by Toussine and Jeremiah continues to be impossible for the island's peasantry and is still considered a status open only to whites or light-skinned people.

It is Toussine's rising from the embers of this tragic conflagration, wounded in spirit but ready to face her adversity and nurture a new daughter, Victory, which reverses the community's jealousy and makes them confer on her the heroic appellation of "Queen without a Name." She becomes, in her triumph against misfortune, "a bit of the world, a whole country, a plume of a Negress" (14). The tale of Toussine offers a paradigm of Guadeloupean womanhood that is also linked to a notion of nationhood; the narrator will measure her own struggle against "that madwoman bad luck" throughout her own life.

Chapter 2 of part 1 focuses on the death of Telumée's father. Unlike Toussine and Jeremiah's life together, which is portrayed as disconnected from the world or the plantation—Edenic in its isolation, except for the community's ingrown malice—Victory and Angebert's lives revolve around the seasonal cycle of sugar cultivation and are at the mercy of its patterns of oppression. The confrontation that ends with Angebert's death comes directly out of the despair that follows the end of the harvest, when the peasants were "reduced to eating roots from the forest" and relied on catching crayfish (21). Germain is hurled by his madness into the murder of Angebert, someone who had attempted to survive in the world of the plantation by "effacing himself" and not offering "the slightest resistance" (23).

Part 2, "The Story of My Life," opens with Telumée's leaving L'Abandonnée after her mother finds love and passion with a Carib from the Côte-sous-levent, the western coast of Basse Terre in Guadeloupe. Sent to live with her grandmother Toussine and her old friend Ma Cia, Telumée crosses the Bridge of Beyond (which gives its name to the English translation of the novel) into a life steeped in the narrative traditions of Guadeloupe. From Queen without a Name and Ma Cia, Telumée will learn the tales, legends, and songs of the Guadeloupean past, especially of its history of slavery and its impact on the peasantry. As Gil Zehava Hochberg argues, "It is the mystery of the images circulating in the stories that compels Télumée to later re-inscribe these images 'back' into history, understood *not* as the story of the past, but as the hidden reality of the present" (6).

In chapter 1 of part 2, Telumée's life with Queen without a Name brings her directly into the world of the plantation, where she joins the "little bands" of children that follow in the wake of cane workers doing menial jobs for little pay. It also brings her into a world where wisdom is conveyed through song. The chapter works through a succession of songs that encompass true and false wisdom, from the painful songs of the cane fields, through "beguines from the old days" (30), slow mazurkas, waltzes, and slave laments. The songs are meant to teach Telumée to disregard the laundry women's view of life as "a torn garment, an old rag beyond all mending"—to look on their pessimism as "null and void" (30). This pessimism, rooted in the daily experience of the sugar plantation, brings darkness into Telumée's life, leaving her hoping for some path out of the life history has imposed on blacks. As the distilled essence of Toussine's own experience with adversity and tragedy, the wisdom of these songs is summed up in her advice to Telumée about the three paths to be avoided in life: "to see the beauty of the world and call it ugly, to get up early to do what is impossible, and to let oneself be carried away by dreams" (30).

Toussine's advice is echoed in chapter 2 of part 2, when the focus shifts to Ma Cia, who encourages Telumée to be "a real drum with two sides" (39) and foretells that the young girl will "rise over the earth like a cathedral" (35). Ma Cia, respected and feared as a witch by her community, is a practitioner of Quimbois, a variation of West Indian Obeah. Like Obeah, it represents "a set of practices related to magic and sorcery with roots in African religiosity" (Olmos and Paravisini-Gebert 150). Quimboiseurs like Ma Cia are herbalists by training and function primarily as

healers and counselor with powers to call upon the supernatural, for good or evil, to help the living reach their goals and settle disputes. They can read the past, present, and future through divination practices such as interpreting the patterns of flames or the designs made by melting candlewax. They use magic to solve problems of the heart, help with business decisions, and prescribe treatments for physical maladies. (Olmos and Paravisini-Gebert 151)

Ma Cia, as her conversations with Toussine reveal in the text, is also skilled in interpreting dreams, forecasting the future, and communicating with the dead, as she does nightly with her now dead husband, Jeremiah. Her intentional spilling of some of her gravy onto the ground is part of an African-derived practice throughout the Caribbean of making an offering to the earth, where the spirits of the ancestors reside. (The relationship with the African spirits is one of reciprocity; they guide and protect the living, who in turn will feed them their favorite foods.) Ma Cia is also believed by the villagers to be able to leave her human form and fly about at night. This conviction, which Toussine dispels by reminding Telumée that the villagers come to Ma Cia for help with physical and spiritual complaints, is rooted in animistic notions of spirits who can live within animals or humans who can metamorphose into animals, usually to inflict harm on those venturing out at night. Stories of spirits and spells, which in Guadeloupe include legends of *soucouyants* (vampires), *dorlis* or *homes au baton* (who abuse women sexually while they sleep), and *djablesses* (who seductively lure men into harm), fascinate Telumée as a child and represent her entry into the supernatural world that will be part of her education in Fond Zombi.

Telumée's meeting with Ma Cia—together with her encounters with the residents of a village still fully dependent on the sugar plantation for their livelihood—underscores the permanence of the social, economic, and racial structures of Caribbean slavery. She would like to understand the "secret that enabled [the grown-ups] to stay on their feet all day without collapsing" (32), inquiring from Ma Cia about the nature of slavery: "What *is* a slave," she asks the old woman, "what *is* a master?" (37). The replies bring her for the first time to an understanding that "slavery was not some foreign country" but that it had happened in Guadeloupe and, more explicitly, in Fond Zombi.

Chapter 3 narrates Telumée's entry into puberty, which in the community of sugar cutters of Fond Zombi means that she becomes potential prey to the rampant sexual exploitation that is part of Guadeloupe's postslavery peasant society. Referring to the plantation foremen who were "connoisseurs of feminine flesh," Toussine vows that Telumée's 16 years were not going to be served up "as a dainty morsel for a foreman" (56). The sexual exploitation of young women in the cane fields has been a theme in a number of West Indian novels, as it is in Raphael Confiänt's *Mamzelle Dragonfly* (see chapter 6 in this volume). The tension in this chapter stems from the juxtaposition of the joy at Telumée's incipient womanhood (the neighboring women come to admire her budding breasts) and Toussine's efforts to keep her granddaughter "as white as a tuft of cotton" (42). The chapter, which opens with Victory's visit to Fond Zombi with news of her impending departure for Dominica with her Carib lover, looks at the fate of women who become too dependent on men for their sense of identity and self-esteem, like Victory, who comes "bearing about her the signs of love and its pangs" (40) and leaves everything behind to follow her Zambo-Carib (the child of a Carib Indian and someone of African descent), despite his womanizing ways. Her oldest daughter, Regina, in turn, trades her connection to her mother's family and traditional Guadeloupean culture to receive the kind of education to which Telumée has only limited access, make a respectable marriage in Basse-Terre, and become "an elegant lady" (41). These departures take them in a direction that is the very opposite of the one open to Telumée, who, on moving into Fond Zombi to live with her grandmother, has moved deeper into the African-derived core of French Antillean culture. She will move deeper still into this Guadeloupean hinterland before her destiny is accomplished.

Toussine's fears for Telumée as she reaches adolescence point to an understanding that the adversities women face—including those tied to the plantation system—are directly related to gender issues. In Telumée's understanding, men "broke bones and wombs" (44). At the center of Telumée's adolescent development is her relationship with Elie, the son of Old Abel the shopkeeper, through whom Schwarz-Bart explores the idyllic possibilities of adolescent love before sexual awareness surfaces. Their first meeting is full of sexual tension, of which the narrator declares herself unaware, "not suspecting [her] first star had appeared in the east" (43). Still children in the eyes of adults, their Thursday afternoons spent at the river leave them "floating in the air" (48). This poetic assessment of their time together, which underscores their innocence and pleasure in everyday things, parallels the Edenic moment that follows the creation of the world in the story Queen without a Name tells Telumée and Elie close to the end of the chapter, when newly created men "lifted their heads and saw a rosy sky, and were happy" (49). The tale of "The Man Who Tried to Live on Air," however, strikes a cautionary note that encapsulates Toussine's feelings about love becoming a woman's master: "the horse musn't ride you, you must ride it" (51).

In chapter 4, which opens with a reference to the start of Telumée's menstruation, she is introduced to the world of the zoreilles, the descendants of the white colonizers who still control most of the arable land and the wealth of Guadeloupe. Like in nearby Martinique, contemporary Guadeloupean society is still marked by social divisions stemming from plantation life, with the zoreilles, the large landowners, still controlling most of the best land, the light-skinned mulattos controlling the professional and merchant class, and the dark-skinned blacks still working the land or occupying the lower employment rungs in the tourist industry. To reach the town of Galba, where she is to work for the Desaragnes, Telumée has to cross the Bridge of Beyond.

The emotional, cultural, and economic distance she must traverse from one world to the other is narrated through the endless and desolate cane fields that separate her village from what is literally "another world" (58).

Her departure, prompted by their worsening destitution after Queen without a Name becomes ill and frail, is also ushered by her need to escape the cane fields, not only because of the sexual exploitation involved, but also because it only offers seasonal work and a future of continued exploitation. Elie, his hopes of a clerical job faded after the end of their substandard education, opts for the work of a tree sawyer. Telumée explores the world of servitude as an alternative to the plantation and to the fate of her peers, depicted here as prematurely pregnant, already "carrying before [them] a little calabash of trouble" (53).

Telumée's entry into the world of the zoreilles or Grand Békés allows Schwarz-Bart to address the racial prejudices characteristic of this class, which maintained its ascendancy until well into the twentieth century through its imposition of strict hierarchies based on the racist notions mouthed here by Madame Desaragne. Telumée's weapon against this world is to retreat into an inner world in which she is "like a pebble in the river just resting on the bottom" (60), hoping her new situation—being in a white world—will not come to master her.

Telumée's brief return to Fond Zombi, where the villagers are full of curiosity about the world in which she now lives, shows how her social status has risen as a result of this contact. As narrated in chapter 5, these returns are punctuated by Elie's growing resentment at the perceived freedom her employment and comparative prosperity gives her. His plans for their future together once he completes his apprenticeship as a sawyer and builds their new house are curiously overshadowed by a growing hostility that manifests itself through contempt for the work she does and pronouncements about his control over her. He describes her work—which for the villagers is symbolized by her ability to make excellent béchamel sauce—as "shaking the white men's doormats" (70) and jokingly refers to controlling the rope around her neck.

The rope will begin to shorten in chapter 6, which opens when Telumée, having reached her full bloom as a woman, must confront her master when he comes to her bedroom at night bearing gifts in exchange for what he expects will be sexual favors. Telumée, proving that the "Loungadors are not pedigree cocks…[but] fighting cocks" (80), fends him off. The episode, a de rigueur scene in novels about servant girls (black or white), signals the end of Telumée's servitude, as it comes right before the completion of the house Elie has been building for their life together.

Telumée's return to Fond Zombi to begin her life with Elie is marked by two ceremonies, one in which they consummate their relationship, the other a communal blessing of their home and new partnership that replaces a traditional marriage ceremony. The latter, which comes at the very center of the novel, is marred by several instances of foreshadowing that speak to the troubles to come for Telumée. From Elie's assertion that is it "a common sight, here in Fond Zombi, the sight of a man being transformed into a devil" (79), to Toussine's advise to Telumée to "find your woman's walk and change to a valiant step" (80), the chapter provides the pivotal move from adolescence to adulthood, from innocent strength to the sort of adversity for which Toussine has been educating Telumée throughout the first half of the novel.

Telumée's brief transition from total happiness to bourgeoning unhappiness takes place in chapter 7, which is constructed through parallels between her romance with Elie and that of her grandmother Toussine's with her husband, Jeremiah. The period when their love blossoms brings prosperity to the entire village: bananas grow aplenty, the sugar plantation expands and unemployment disappears, more houses are built so that Elie's lumber business prospers, and Toussine feels that "good luck had descended on [her] body and into [her] bones" (88), just like "a little wind of prosperity blew over the village" (90). Like in Toussine's own story, Telumée and Elie's happiness is threatened by gossip and jealousy, both stemming from Schwarz-Bart's understanding of Guadeloupe's peasant society as fundamentally patriarchal.

Schwarz-Bart had alluded to this patriarchal foundation and the ways in which it threatened Telumée's happiness earlier in the novel, when Telumée narrates the scene in which Elie describes his hold on her as a rope around her neck that he can tighten at will. In chapter 7, the villagers, jealous of their close attachment, goad him with the idea that Telumée is in control of their relationship, forcing him into a defense of his relationship and planting the seeds of resentment at being seen by the community as unmanned by his lover. Telumée, on her part, fears her erstwhile friend Letitia's growing hold on Elie and has to contend with a jealousy that "crept into the sea breeze" until her soul "could no longer find rest" (92).

These tensions come to full fruition in chapter 8, which opens ominously with Telumée's fears that her quick rise to perfect happiness will be paid for in misery of the acutest kind: "I was puzzled at having obtained, all at the same time, the three crowns that can usually be hoped for only at the end of a long life" (95). This preface to the narrative of Telumée's coming trials points to the biblical roots of the second part of the text, which draws on the book of Job to describe how Telumée's easily achieved prosperity—which incites, in this case, the jealousy and ill will of her neighbors—will be paid for in painful and humiliating trials that will bring her down to the edge of despair before she can rise again to her full womanhood.

Despite the biblical resonances of Telumée's forthcoming trials, *The Bridge of Beyond* is not a novel with an avowedly Christian foundation. Whereas spirituality plays a central role in the development of the characters and in their approach to life, the life of the spirit is modeled on creolized practices that blend Christian elements with African-derived beliefs. The latter is dominant in day-to-day life, although the community organizes socially around a Catholic church that draws them to worship on Sundays.

This blend of Christian and African-derived spiritual elements is evident in the conflation of notions of zombification and resurrection in chapter 8. Zombification—a process through which a person achieves a state similar to death, only to be brought back to life in a traumatized, so-called zombified state—is here presented as a metaphor for the mental, physical, and emotional collapse Telumée will undergo after Elie very publicly and humiliatingly forces her to leave their home to install Letitia in her place. Telumée's Job-like trial, which is represented here as a form of zombification—which leaves her with "half of [her] soul...broken and the other half debased" (112)—becomes a process from which she will emerge reborn.

Throughout the text, Schwarz-Bart identifies Guadeloupean identity with the strength of Afro-Caribbean women, whose power to endure stems from a history of survival through the Middle Passage, slavery, and the harshness of postslavery conditions for the peasantry in the region. In chapter 7, the community of Fond Zombi's prosperity was linked to Telumée's happiness with Elie; in chapter 8, the community shares Telumée's fate. As Telumée's spirit succumbs to the humiliation and ill treatment she receives from Elie, Fond Zombi becomes "like a desert": "Evil seemed to hang in the air, the only tangible thing there was" (97).

In chapter 9, which details Telumée's degradation, Schwarz-Bart explores the nature of gender relations among the peasantry in Guadeloupe, focusing on how they are dependent on economic conditions of oppression and lack of opportunity. Her mortification is shown as a process that parallels Elie's own collapse. Although Elie is the agent of Telumée's breakdown, he is himself a victim of the circumstances that control peasant life in Guadeloupe. As such, he is as much a victim of circumstances as Telumée is, although she is the only one of the characters willing to acknowledge her double victimization.

Chapter 10 narrates how Telumée is healed by the support of her community, which sees in her health and recovery the key to its own well-being. The chapter underscores the self-community-nation link that Schwarz-Bart has explored tangentially throughout the text and that makes of Telumée an emblem of Guadeloupean womanhood. It stresses the notion that true nationhood is linked to the peasantry, and especially to the strength of Creole peasant women. Here, her cure is depicted as "proof that a Negro has seven spleens" (115). In her description of Telumée's cure, Schwarz-Bart returns to the notion of life as a horse that must be controlled by the rider, which she introduced in chapter 3. Her community's support, Telumée explains, "helped to lift me back in the saddle, to hold my horse's bridle with a firm grip" (115). Telumée, in turn, gains stature as an emblem of her community, a model to be emulated.

Telumée's healing leads indirectly to the death of Queen without a Name, who, although frail and ill, remains in this life until assured that her granddaughter does not need her anymore. "Now that I've seen you suffer," Toussine tells Telumée, "I can close my eyes in peace" (120). She also points Telumée toward a new path, counseling her to leave Fond Zombi so that "the root of your luck will grow and bloom again" (117). That path, as Schwarz-Bart will develop in chapter 11, leads first toward the forest and the development of her spiritual powers with Ma Cia, and second to love again with Amboise.

Telumée's time with Ma Cia deepens the former's knowledge of "the secrets of plants," a central attribute of the Obeahwomen who fulfill the role of healers in the Caribbean. Her sufferings—and the way in which she has surmounted her troubles—are a sign that Telumée is ready for this level of initiation, through which she learns about the "human body, its centres, its weaknesses, how to rub it, how to get rid of faintness and tics and pains" (130). However, Ma Cia, unlike Telumée, has reached a moment in her life at which the burden of her community's history of oppression has grown too heavy to be borne. "We have been goods for auction," she tells Telumée, "and now we are left with fractured hearts" (130). Although Ma Cia has mastered the secrets of metamorphosing into a variety of animals and ultimately takes the shape of a dog permanently, Telumée refuses this knowledge, a refusal that points to a desire to remain in her human form and fulfill her fate in this life.

This fate, as narrated in chapter 12, takes Telumée to La Folie (the madness), known as the Brotherhood of the Displaced (127–28). Here Telumée must undergo a further trial, that of entering the world of the cane plantation, which she had feared "worse than the devil" (133). This experience, which Telumée describes as an "affliction," links the character directly to the history of the plantation that had forced Ma Cia into finally abandoning her human shape. This affliction, this entering into "the malediction" of the cane fields, signals Telumée's ultimate debasement, leaving her "a woman without hope," waiting the wind to "set it afloat again" (139).

Telumée's acceptance of Amboise's love brings her full circle to the cultivation of a joint garden that had been the basis of Toussine and Jeremiah's happiness together. Together, they share years of "contentment, good words, and kindness," during which the food made from their crops became "an argument for the continuation of life" (148). Telumée moves from deep abjection to congratulating herself every day "on being of this world" (152).

Surprisingly, for a novel that places such emphasis on the importance of maternal genealogy, Telumée's "satisfied belly" does not produce a child. Hochberg argues that "the inclusion of this negation of motherhood *within* matrilineal narratives functions as an inner disruption; breaking the coherence of the framing maternal narrative directs our attention to the limitations of these narratives as a source of women's liberation" (9). Schwarz-Bart underscores these limits through the sad narrative of Telumée's adoption of Sonore, a child brought to her on the verge of death who she restores to life.

Sonore enters Telumée's life after Amboise's death, which takes place during a labor strike that could refer to general labor strikes in Guadeloupe and Martinique in 1951. This period, during which Telumée gains a reputation as a healer and grows to be feared for the power her knowledge of herbs gives her, is one of happiness in the nurturing of Sonore and of renewed pain as the young woman is torn from her by the wickedness of Angel Medard. Medard had "assumed the appearance of a man in the world" but could not be a man since he lacked a soul. As Schwarz-Bart prepares to close her narrative, we will find Telumée occupying a space similar to that inhabited by her grandmother Toussine at the end of her life—contented in her garden, having had the strength to transcend the trials life had presented her. To reach that contentment, however, Telumée, like Toussine, will face the loss of a "daughter" through the malice of Medard. Through her ill-paid generosity toward Medard, nonetheless, she will, like her grandmother, receive an honorific title, that of Telumée Miracle.

Schwarz-Bart closes Telumée's story by placing her in the town of La Ramée, amid a rapidly changing society moving quickly toward modernization. Here she will live through her last confrontation with Elie, during which she cannot offer the words of kindness that would have closed that chapter of her life with saintly generosity. The words she cannot say become "the only thing I regret in my whole life" (171). Telumée—now Telumée the Miracle Woman—sums up in her narrative Schwarz-Bart's views on the role of Creole peasant women as the cornerstone of Guadeloupean culture. Telumée speaks of the "rains and winds" that have buffeted her throughout her life (the French title of the book, *Pluie et vent sur Telumée Miracle,* is literally "Rain and Wind on Telumée the Miracle Woman") as the fate of those who are "still suffering and dying silently of slavery after it is finished and forgotten" (169). Her triumph, Schwarz-Bart would argue, is that she is "still a woman standing on [her] own two legs," who knows that "a Negro's not a statue of salt to be dissolved by the rain" (172).

Chapter 16

Derek Walcott's Omeros

Derek Walcott, winner of the 1992 Nobel Prize in Literature, was born on January 23, 1930, in Castries, capital of the Caribbean island of St. Lucia. His father, Warwick, a painter, died when Derek and his twin brother Roderick were just a year old. Their mother, Alix, was a teacher at the town's Methodist school. Walcott attended St. Mary's College in Castries and the University of the West Indies in Mona, Jamaica, where he studied French, Spanish, and Latin. His mother is credited with supplementing his education by instilling in him a love of poetry and of the classics of European literature. In 1958, having already published a number of dramas and collections of poetry, he was awarded a Rockefeller Foundation Fellowship to study theater in New York City.

Walcott began his literary career while still an adolescent, publishing his first collection of poetry, *25 poems,* with the aid of his mother in 1948. Two other collections, *Epitaph for the Young: XII Cantos* and *Poems,* were published in 1949 and 1951, respectively, although he would not gain international recognition until the publication of *In a Green Night* in 1962. While still in his early twenties, Walcott began what would become a very successful career as a dramatist. In 1950 he founded the St. Lucia Arts Guild, a theater organization, the same year he completed his first play, *Henri Christophe,* based on the life of one of the leaders of the Haitian Revolution. A number of plays followed in quick succession: *Harry Dernier: A Play for Radio Production* (1951), *Wine of the Country* (1953), *The Sea at Dauphin* (1954), *Ione* (1957), *Drums and Colours: An Epic Drama* (1958), and *Ti-Jean and His Brothers* (1958).

Following his graduation from the University of the West Indies, Walcott worked as a teacher and journalist throughout the Caribbean, in St. Lucia, Jamaica, Grenada, and Trinidad. He worked as a journalist for *Public Opinion* in Kingston, Jamaica, and for the *Trinidad Guardian* in Port of Spain. In 1959 he became founding director of the Little Carib Theater, later known as the Trinidad Theatre Workshop, where he coordinated projects until 1976. His career as a dramatist reached international fame when he was awarded an Obie Award in 1971 for distinguished foreign play for *Dream on Monkey Mountain*. More than a dozen additional plays have followed, among them *The Joker of Seville* (1974), *O Babylon!* (1976), *The Isle Is Full of Noises* (1982), *Odyssey: Stage Version* (1993), and *The Capeman* (1997, in collaboration with Paul Simon). His growing fame led to a number of positions in creative writing at prestigious American universities such as Columbia, Yale, and Harvard. Since 1981, he has been a professor of English at Boston University, and he divides his time between Boston and St. Lucia. At Boston University, he founded the Boston Playwrights' Theater, which presents original works by local, national, and international writers and which maintains an exchange program with the Trinidad Theatre Workshop.

In the early 1960s, Walcott returned to poetry as his preferred medium for literary expression. His 1962 collection *In a Green Night* became his breakthrough book, establishing him as a poet of note. More than a dozen volumes of poetry have followed, among them *The Castaway* (1965), *The Gulf* (1969), *Another Life* (1973), *The Fortunate Traveler* (1981), *Omeros* (1990), *The Bounty* (1997), *Tiepolo's Hound* (2000), and *The Prodigal* (2004). Walcott's poetry explores the disjuncture between the colonized and the colonizer, seeking to help us understand the personal and political implications of the Caribbean's cultural, racial, and social hybridity. In his poetry, he seeks to reconcile the seemingly irreconcilable strands that make up postcolonial Caribbean cultures in a language that reflects the richness and variety of cultures that, in his eyes, have been enriched by creolization and transculturation.

Walcott's first collection of essays, *What the Twilight Says,* which includes his Nobel Prize acceptance speech, was published in 1998. As his Nobel address shows, Walcott has emerged as a strong advocate for a Caribbean environment threatened by unrestrained tourism development, a subject to which he has returned with poignant urgency in subsequent essays and interviews. Walcott was very vocal in opposition to the building of the Hilton Jalousie Plantation resort in the valley sloping down to the sea between the Pitons, the two great volcanic cones on the west coast of St. Lucia and now a UNESCO World Heritage site. Writing in a local paper, he equated the economic arguments in favor of the resort—that it would provide extra income and jobs—to proposing building "a casino in the Vatican" or a "take-away concession inside Stonehenge" (Pattullo 4).

Walcott is also an avid watercolorist, whose work has been exhibited in galleries throughout the West Indies and has served to illustrate his published work, particularly *Tiepolo's Hound* (2000). He has explored the relationship between art and poetry in works such as his essay "As the Twilight Says," his autobiographical poem *Another Life,* and his exploration of the work of Caribbean-born artist Camille Pissarro in *Tiepolo's Hound.*

Throughout his long career, Walcott has been awarded numerous prizes. In addition to his Nobel Prize, he has won the Queen's Medal for poetry in 1988, the W. H. Smith Literary Award for *Omeros* in 1990, a MacArthur Foundation genius award, and a Royal Society of Literature Award. He is an honorary member of the American Academy and Institute of Arts and Letters.

Omeros

The national anthem of the island of St. Lucia speaks of the days "when nations battled for this Helen of the West...the days when strife and discord, dimmed her children's toil and rest," a reference to the bitter rivalry between England and France during the eighteenth century for possession of the island. In *Omeros,* Walcott's longest and most ambitious poem, he brings the lines of the anthem to life by focusing on the struggle of two fishermen for a Creole Helen. The poem, widely believed to have been the achievement that secured Walcott the Nobel Prize in literature in 1992, draws on characters and plotlines from Homer's *Iliad* and *Odyssey,* but transposed here to a twentieth-century Caribbean reality, firmly planted in the specificities of life in St. Lucia, particularly in the northern coast towns of Castries and Gros Ilets.

In *Omeros,* Walcott follows a poetic tradition that links, among others, Homer, Dante's *Divine Comedy* (1321), and John Milton's *Paradise Lost* (1667):

The meter is a loose hexameter, approximating Homer's, though it contracts occasionally to five or even four-beat lines, as if to acknowledge also Miltonic blank verse, the accentual tetrameter of *Beowulf* or *Piers Plowman,* and the folk music of both Europe and the Caribbean. The *Omeros* stanza, with the exception of one section (Book Four, Chapter XXXIII, iii) in tetrameter rhymed couplets, is the tercet of Dante's *Divine Comedy.* But Walcott adapts the stanza freely, departing from Dante's strictly-linked rhyme to accommodate ad-hoc variations on *terza rima.* (Breslin)

There are a number of parallel plots in the poem, leading to a complicated narrative structure. The poem is divided into seven books with 64 chapters and four major plot threads, all closely interrelated. They, and the characters that play them out, are introduced in book I. The first of these is the rivalry of fishermen Achille and Hector over Helen, who is identified with St. Lucia itself. Closely related to this plot is the story of Philoctete and his search for a cure to a festering wound, eventually healed by Ma Kilman, the bar owner and healer. The third is the story of two British ex-patriates in St. Lucia, Sergeant Major Dennis Plunkett and his Irish wife, Maud, who have settled on the island as farmers and are seeking to reconcile themselves, as whites, to the story of British colonization in St. Lucia. The fourth, the story of the poet-narrator wandering around the world, haunted by the memory of lost love, is closely related to the Ulysses of *The Odyssey*.

The poem opens (part I of chapter I) with Philoctete explaining to a group of tourists how the gommier tree *(Dacryodes hexandra)* has traditionally been cut to carve out canoes in Dominica and St. Lucia. The tree has an easy-to-carve soft center and secretes a resin that serves as a protection from seawater. The character of Philoctete is based on that of a Greek hero, mentioned in Homer's *Iliad,* who was exiled on the island of Lemmos, where he suffered a wound on his foot that festered and from which emanated a foul smell. The Philoctete of *Omeros,* at once vulnerable to the tourists' gaze and protected from the soul-stealing power of their cameras by his connection to the ancestral power of the trees, opens the narrative by invoking the history of his home island, which ties the tourists to the race of conquerors that came to displace the indigenous Aruacs.

The ritualistic cutting of the trees, in which the trees are personified, is depicted in the text as symbolic of the exploitation of nature by the conquerors that followed on the discovery of the island by Europeans in 1500. The destruction of the Aruacs ushers in not only a new religion, in which the trees are no longer sacred, but leaves them exposed to a deforestation for profit that is far from the ceremonial cutting of the gommiers to build boats. Under this exploitation the generator works on destroying the forest, much faster an evenly than the fishermen could.

In part II of chapter I, Walcott underscores the idea of the sacred nature of the trees, a notion that is akin to that expressed by Jacques-Stephen Alexis in his novel *Les Arbres musiciens,* where he speaks of the trees of Haiti's embattled forests "as a great pipe organ that modulates with a multiple voice... each with its own timbre, each pine a pipe of this extraordinary instrument" (qtd in Benson 108). Here the voice of the trees has been silenced, as it belongs to an ancestral history before that of man. They retain, however, a thirst for the sea—a sort of communion with the fishermen who come to cut them with ceremonial respect—which is rooted in the link that the poem assumes between the present-day fishermen and the Aruacs who first populated the island. "Now the trunks in eagerness to become canoes/ploughed into breakers of bushes—" (7).

The section also introduces the character of Achille, one of the two sailors around which the main narrative plot will revolve. The ritualistic cutting of the tree is partially seen through his gaze, telescoping through his gaze the process of turning a tree trunk into a canoe. Achille moves from looking on the hole left in the ground by the roots of the laurel, through his being one of the men participating in the ceremonial cutting if the trees (7), to the naming of his own canoe, *In God We Troust*. The chapter ends with Achille leaving his hut in the early morning light to join the fishermen going out to sea.

Chapter II follows as the village fishermen set out past the wistful Philoctete, who must remain on land because of his festering wound. Walcott compares the group to warriors from a battle waged in a faraway place, in his first implied connection between the world of these fishermen in St. Lucia and the Greek warriors of Homeric Greece. Chief amid these fishermen/ warriors stands Hector, his presence underscoring the Homeric connection.

Chapter II also introduces Seven Seas, a former fisherman who has gone blind but who claims the wisdom of one who has sailed around the world. Introduced in his hut as he makes coffee, envying the fishermen in their canoes out at sea, he envisions "the past of another sea" (12). Like Philoctete, Seven Seas marks the rhythm of the day at sea, invoking Omeros the epic bard as he marks its beginning: "O open this day with the conch's moan, Omeros" (12).

Omeros the bard—the voice of the poet—enters the poem in part III of chapter II, where his name is linked to the development of Antillean patois: the *O* for the call of the conch shell, *mer* for both mother and the sea, *os* for the gray bones of the many dead. As a poet with the gift of seeing the past (a gift he shares with Seven Seas), Omeros invokes the legacy of slavery that forms the bridge between Homeric and Antillean histories, turning his poetic gaze onto the everyday lives of the fishermen around him. Like Seven Seas, who, blind like Homer, sits by the drying fishnets listening to the sounds of the shore, Omeros hears the voices of the fishermen quarreling over the "shadow" whose name was Helen.

Part II of chapter III introduces Ma Kilman, whose bar—the oldest in the village—occupies one of the gingerbread cottages characteristic of St. Lucian coastal towns such as Gros Ilet. The description of the bar situates it firmly within St. Lucian village life, with its tables for playing dominoes, its beaded curtain and Coca-Cola neon sign, and surrounded by the typical small shops, clubs, and pharmacies. The two men who make the bar their place of awaiting during the day—Seven Seas and Philoctete—both seek her for the mysterious powers she is said to possess. She is a healer in the tradition of West Indian Obeah practitioners and has intimate knowledge of the afterlife.

Here Walcott underscores the links between Seven Seas and the figure of Homer as a blind singer, describing him as sometimes singing in unclear words—perhaps Greek, or perhaps and old African tongue—unintelligible to Ma Kilman. The reference to Old St. Omere, linked here to Seven Seas, could be read as an allusion to Dunstan St. Omer, the acclaimed St. Lucian artist who was Walcott's childhood friend and whose work decorates many churches throughout St. Lucia, including the one in Gros Ilet.

In part III of chapter III, Walcott links Philoctete's wound to the legacy of slavery—and therefore not easy to cure. The festering injury stands as a symbol of the wounds of a colonial history founded on slavery and exploitation. The search for a cure for this cultural wound, Ma Kilman suggests, is to be found in nature and the practices of their ancestors. She proposes to seek a medicinal flower to prepare in a tisane in the ancestral way she had learned from her grandmother. She articulates this search through a return to the image of the wounded tree that opens the narrative, which underscores the connection between Philoctete's wound and ancestral grievances linked to the colonial encounter.

Chapter IV finds Philoctete in the forest, walking past an old ruined sugar estate, with its rusted cauldrons and boiling vats—the only remains of the island's plantation history. The image of woods growing to cover the remnants of the sugar plantation is a familiar one in Walcott's poetry, one that appears also in more recent collections of poems, such as *The Prodigal*: "What if our history is so rapidly enclosed/in bush, devoured by green, that there are no signals" (99) now that the memories of events have not been recorded anywhere but in memory and the trees are "sworn to ancestral silence" (99).

The ruined plantation, however, continues to impose its presence in the lives of the descendants of slaves, like Philoctete, who uses the collective wisdom of the St. Lucian people, as evident in their proverbs, to summarize the burden of hard and poorly rewarded labor left as a legacy of the plantation economy: *"When cutlass cut smoke, when cocks surprise their arseholes/by shitting eggs,* he cursed, *black people go get rest from God"* (21).

Part III of chapter IV introduces Helen, who, like Philoctete, is first seen in the context of St. Lucia's tourist landscape. Described first by the poet's gaze—his sections are the only ones narrated in the first person—she emerges amid tourists baking in the sun. The poet shows Helen, in her traditional madras head-tie, proud and queenly against the background of bad-tempered tourists and locals in the uniforms of servitude of the tourist industry. Later, pregnant but not knowing by whom, she is rejected in her search for a job as a waitress. She is too outspoken, too unwilling to submit herself to the debasement required by tourist service.

Chapter IV introduces the Plunketts—the Major and his wife Maud—as British ex-pats, whose uncompromising anticolonial stance sets them aside from the more typical colonialist mind-set of their kind. Tied to the history of the "ebbing" British Empire through his service under Field Marshall Bernard "Monty" Montgomery, the hero of El Alamein, the couple has opted to live as farmers in St. Lucia, one of the sugar islands inhabited by people without history. Devoted to the island and its people, and critical of the local ministers who are profiting form the wealth brought in by tourism and gambling, they are not without their share of romance. It is the major who seeks to impose over the figure of their former maid Helen the

burden of Homeric significance, setting her as the prize in the struggle between Achille and Hector. Helen resists that portrayal of herself, remaining
oblivious to anything beyond her struggle for survival, which she is prone
to acknowledge openly and seemingly casually through the singing of the
Beatles's song "Yesterday."

Part II of chapter IV includes an intervention from the poet—the narrative
I—pointing to the fact that Major Plunkett had been wounded during the
war and linking this wound to the overall theme of the narrative. The poet-
narrator will intervene directly in the text again in part III of chapter VI,
picking up on Helen's Beatles reference to offer a meditation on Homeric
history introduced by a series of "yesterdays" and interrupted by the sight of
Helen at the beach. She has set up a hair-braiding table for tourists, since she
is unable to find work as a waitress. The narrator, in his own fascination with
Helen, identifies with Achille, who has been abandoned in favor of Hector.

The rivalry between Hector and Achille—the subject of chapters VII–X
of book I—is presented here as deeply tied to their ability to provide for
Helen's needs within the limited opportunities offered in a postcolonial,
underdeveloped economy such as that of St. Lucia. Achille, in his struggle
for quick money, looks to the sea as his only source of possible wealth, il-
legally diving for coral and conch shells and for the illusory gold from a
sunken Spanish ship with the "ransom of centuries" waiting behind its cabin
doors. The mirage of the Spanish galleon vanishes "with all hope of Helen"
(46), underscoring the futility of Achille's search, but offering nonetheless a
confrontation with the history of slavery that still determines his chances of
survival and happiness.

Philoctete's failed efforts at making peace between Achille and Hector—
founded on the notion that the two men share a common bond through
the sea—precedes the start of the hurricane season. Walcott offers the reader
two viewpoints on a tropical tempest. Achille, caught in the storm, barely
makes it to shelter, where he hears the clang "of thousands of iron nails
poured in a basin/of rain on his tin roof" (50). Hector, trying to save his
canoe, gets caught in the waves, fighting the sea until he is able to gain the
sandy shore.

The power of the Cyclone is described by Walcott in part III of chapter IX
as a wild fête jointly celebrated by the Yoruba-derived gods of the Caribbean
religions of Santería and Vodou and the ancient Greek gods of the Homeric
tradition: "the abrupt Shango drums/made Neptune rock in the caves" (52).
Oblivious to human prayers and to the devastation below, the gods hold a
"hurricane-party," brought close by the "thunderous weather,/where Ogun
can fire one with his partner Zeus" (53).

The impact of the hurricane—seen briefly through Achille's retrieving of
his canoe—is presented primarily through the despair under which Major
Plunkett sinks because of the weather, which has destroyed crops and gar-
dens. His reconnaissance drive around the island to look at the damage

allows Walcott the opportunity to offer the reader a survey of his home island that encompasses both the cloud-covered mountain of La Sorcière ("the sorceress," with its allusion to the West Indian practice of Obeah), through the fishing village of Anse La Raye and the massive Pitons, to the Soufrière volcano. Seen through the eyes of the Major as a process of rediscovery, the features and beauty of the island here help explain the Major's deep commitment to the island, his preference for the forests and springs speaking in the island's dialect.

This sense of commitment leads Major Plunkett to an obsession with writing the history of the island. For Walcott, the writing of history in the Caribbean region has always been a complex exercise. In his essay "The Muse of History," he writes that "in the New World, servitude to the muse of history has produced a literature of recrimination and despair, a literature of revenge written by the descendants of slaves or a literature of remorse written by the descendants of masters" (354). Major Plunkett's exploration of Caribbean history throughout the narrative will strive—not always successfully—not to fall into the pitfalls of history as seen by Walcott in this early essay, where he poignantly argued that "as we grow older as a race, we grow aware that history is written, that it is a kind of literature without morality, that in its actuaries the ego of the race is indissoluble, and that everything depends on whether we write this fiction through the memory of hero or of victim" (354).

In chapter XII, the final chapter of book I, the narrator—now identified with Walcott himself through the identifying of his father's first name as Warwick—delves into his own personal history. Visiting his childhood home—now a printer's shop—he embarks on a leisurely walk through his native city, Castries, with the ghost of his father. A lovely, bustling Caribbean hamlet, it is evoked here first in the early years of the twentieth century, when it was still inhabited by colonial officials with their white suits and pith helmets, and later in a present of tourists with soul-stealing cameras throwing coins to diving boys from luxury cruise liners. A follower of Marcus Garvey and his pan-Africanist movement, the ghost of the poet's father addresses the question of his son's seeking immortality through writing. Pointing to the women balancing loads of coals on their heads, he counsels his son to remain on task, since only hard steady work, like that of the women who make their way from country to market, will bring his dreams to fruition. The poet's paternally assigned task, therefore, is to give voices to the likes of those women.

In book II of *Omeros*, Major Plunkett's research into the Battle of the Saintes reveals the presence of a namesake, Midshipman Plunkett, killed in the battle at the age of 19. The battle, fought from April 9 to April 12, 1782, and named after a group of islands between Guadeloupe and Dominica, was a salient moment in the history of the struggle between England and France over control of the Lesser Antilles. Led by Admiral Rodney, it is commemorated in the St. Lucian national anthem, which alludes to the time when European powers fought for this "Helen of the West." The young midshipman's career, which included a stint as a spy in Holland, allows Walcott to swiftly trace the history of the interconnections between European politics, the American Revolution, and developments in the Caribbean. The ancestral lines of Major Plunkett and Achille meet at Fort Rodney (Pigeon Island), where Achille's ancestor is a slave building the fort on the hill overlooking the sea from the small island off the northwestern coast of St. Lucia, across from Gros Ilet, the very fort in which Midshipman Plunkett will die in battle. The connection is underscored by the fall of a bottle of wine into the sea from the midshipman's ship—the very same bottle which, encrusted with fool's gold, Achille had seen in the islet's museum.

The trajectory of the Major, from finding out in his research about the death of his namesake on Pigeon Island to his finding himself living two centuries later within sight of the latter's place of death, points thematically to the end of British rule over the island and to the futility of seeking to expiate the guilt of that empire through a "pious pilgrimage" through the sites of its grandeur. Although Plunkett finds through his research one he can claim as "a namesake and a son" (94), he is left with no idea of how to accomplish the task of historian in a place like St. Lucia.

In his efforts to find a way to reword the history of the region, Major Plunkett builds on the explanation offered by some historians that the Battle of the Saintes was fought for possession of the island of St. Lucia. From Major Plunkett's perspective, Helen/St. Lucia, as a desired object, stood for a variety of intangible connections that had little to do with the island itself. He finds, when looking at the accumulation of research materials on his desk, that he has learned to distrust their truth.

Looking beyond "factual fictions" for the truth behind history, Major Plunkett finds desire—the desire of Great Britain and France for St. Lucia and its surrounding islands, on one hand, and his own desire for Helen, on the other. Catching Helen (when still working as their maid) trying on a bracelet from Maud's jewelry box, he finds himself transfixed by her scent and closeness. The encounter brings to the fore the limitations of the writing of academic history in fostering a true understanding of the past. The sexual desire explicit in the encounter also brings into question the sincerity of the major's commitment to the island and its people. Betrayed by sexual desire, he ponders the lasting power of the desire of empire.

Chapter XX (book II) returns to the figure of Philoctete to offer us a glimpse of history in the making through his involvement in Prof. Statics's political campaign. The insight into local politics allows Walcott to return to his depiction of tourism work as a slavery-prolonging type of servitude, a theme he had introduced earlier in the poem through his description of hotel workers mortified by boorish tourists and through the industry's rejection of Helen as a potential worker because of her outspokenness and haughty manner. Tourism is akin to slavery, a return to servitude, to dividing the island into spaces into which St. Lucians can only enter as servant. Later, as

Helen walks amid tourists through Gros Ilet's Friday night jump-up, Walcott underscores the theme of the island's problematic dependence on tourism, seeing Helen as offering himself like the island, sacrificing (whoring) a way of life about to disappear.

Gros Ilet's famous Friday night jump-up, a weekly street party that brings together islanders and tourists alike, is an ideal setting for Walcott's meditation on the threat posed by tourism to the culture and mores of the St. Lucian people. Sandwiched tightly between the luxury hotels, expensive foreign-owned condominiums, and yachts of fashionable Rodney Bay and the all-inclusive offerings of one of several Sands resorts on the island, the small, traditional fishing village with its colorful cottages decorated with lacelike woodwork looks like a slice of island life whose days are numbered. Achille, stargazing on his canoe, deplores the disappearance of a way of life he loves. The Major, likewise stargazing, underscores the tension between village and tourists as he describes the contending styles of music (local and international) that fight for attention. It is not surprising, then, given that the tensions that enter the narrative through the depiction of the threat posed by tourism are filtered through Achille, that the section ends with his repudiation of a Helen (the island) who has eagerly participated in this tourist-accepting jump-up. The section will end with a rupture between them that leads her into the arms of Hector, who has sold his canoe to buy a passenger van with leopard skin coverings and flames painted on the sides, giving up the sea. Named the "Comet," it will help him fly down the roads, believing that despite all, Helen still loved Achille, eventually to his death. It makes Hector the counterpart of Helen, who had been described by Achille as "Bright Helen," who "was like a meteor" as he watched her "falling arc" crossing the village (112).

The conclusion of book II finds Achille lamenting his fate after Helen's departure. Walcott dwells here on the theme of the wound, comparing Achille's emotional wound to Philoctete's. Steeped in his grief, he sets out to sea, glimpsed by Maud from her garden, following a sea swift—a *hirondelle des Antilles*—as a "bait of the gods" that draws him toward the open Atlantic, the space of the triangular trade responsible for the institutions of slavery and the plantation. A victim of sunstroke, Achille sees the ghost of his father coming to guide him into a questioning of his identity.

In book III, Achille, suffering from sunstroke-induced delirium, travels back to Africa to find himself in his father, retracing the route of the Middle Passage. This imaginary return is to a point in the past that allows Achille to encompass the significance of the enslavement and transportation of African peoples to the New World. From not being able to tell his father the meaning of his name to having to learn anew the names and deeds of the African gods his ancestors venerated, Achille embarks on a voyage of memory and retrieval that can help him understand who he is and his position in a postcolonial world. He will witness the grief brought on villagers by a slave raid, walking through the dusty village with its doors "like open graves" (145). Prodded into violence by his rage and grief, he kills one of the raiders, only to end in spasms of grief as if confronting the death of a brother. His hope is to deliver the captives so as to change the whole course of Antillean history, to stop the islands' painful encounter with slavery. Through this voyage, Achille is able to retrieve his history and that of his people, healing thereby from the devastating pain of losing one's homeland.

Achille's return from his sunstroke voyage is marked by a swift run through the history of colonial exploitation that telescoped the time between the moment in Africa he has visited and his twentieth-century present in St. Lucia. This hurried historical voyage takes him past debates about manumission; the madness of George III; the burning of a Jesuit mission in Veracruz; Jews fleeing from the Inquisition to the New World; the death of Toussaint L'Ouverture in France; the deadly tsunami that hit Port Royal in 1692; the careers of Queen Victoria, abolitionist William Wilberforce (1759–1833), and Charles Darwin (1809–1882); and the departure for the Caribbean of thousands of Indians as indentured servants. Achille will confront another history on his return to Gros Ilet, when, raking the leaves in Seven Seas's yard, he finds an Arawak totem, a frightening reminder of the native inhabitants of St. Lucia that Achille hurled away from him. As a symbol of a destroyed people, the totem stands for thousands of souls lost to history in St. Lucia.

Walcott is as interested in the voyage as he is in Achille's return to Gros Ilet. Given up for dead, he is apprehensively wished for by Helen, who, like Penelope, is made to suffer the grief of uncertainty while she waits for news. Like Odysseus, Achille is returning from an epic voyage, ready to shout from happiness at the first sight of home. His return is witnessed by Helen and sensed by Seven Seas, who, with clairvoyance, had known his whereabouts when everyone thought him dead. It is moreover witnessed by the narrator, who, fresh from a visit to his "amnesiac" mother, watches his canoe nearing the island.

Book IV find the narrator-poet in the United States, where, through his meditation on the fate of the Native American tribes and the impact of slavery on contemporary racial attitudes, he links the deaths of the Arawaks and Caribs in the Caribbean to the larger history of the genocide of native peoples in the Americas. Opening with the narrator on the shores of Long Island Sound and moving to Brookline, Massachusetts (Walcott has long held a position as professor at Boston University), where he is mourning his "abandonment in the war of love" (171), the poet presents himself to the reader as another wounded, lost Philoctete. The wound is exacerbated by the emptiness of the house, which he describes as "less a mystery that the *Marie Celeste,*" the classic ghost ship, a brigantine found in the Atlantic in 1872 under full sail but without a single member of its crew (171). "House Chant" (chapter XXXIII, part III), written in rhymed couplets that set it apart from the rest of the poem, underscores thematically his refusal to accept it as a home and provides a transition to a section of the narrative poem that addresses the history of exploitation of Native American peoples.

Chapter XXXIV opens with a series of Native American images, among them that of the building of the Union Pacific railroad across the United States, described as a spike driven into the heart of lands that once belonged to Native American tribes like the Sioux. As his guide into the history of the genocide of Native Americans, the poet chooses Catherine Weldon, a widowed artist from New York and member of the National Indian Defense Association, whose commitment to the defense and protection of the Native American tribes led her to venture into Lakota territory in the 1880s. She settled in the Standing Rock Reservation in Dakota Territory, where she worked closely with Sitting Bull as his secretary. In chapter XXXIV, part III, Walcott describes her mulling over the pleasures of a late summer in the plains, thinking of her late husband and of her young son's death after stepping on a rusty nail. Here the notion of wound moves from the personal (the poet's as well as Weldon's) to encompass that of the Native American nations losing rights to land and freedom. In Weldon's soliloquy, which follows in chapter XXXV, Walcott uses smoke, a leitmotif, to convey inner feelings throughout the text, to explain her deep identification with Native Americans, which the poem claims began when she worked in Buffalo Bill Cody's circus. John van Sickle has argued that "smoke with its shifting forms serves Walcott . . . to describe his mind's workings as associative and metaphoric. Nothing in her fragmentary history shows that *Catherine Weldon* actually joined Buffalo Bill's circus, but Walcott seizes the occasion to recall how the Native Americans were turned into a degrading spectacle in the eastern cities, masking their suffering in the West" (40).

Walcott will underscore the theme in chapter XXXV, where he is led by a guide to the starting point of the Trail of Tears in Georgia, a reference to the forced relocation of the Cherokees to the west of the Mississippi in 1838 (the march took a heavy death toll, leading to the death of some 4,000 Native Americans). Walcott links this genocidal march to the persecution and lynching of African Americans by the Ku Klux Klan in the twentieth century. Against this calendar image stand "Negro shacks" that move "like a running wound" (178). Walcott will return to the church image toward the conclusion of book IV, pondering on the mistreatment of Native Americans.

As book IV closes, Walcott seeks to establish the connections between the poet's emotional wounds, Catherine Weldon's personal and national anguish, and the history of his home island. Depicting Weldon looking at dancers reminiscent of the Ghost Dance—a reference to a religious movement, centering on a circle dance, that incorporated elements of the belief systems of a number of Native American nations and which is linked to the Wounded Knee massacre—Walcott addresses the notion of the sublimation of personal pain through commitment to a larger cause. The poet had found

Weldon as he was looking for characters for his poem, and her plight made her rise in marked relief in part because her sufferings put to shame his own pain at the loss of his love. The narrator will find his central character, Achille, during a visit to a museum, vividly rendered in Winslow Homer's *The Gulf Stream,* which depicts a young black man on a broken boat surrounded by sharks in the middle of a tumultuous sea. The painting, owned by the Metropolitan Museum of Art in New York City, strikes the narrator as that of a man heading toward Africa. The presence of the threatening sharks, however, reminds him of the racism that pervades U.S. society, depicted here in three examples: the swelling sea reminds him of Herman Melville's thought on the whiteness of the whale; he fails to find a cab since they will rarely stop for a black man in solitary spaces late at night; and when he moves to a bus stop where a woman awaits, she gives him a look of alarm that seems to stem directly from Melville's novel. Book IV will close as it opened, with the poet on a cold beach, where he meets once again the ghosts of his father, advising him to see the world and go everywhere, but to return to reencounter and value the simplicities of life in his home island.

In book V, the narrator—as suggested by his father—travels far and wide: London, Port of Spain, Greece, Dublin, Istanbul, Venice, Rome, Concord, Boston Harbor, Toronto, and the American Great Plains. The focus of the section is the history and impact of imperial exploitation and genocide. His voyage takes him past the ports of the triangular slave trade, the slave market of Trinidad, the monuments built to imperial expansion from the Greeks to the United States, and ultimately to the site of his own personal loss, the new home of his failed love, whose address he has now lost.

The section looks critically at the power of Europe and its New World descendants over peoples of color in the Americas, a power manifested by Pope Alexander, whose bull *Inter Caetera* of May 4, 1493, divided the newly discovered lands between Spain and Portugal. The metropolises of empire, such as London, are depicted in this section as places at the center of the international trade in which sugar was a major player until the middle of the twentieth century—a trade "stirred" with the sweat and toil of West Indian slaves and cane workers. Their claims to democratic ideas, such as those that form the basis of the U.S. Constitution, emerge out of small towns that stress their links to Western civilization through names such as Athens and Troy, but which are peopled by convicts and immigrants whose notion of democracy was built on the dispossession of Native Americans and African slaves. They are also evident in their betrayal of treaties with the Native American population—snow blows over the Great Plains in the form of bits and pieces of paper blown to the wind, representing the many dishonored agreements that marked the western expansion in the United States.

In book V, Walcott underscores above all the complexities of the meaning of history for Native Americans and the descendants of African slaves, who have no documents or ruins to chronicle their history of oppression.

His own journey through cities laden with monumental ruins (which includes James Joyce's Dublin) leads him to a rejection of monuments and ruins as embodiments of history. Visiting Venice, the history of which seems encapsulated in sighing bridges over ancient canals, the narrator claims that, like his father had counseled, what he preferred was not the history frozen in this ancient monuments but the birds fluttering in the sky, alighting briefly on the heads of statues.

Book VI—narrated by the poet after his return to St. Lucia from his travels—tells of the deaths of Hector and Maud and the healing of Philoctete after Ma Kilman finds the curing herb whose name she had forgotten. It ends with Helen's return to Achille after Maud's funeral. The book opens with a meditation on the "bitter history of sugar" that links the Caribbean islands from San Fernando in Trinidad to Mayagüez in Puerto Rico. Like his father had advised, he has returned to embrace the beauty and freshness of the island, its sense of eternal renewal that can set aside the claims of a history of exploitation.

Anticipating his interpretation of Hector's death as stemming from his abandonment of the sea, the poet will question his own devotion to his craft, wondering if he, like Plunkett, is not attached to the surrounding scenes in the same way Plunkett is determined to fixate the past through his historical research. His craft, which he describes as requiring the same artistry that can stencil a window frame or carve a wooden canoe, may be too wedded to depicting the natural and human landscape of St. Lucia as transfixed in the embers of empire. Has he turned the poverty of his fellow islanders into the source of his sense of paradise—their continued poverty the only way of nostalgically preserving the past—the poet wonders, a questioning of his own motives that stems from a fear that art is only a way of reconstructing the nostalgia of history and he, as a poet, is no different than his own history-obsessed creation, the Major. Hector, then, functions as a cautionary figure that reminds him of his father's advice to stay true to the island. Having died sighing for a lost connection to the sea after having been corrupted by the urban life of Castries, his funeral is a ritual of reinsertion into the life of the sea. This represents a return to the natural rhythms of the culture of the island, as St. Lucia's culture has developed around the coast, its interior largely forest covered and undeveloped. Mourners were called to the funeral by the conch shell, his body was lowered into the earth in the traditional hand-carved wood canoe. Achille, in a gesture of reconciliation, carried an oar into the church, together with the red tin that had been the symbolic object of their rift. His words of farewell are words of admiration for his later rival's seafaring skills.

Hector's funeral has its counterpart in Maud's, which is also narrated in book VI. The Plunkett's creolization is signaled before her death by the disappointment of their return visit to England, where he missed the sounds of the island's market and of the palm fronds swaying in the breeze in a heard but not understood dialogue. Her funeral, attended by the narrator, marks the reconciliation of Achille and Helen. It also allows the narrator to remind the reader that he is attending the funeral of his creation—inserting himself into his own narrative, stepping into his fiction. Walcott here plays with the complexities of the levels of interaction between reality and fiction, and between author and narrator. The day after the funeral, for example, the author-narrator (a line that has been blurred in the narrative of the funeral) has an encounter with Major Plunkett at the bank in which the Major's thin veneer of island identity is momentarily erased, becoming, before his own narrator-creator, a representative of the history of empire the Major has tried to rewrite.

In the closing pages of book VI, Walcott rejects both the Major's conceit of seeking to turn history into myth and his own attempts at superimposing over that history the structures of the Homeric epic. The literary representation of the ethos of the St. Lucian people—a reading of the text would suggest—requires these attempts to bring it into the parameters of established Western classics before rejecting them as unnecessary for the true portrayal of a people and its culture. In his reconsideration of his own mythologizing, the narrator will question both approaches as failed attempts to grasp the realities of St. Lucian life.

Inserted between these two funerals is the tale of Ma Kilman's discovery of the herb needed to cure Philoctete's wound. The tale allows Walcott to bring together four narrative strands—the wound itself, which has functioned as a foundational metaphor throughout the entire poem; the flight of the sea swift, which had led Achille to his African voyage and here is seen as having carried the seed that produced the plant that heals Philoctete (238); the language of the ants, whose presence has graced the entire text, but which now invokes the language of Ma Kilman's grandmother, her path back to the gods she has forgotten in her half-assimilation into the Catholic Church; and the poet's identification with Philoctete. Restored by the healing powers of the sybil, the Obeahwoman, from the shared strains of their cultural heritage, both poet and character are healed from the damages of history.

Book VII, the final book of *Omeros*, finds the narrator-poet reenvisioning St. Lucia and its history as he walks the paths of the island with Omeros (sometimes in the guise of Seven Seas, his blind alter ego). As his guide, Omeros also assumes the guise of Virgil, in the narrator's *Inferno*-like voyage to the Soufrière volcano, now one of St. Lucia's most popular tourist attractions.

Throughout book VII, Walcott is focused on the theme of the selling of the island to tourists to the benefit of a few. At the volcano/hell, he sees the impact of the kind of political speculation that has seen the enrichment of many on the island at the expense of the people's welfare, a topic that has fueled his critique of tourism in and out of his poetry. The impact of tourism, which threatens the traditional ways of the island and puts its people at peril (this is, after all, the lesson of Hector's death), is presented again as the poem closes through the essentializing power of the tourist's camera as it focuses on the islander. The poem opened with Philoctete smiling for the tourists, who attempted to take his soul in their photographs. Helen, in turn, forced to work as a waitress, is served to her customer in traditional costume—now in full madras—with its sensual low-cut bodice and frilly allures. In his critique of tourism and industrialization in the region, Walcott introduces the environmental perspective that has seen him take an active part in antidevelopment efforts in St. Lucia. Philoctete wonders if, given the changes brought to the island by tourism development and the greed that has brought industrial fishing to the region, he was the only fisherman left who believed in the spiritual connection between work and nature, between the fisherman and the sea that gives him life. Walcott encapsulates his view of the impact of tourism on Gros Ilet through his description of the village as "a souvenir of itself" (310).

As he closes his poem, the narrator assumes a Homeric voice to remind us that he "sang of quiet Achille, Afolabe's son," followed the sea swift, whose "wing-beat carries these islands to Africa," and "sang our wide country, the Caribbean Sea" (320, 319). The poem's most enduring metaphor—once the Homeric mythologizing is found to be empty of meaning—is that of the sea that both separates the islands from Africa and make a return to the ancestral world possible. "Let the deep hymn/of the Caribbean continue my epilogue," the poet entreats, as regardless of the vicissitudes of its islands, the healing sea "was still going on" (325).

Works Cited

"Aimé Césaire passe la relève au Parti progressiste martiniquais." *Culture Femme* (2005), June 14, 2005. http://www.culturefemme.com/actualites/detail. php?id=820.

"Airtalk." Narr. Larry Mantle. KPCC, Pasadena, February 17, 1996.

Amnesty International USA. "'Battybwoys Affi Dead': Action against Homophobia in Jamaica," 2007. http://www.amnestyusa.org/outfront/jamaica_report.html.

Anthony, Michael. *The Year in San Fernando*. London: Heinemann, 1997.

Bawer, Bruce. "Civilization and V. S. Naipaul." *Hudson Review* 55.3 (2002): 371–84.

Beck, Ervin. "Social Insecurity in Beka Lamb by Zee Edgell." http://www.goshen. edu/english/ervinb/BekaLamb.htm.

Benson, LeGrace. "A Long Bilingual Conversation about Paradise Lost: Landscapes in Haitian Art." *Caribbean Literature and the Environment: Between Nature and Culture*. Ed. Elizabeth M. DeLoughrey, Renée K. Gosson, and George B. Handley. Charlottesville: UP Virginia, 2005. 99–109.

Breslin, Paul. "Omeros." *The Literary Encyclopedia*, February 6, 2004. http://www. litencyc.com/php/sworks.php?rec=true&UID=3088.

Capote, Truman. *Music for Chameleons*. New York: Vintage, 1994.

Carpentier, Alejo. *The Kingdom of This World*. 1949. Trans. Harriet de Onís. New York: Noonday Press, 1957.

———. *El reino de este mundo*. Mexico City: Compañía General de Ediciones, 1969.

———. "Leyes de Africa." *Carteles*, December 27, 1931: 46.

Cliff, Michelle. *Abeng*. New York: Plume, 1995.

Condé, Maryse. *I, Tituba, Black Witch of Salem*. Trans. Richard Philcox. New York: Ballantine Books, 1992.

Confiänt, Raphael. *Mamzelle Dragonfly*. Trans. Linda Coverdale. Lincoln: U Nebraska P, 2001.

Cudjoe, Selwyn. *V. S. Naipaul: A Materialist Reading*. Amherst: U Massachusetts P, 1988.

Danticat, Edwidge. *The Farming of Bones*. New York: Soho Press, 1998.

Davis, Angela. "Foreword." *I, Tituba, Black Witch of Salem*. By Maryse Condé. Trans. Richard Philcox. New York: Ballantine Books, 1992. i–xi.

Dawson, Ashley. "Squatters, Space, and Belonging in the Underdeveloped City." *Social Text* 81 (2004): 17–34.

Dayan, Joan. *Haiti, History, and the Gods*. Berkeley: U California P, 1995.

Deen, Shamshu. "Michael Anthony: A Giant among Us." *Independent* [London], July 28, 2000: 1.

Edgell, Zee. *Beka Lamb*. London: Heinemann, 1986.

Edwards, Paul, and Kenneth Ramchand. "Introduction." *The Year in San Fernando*. By Michael Anthony. London: Heinemann, 1997. vii–xxvi.

Esteves, Carmen C. "Afterword." *Happy Days, Uncle Sergio*. By Magali García Ramis. Trans. Carmen Esteves. Fredonia, NY: White Pine Press, 1995. 169–75.

———. "Literature/Journalism: The Frontier (An Interview with Magali García Ramis." *Callaloo* 17.3 (1994): 862–69.

Evaristo, Bernadine. "Zee Edgell." *Bomb* 82 (2002): 54–59.

Frye, Karla. "'An Article of Faith': Obeah and Hybrid Identities in Elizabeth Nunez-Harrell's *When Rocks Dance*." *Sacred Possessions: Vodou, Santería, Obeah, and the Caribbean*. Ed. Margarite Fernández Olmos and Lizabeth Paravisini-Gebert. New Brunswick, NJ: Rutgers UP, 1997. 195–215.

García Ramis, Magali. *Happy Days, Uncle Sergio*. Trans. Carmen Esteves. Fredonia, NY: White Pine Press, 1995.

Heinemann, Lynn. "Art Talk: Patricia Powell, Author." Massachusetts Institute of Technology. September 17, 2003. http://web.mit.edu/newsoffice/2003/powell-0917.html.

Hochberg, Gil Zehava. "Mother, Memory, History: Maternal Genealogies in Gayl Jones *Corregidora* and Simone Schwarz-Bart's *Pluie et vent sur Télumée Miracle*." *Research in African Literatures* 34.2 (2004): 1–12.

Hoetink, H. "'Race' and Color in the Caribbean." *Caribbean Contours*. Ed. Sidney W. Mintz and Sally Price. Baltimore: John Hopkins University Press, 1985. 55–84.

Human Rights Watch. "Homophobia in Jamaica and Its Role in Driving the HIV/AIDS Epidemic." *Hated to Death: Homophobia, Violence, and Jamaica's HIV/AIDS Epidemic* 16.6b (2004), November 2004. http://hrw.org/reports/2004/jamaica1104/.

Jaggi, Maya. "Island Memories." *Guardian* [London], November 20, 2004. http://books.guardian.co.uk/review/story/0,,1354314,00.html.

"Jean Rhys (1890–1979)." Books and Writers. 2003. http://www.kirjasto.sci.fi/rhys.htm.

Kenney, Susan. "Paradise with a Snake." *New York Times*, April 7, 1985.

Kincaid, Jamaica. *Annie John*. New York: Noonday Press, 1997.

Knight, Franklin W. *The Caribbean: The Genesis of a Fragmented Nationalism*. New York: Oxford UP, 1978.

Kreilkamp, Ivan. "Jamaica Kincaid: Daring to Discomfort." *Publishers' Weekly* 243, January 1, 1996: 54–55.

Labat, Jean-Baptiste. *Labat's Nouveau Voyage aux isles Françaises de l'Amérique.* La Haye: P. Husson, 1724.

Laguerre, Michel. *Voodoo and Politics in Haiti.* New York: St. Martin's Press, 1989.

Lans, Cheryl. *Creole Remedies of Trinidad and Tobago.* n.p.: lulu.com, 2006. http://books.google.com/books?id=-G0OyfnZd58C&dq=creole+remedies+of+trinidad+and+tobago&pg=PP1&ots=VfxbrEZntT&sig=ZbIIuBbiwh4xYu95hF8VHkotiQA&hl=en&prev=http://www.google.com/search%3Fsourceid%3Dnavclient%26ie%3DUTF-8%26rls%3DSUNA,SUNA:2006-51,SUNA:en%26q%3Dcreole%2Bremedies%2Bof%2Btrinidad%2Band%2Btobago&sa=X&oi=print&ct=title&cad=one-book-with-thumbnail#PPP1,M1.

Lehmann-Haupt, Christopher. Rev. of *Music for Chameleons,* by Truman Capote. *New York Times,* August 5, 1980. http:www.nytimes.com/books/97/12/28/home/capote-music.html?_r=1&oref=slogin.

Lightfoot, Judy. "Tree of Life: A Florid Coming-of-Age Novel Set in Martinique." Rev. of *Tree of Life,* by Raphael Confiänt. *Seattle Weekly,* July 26, 2000. http://www.seattleweekly.com/2000-07-26/arts/tree-of-life.php.

Márquez Rodríguez, Alexis. *La obra narrativa de Alejo Carpentier.* Caracas: Biblioteca de la Universidad Central de Venezuela, 1970.

Matibag, Eugenio. "Ifá and Interpretation: An Afro-Cuban Literary Practice." *Sacred Possessions: Vodou, Santería, Obeah, and the Caribbean.* Ed. Margarite Fernández Olmos and Lizabeth Paravisini-Gebert. New Brunswick, NJ: Rutgers UP, 1997. 151–70.

McCluskey Jr., John. "Review of *A Small Gathering of Bones by Patricia Powell.*" *Journal of Third World Studies* 13.1 (1996): 310–17.

Métraux, Alfred. *Voodoo in Haiti.* Trans. Hugo Charteris. New York: Schocken, 1972.

"Michelle Cliff." *Dictionary of Literary Biography.* 3rd ed. Vol. 157. Detroit: Gale, 1996. 49–58.

"Michelle Cliff." VG: Voices from the Gaps. Women Artists and Writers of Color, an International Website. 2006. http://voices.cla.umn.edu/vg/Bios/entries/cliff_michelle.html.

Mintz, Sidney W. *Caribbean Transformations.* Baltimore: John Hopkins UP, 1974.

Moller, Jan. "Cockfighting a Grand Tradition, Owners of Raided Club Say." *Times-Picayune,* April 25, 2007. http://blog.nola.com/times-picayune/about.html.

Montero, Mayra. "The Great Bonanza of the Antilles." *Healing Cultures: Art and Religion as Curative Practices in the Caribbean.* Ed. Margarite Fernández Olmos and Lizabeth Paravisini-Gebert. New York: Palgrave, 2001. 195–201.

———. *The Messenger.* Trans. Edith Grossman. New York: HarperFlamingo, 1999.

Morales, Ed. *The Latin Beat.* New York: Da Capo Press, 2003.

Mosher, Howard Frank. "Staying Alive." Rev. of *I, Tituba, Black Witch of Salem,* by Maryse Condé. *New York Times,* October 25, 1992. http://query.nytimes.com/gst/fullpage.html?res=9E0CEEDD103ff936A15753C1A964958260&partner=rssnyt&emc=ss.

Murphy, Joseph. *Santería: African Spirits in America.* Boston: Beacon Press, 1993.

Mustafa, Fawzia. *V. S. Naipaul.* New York: Cambridge UP, 1995.

Naipaul, V. S. *The Mystic Masseur.* New York: Vintage International, 2002.

Olmos, Margarite Fernández, and Lizabeth Paravisini-Gebert. *Creole Religions of the Caribbean: An Introduction from Vodou and Santería to Obeah and Espiritismo.* New Brunswick, NJ: Rutgers UP, 2003.

Ormerod, David. "In a Derelict Land: The Novels of V. S. Naipail." *Contemporary Literature* 9.1 (1968): 74–90.

Parkinson, Wenda. *This Gilded African*. London: Quartet Books, 1978.

Pattullo, Polly. *Last Resort: The Cost of Tourism in the Caribbean*. 2nd ed. New York: Monthly Review Press, 2005.

Powell, Patricia. *A Small Gathering of Bones*. Boston: Beacon Press, 2003.

Prieto, José Manuel. "Mayra Montero." *Bomb* 70 (2000). http://www.bombsite. com/montero/montero.html.

Ramchand, Kenneth. "Preface to the 1970 Edition." *The West Indian Novel and its Background*. Kingston, Jamaica: Ian Randle Publishers, 2004. xxxiv–xliv.

Rhys, Jean. *Wide Sargasso Sea*. New York: W. W. Norton, 1999.

Richardson, Alan. "Romantic Voodoo: Obeah and British Culture, 1797–1807." *Sacred Possessions: Vodou, Santería, Obeah, and the Caribbean*. Ed. Margarite Fernández Olmos and Lizabeth Paravisini-Gebert. New Brunswick, NJ: Rutgers UP, 1997. 171–94.

Rodríguez Monegal, Emir. "Lo real y lo maravilloso en *El reino de este mundo*." *Asedios a Carpentier*. Ed. Klaus Muller-Bergh. Chile: Editorial Universitaria, 1972. 39–48.

Rohlehr, Gordon. "The Ironic Approach: The Novels of V. S. Naipaul." *The Islands in Between*. Ed. Louis James. London: Oxford UP, 1968. 121–36.

Schwarz-Bart, Simone. *The Bridge of Beyond*. London: Heinemann, 1982.

Shaw, Donald. *Alejo Carpentier*. Boston: Twayne, 1985.

Silenieks, Juris. "Martinique: *Mamzelle Libellule* by Raphael Confiänt." *World Literature Today* 69.4 (2002): 854.

Simpson, Louis. "Disorder and Escape in the Fiction of V. S. Naipaul." *Hudson Review* 37.4 (1984): 571–77.

Smith, Faith. "An Interview with Patricia Powell." *Callaloo* 19.2 (1996): 324–29.

Speratti-Piñero, Emma Susana. "Creencias afro-antillanas en *El reino de este mundo* de Alejo Carpentier." *Nueva Revista de Filología Hispana* 29.2 (1980): 574–96.

Thieme, John. "Searching for a Centre: The Writing of V. S. Naipaul." *Third World Quarterly* 9.4 (1987): 1352–65.

Torres-Rosado, Santos. "La mujer como referente estético-literario en *El reino de este mundo* de Alejo Carpentier." *Cincinnati Romance Review* 10 (1991): 208–16.

Valens, Keja. "Obvious and Ordinary: Desire between Girls in Jamaica Kincaid's *Annie John*." *Frontiers* 25.2 (2004): 123–49.

Van Sickle, John Babcock. "Virgilian Reeds: A Program Cue in Derek Walcott's *Omeros*." *Vergilius* 51 (2005): 32–61.

Walcott, Derek. "The Muse of History." *The Routledge Reader in Caribbean Literature*. Ed. Alison Donnell and Sarah Lawson Welsh. London: Routledge, 1996. 354–58.

———. *Omeros*. New York: Farrar, Straus, Giroux, 1990.

———. *The Prodigal*. New York: Farrar, Straus, and Giroux, 2004.

Younge, Gary. "Chilling Call to Murder as Music Attacks Gays." *Guardian* [London], June 26, 2004. http://www.guardian.co.uk/world/2004/jun/26/ gayrights.arts.

Index

About the Author

LIZABETH PARAVISINI-GEBERT is Randolph Distinguished Professor of Hispanic Studies at Vassar College.